A MAP TO HEALING AND YOUR ESSENTIAL DIVINITY THROUGH THETA CONSCIOUSNESS

The Physics of the Immortal "Light Body" and the Creator's Template of Perfection and Abundance for His People

Dr. Robert J. Newton, J.D., N.D.

BALBOA.
PRESS

A DIVISION OF HAY HOUSE

Balboa Press books may be ordered through booksellers or by contacting:

Balboa Press
A Division of Hay House
1663 Liberty Drive
Bloomington, IN 47403
www.balboapress.com
1-(877) 407-4847

ISBN: 978-1-4525-4445-8 (sc)
ISBN: 978-1-4525-4461-8 (hc)
ISBN: 978-1-4525-4446-5 (e)

Library of Congress Control Number: 2011963414

Printed in the United States of America

Balboa Press rev. date: 02/17/2012

TABLE OF CONTENTS

PRE-PROLOGUE DISCLOSURE

The author of this book RECEIVES NO COMPENSATION from any source, organization or person listed in this book EXCEPT FROM HIS OWN SEMINARS AND CLASSES AND THE BOOK! Specifically, he has not been commissioned by "Babji's Kriya Yoga" or Marshall Govindan Satchidananda, "The Kabbalah Center" or the Berg family, "The First Church of Christ Scientist" in Boston Massachusetts or any other Christian Science branch church, Hinduism or any Hindu group including "The Kauai Hindu Monastery"(including "Hinduism Today"), Buddhism or any Buddhist group, The Builders of the Adytum", "The Self Realization Fellowship", Dane Spotts and "Ultra Meditation", "Q-Laser" and "Laser Wellness", "Pyradyne", "Metaforms", the "John Ellis Water Machine" and any Tai Chi organization, David Wilcock, Jay Lakhani, Robert Temple, Zecharia Sitchin, Louise L. Hay or Hay House, Tim C. Leedom and Maria Muroy, Dr. Rocco Erico, Fetzer and Tolman of "www.a3dmind.com"., Peter Caddy, Michaelle Small Wright, Julio Rivas, Mitch Battros, Dr. John Bradenbury, Richard De Wolf, William Haney, Jack Davis, Jasmuheen, "The American Free Press" and "Liberty Lobby", Craig Biddle and "The Objectivist Journal", Rudolph Steiner and any organization related to him or his teachings, Linda Joy Rose, Dr. Robert Becker, Dr. Samuel West, Dr. Leonard Caldwell, Dr. Fred Bell, Dr. Johanna Budwig, Steven Lewis and the "AIM program", the Dinsbaugh organization, Astropysicist Dr.Hugh Ross, Valery P. Kondratov, Dr. Yockey, Alain Contant, William Henry, and Swami Saraswati and his ashram!

By this true proclamation you can be assured that the AUTHOR DOES NOT HAVE A HIDDEN AGENDA OR IS AN AGENT REPRESENTING ANYTHING OR ANYONE WHO IS INCLUDED

IN THE CONTENT OF THIS BOOK. The author is humbled and honored to be the channel through which this book is revealed. THERE IS NO INTENTIONAL ARROGANCE ON THE PART OF THE AUTHOR ALTHOUGH THERE MAY BE THOSE PEOPLE WHO CLAIM SUCH! He knows THAT ALL INTELLIGENCE EMANATES FROM THE CREATOR through Divine Mind/Akashic Concsiousness/ Cosmic Consciousness and from nothing else—certainly not a puny Brain, which is nothing more than a "personal", personal computer which stores and retrieves information from your Brain!

This "personal", personal computer DOES NOT HAVE POWERS OF CREATIVITY, INTELLIGENCE, WISDOM AND INSIGHT, BUT IT DOES AN OUTSTANDING JOB OF STORING INFORMATION AND KNOWLEDGE!!!!

THE AUTHOR also IS NOT AN ACTIVE MEMEBER OF ANY BOARD OF DIRECTORS OF, OR HAS AN ACTIVE INTEREST, FINANCIAL OR OTHERWISE, IN ANY RELIGION OR GROUP LISTED WITHIN THIS BOOK!!!!

There is NO DELIBERATE INTENTION OR HIDDEN AGENDA TO UNFAIRLY DEMEAN ANY PERSON OR GROUP. Any evaluation made by the author is from decades span of perspective, legally admissible evidence, including anecdotal evidence—not just an arbitrary opinion, which is essentially worthless. HOWEVER, SOMETIMES THE TRUTH CAN SEEM DEMEANING, RATHER UGLY AND UNSETTLING TO THOSE PEOPLE WHO DO NOT UNDERSTAND IT OR THOSE PEOPLE WHO DO NOT WANT TO LOOK AT IT OR THOSE PEOPLE WHOSE EXISTING BELIEF SYSTEMS ARE THREATENED BY IT! The author does not and will not intentionally criticize anything or anyone but WILL RATHER EXPLAIN WHY SOMETHING IS NOT TRUE and NOT JUST ASSERT SUCH! There must be a PREPONDERANCE OF EVIDENCE BEFORE THE AUTHOR COMES TO CONCLUSIONS. THERE ARE NO

INTENTIONS OF "ASSASSINATING" ANYONE'S CHARACTER OR BELIEFS, although there will be people who, contrary-wise, will state that this is the case!!!! For the author, this is an accepted "price" of being a "pioneer"!

IF YOU ARE NOT FANATICAL ABOUT KNOWING THE TRUTH AND NOT ABLE TO BE FLEXIBLE ENOUGH TO LEARN NEW CONCEPTS, AS IS THE AUTHOR, DO NOT READ THIS BOOK AS IT WILL UPSET YOU BEYOND YOUR POINT OF EQUILIBRIUM!!!! If your balance comes from DEFENDING the "STATUS QUO", be ADVISED TO AVOID READING THIS BOOK since its purpose is to OBLITERATE and VAPORIZE THE PREVAILING UNDERSTANDING OF MAN BECAUSE IT IS MISINFORMED AND MISFORMULATED AND MALFORMULATED in contrast to what will be revealed in this book AND KNOWN TO A FEW PEOPLE FOR THOUSANDS, MILLIONS AND EVEN BILLIONS OF YEARS, first probably known in India around 1.9 billion years ago!!!!

FOR SEEKERS OF TRUTH AND DIVINITY—A STATE OF ONENESS WITH THE CREATOR—THIS BOOK SHOULD INCREASE A CONDITION OF EQUILIBRIUM AND UNDERSTANDING AND UNLOCK THE SHACKLES THAT HAVE BOUND US, as when Jesus stated, "Ye shall seek the Truth and the Truth shall make ye free." If you are a "Theta healer" or a "Reiki healer", your healings will be more complete and occur within a shorter duration. If you are a Christian Scientist, this book, or at least parts of it, will bring you a greater spiritual understanding and appreciation of Mary Baker Eddy's works and will certainly make you a better healer. If you are a Yogi or Yogini, this book should be invaluable in giving insights and direction to your spiritual journey beyond the framework of Yoga, including healing and abundance.

If you are a Christian, Moslem, Jew, Buddhist, Hindu, Theosophist, a Rosecrucian, a Hermeticist, an Ascelpiad, a Mason, a Builder of the Adytum student, a Pantheist or any other seeker of the Truth, this book could PARCH YOUR THIRST BECAUSE IT CONTAINS HIDDEN TRUTHS THAT CAN BE APPLIED IN YOUR EVERYDAY LIFE SO THAT YOU LIVE LIFE AT AN OPTIMUM LEVEL! In fact, if this book could not accomplish greatly enriching your life, the author would not waste his time composing the text and there would be not value in your partaking thereof!!!! If you are an artist or writer, this book can PUT YOU IN A SYNCHRONIZED STATE WITH THE UNLIMITED CREATIVITY AND CLARITY OF THE DIVINE MIND or the AKASHIC FIELD from whence emanates all inspiration and knowledge. If you are a scientist or mathematician, likewise, you can be aligned with all knowledge ensconced in the atomic field of atoms (Akashic Records) and be able to solve complex problems and unearth "new discoveries".

WHAT THIS BOOK HAS THE POTENTIAL TO DO IS TO CREATE A PROCESS OF "SPIRITUAL ALCHEMY" WHEREIN OUR ENTIRE CONSCIOUSNESS IS TRANSFORMED TO A STATE WHERE WE CAN LITERALLY BE ABLE TO SEE AND LIVE IN THE "TRUE AND PERFECT" CREATION OF OUR GOD!!!! And the implications regarding this will profoundly change us in ways we wanted to believe was possible but thought we really did not have any hope of achieving this!

Why this information and its attendant "truths" have been hidden from you will be explicated throughout this book. If you choose to partake of this book, welcome to the OASIS (Over-Arching Spiritually Integrated Sciences)! This is where many different paths come together to create an incredibly delicious casserole or an amazing mélange—where the ingredients are more meaningful and powerful, aggregated together than they are separated!

PROLOGUE

"FROM A 'CLOSED MIND', CONSCIOUSNESS WILL NOT ONLY NOT GROW AND EVOVLE, IT WILL SHRIVEL AND DIE AS A PLANT THAT HAS BEEN DEPRIVED OF WATER! FROM AN 'OPEN MIND', CONSCIOUISNESS GROWS AND EXPANDS LIKE A VIGOROUS VINE AND WILL ATTACH ITSELF THROUGH ITS TENDRILS INTO A DIRECT LINK WITH 'DIVINE MIND' AND WILL EVOLVE INTO THE MAGNIFICENCE OF A DOUBLE PETALLED, FRAGRANT ROSE AND THE LUSTER OF A FLAWLESS, 'BRILLIANT CUT' FACETED DIAMOND!!!!" This is attributed, via "Akashic knowledge", to my beautiful, deceased friend, of many lifetimes, Judith Frankel, who is truly a light of untold brilliance and beauty, both incarnate and discarnate!

This is a book about HEALING, ABUNDANCE and IMMORTALITY. Although it may seem that these things are not connected, at their essence they most certainly are, as will revealed within the pages of this book! IF YOUR LIFE IS ALREADY PERFECT OR AT LEAST VERY GOOD— if you have perfect health and abundance and are personally fulfilled— THEN YOU MOST LIKELY DO NOT NEED TO READ THIS BOOK! IF, ON THE CONTRARY, YOU ARE UNHAPPY or just "so-so" AND WISH THERE WAS "MORE" OR YOU KNOW THERE MUST BE "MORE", THIS BOOK CAN BE YOU MAP THERETO

This is precisely why this book is being written because many of us have become "bogged down" in this "game" we could call "Life". Certainly, this applied to the author at a time in his life also. Rabbi Yehuda Berg in "The 72 Names of God: Technology for the Soul" frames our predicament clearly. He states that WE ARE ALEADY PERFECT but that we agreed to come to planet Earth to play a "game" where we would incarnate here and have the memory of our perfection taken from our consciousness. Then, in this "game" we would search to have this re-revealed to ourselves! THIS SEARCH FOR PERFECTION IS MORE AKIN TO OUR PREDICAMENT THAN OUR BEING "FLAWED SINNERS", as too many of us have been erringly taught and directed to believe BY INCORRECT RELIGIOUS AND POLITICAL INTERPRETATION! The author knows that when we get here to "play the game", it seems to be extremely intense and even worse, CONFUSING AND WAY TOO COMPLICATED!!

And yet in the same vein as Rabbi Berg, the Kriya Yoga Siddha, Patanjali, in "The Yoga Sutras" reveals that Yoga aids in cleansing the subconscious mind. And we do this in layers as in "PEELING AN ONION" with the result that our INHERENT PERFECTION IS EVENTUALLY REVEALED and the author hopes, graciously, with less pungency than our Allium "friend", the Onion! But even if you have to deal with the odor, it is more than worth the effort to reach your REAL AND PEERFECT STATE OF BEING AND CONSCIOUSNESS, which we have been told is "unattainable", here on Earth!

In the "Emerald Tablets" by Hermes Trismegistus, Hermes, who seems to be of extraterestial origin, states that OUR GOD IS A PERFECT GOD which created everything and consumes our entire world. This seems similar to Einstein's "Unified Field Theory" from Physics with the CREATOR being the "CONSUMER/ UNIFIER". And Hermes further says that if we take this "CONSUMING POWER" we can integrate this into our Earth. And so the "UNIFIER"/CREATOR is also the "INTEGRATOR" of itself through an ENDLESS "SEA" OF ATOMS.

So what does this essentially mean? It means that WE HAVE THE ABILITY TO CREATE AND/OR LIVE IN A STATE OF

PERFECTION/HEAVEN OPERATING ON OUR PLANET AND IN OUR EVERYDAY LIVES. Actually this "PERFECT STATE" STATE" IS ALREADY OPERATIONAL but is basically UNPERCEIVED BY THE MASSES of humanity and for good reasons, which will be explained shortly!The first chapter of Genesis in the Bible, says or implies much of the same thing where it discusses a "very good" creation. In "The 72 Names of God" in "Exodus 14 verses 19-21", the PERFECT TEMPLATE of God's CREATION and the perfect quailites of God are revealed and distilled in "Aleph Kaf Aleph" (restoring things to their perfect state). The operative word here again is "RESTORING" and this IMPLIES THAT PERFECTION HAS ALWAYS EXISTED AND DOES NOT NEED TO BE CREATED OR RECREATED BUT RATHER RE-REALIZED! This differs greatly from the prevailing beliefs of orthodox Christianity, Islam and Judaism!

In the "Patterns of the Trestleboard: the Truth About Self", an intense seeker of true knowledge, Paul Foster Case, also reveals a perfect template of creation and reveals that from the exhaustless substance of God ALL OF OUR NEEDS ARE MET! Mary Baker Eddy, in "Science and Health with Key to the Scriptures", also reveals the perfection of our creator who CREATED US IN ITS IMAGE AND LIKENESS as revealed in the "Bible" and "Torah" in the beginning of "Genesis". Mrs. Eddy states that by aligning ourselves with God that ALL OF OUR NEEDS ARE MET.

Plato, the great Greek Philosopher, talked about "perfect forms" which existed behind the various objects on our Earth! This was explained to us about two and a half mellenia ago. Was anybody then paying attention to him? Apparently, few people if any, including his student Aristotle!

The VEDIC TEXTS from ancient India also talk about THE PERFECTION CREATED BY SHIVA (GOD). Additionally, it discusses Maya, the illusion that things seem imperfect even though they are not! This is our oldest known concept of cosmogony (creation) and cosmography (the structure of the Universe). Even the ancient language of India, Sanskrit, means "PERFECT FORM" or PERFECTION IN AND OF ITSELF! In the BHAGAVAD GITA, Krishna reveals in detail the MAGNIFICENCE OF OUR CREATOR'S CREATION which includes us and how we CAN ACHIEVE THIS MAGNIFICENCE THROUGH YOGA, as does Patanjali in "The Yoga Sutras" and Thirumoolar in "Thirumandiram".

Patanjali, the great Kriya Yoga Siddha/MahaAvatar/Satguru stated MANY THOUSANDS of years ago in "The Yoga Sutras" that MAN is made in the IMAGE AND LIKENSS OF GOD. So, through a preponderance of evidence, A RECURRING PATTERN OF PERFECTION HAS BEEN ESTABLISHED HERE FROM MANY DIFFERENT SOURCES! This EVIDENCE has been STARING HUMANITY IN THE FACE for thousands of years or longer—MAYBE EVEN MILLIONS AND BILLIONS OF YEARS!! Why has it gone unnoticed, even today with all of our technological advancements? Unfortunately, these technological advancements have out-paced our spiritual perspective, much as what occurred what occurred to the Atlanteans!

Along the way in human history, which goes back so much farther than what is believed by almost all archaeologists, we have come under a **"VIEL OF IGNORANCE"** which has precluded us knowing and living in our inherently Divine lives!! Unfortunately, THERE ARE PEOPLE AND GROUPS AND RELIGIONS AND GOVERNMENTS THAT WOULD RATHER WE DO NOT KNOW THE TRUTHS OF OUR CREATION OR THE TRUTH ABOUT OUR CREATOR! This is why the underlying perfection of our Creator that we ourselves reflect remains basically unperceived by the masses. Unfortunately, for the vast majority of humanity, THE ILLUMINATI (CABAL) CULT, OBESSED WITH MONEY AND INTOXICATED BY POWER (essentially controlling everything on our Earth, directly or indirectly through interlocking directorates) and the DOGMATIC, UNINSPIRED AND REPRESSIVE MENTALITY OF SOME ORGANIZED RELIGIONS, with possibly four exceptions (Christian Science, Buddhism, Hinduism, Kabbalistic Judaism), have kept the MASSES of humanity "UNDER THEIR

THUMB", subjugated by sophisticated PROPOGANDA, outrageous UNTRUTHS, "PRETZEL AND CIRCUITUS LOGIC" and FANTASY ASSERTIONS and scenarios which have SCANT OR NO EVIDENCE TO SUPPORT THEM.

These malformulated ideas have NO RELATION TO THE TRUTH OF THE CREATOR/God such as DISTORTED DECLARATIONS that "you will go to hell if you are not saved by Jesus before you die". Also, "you are a flawed, imperfect sinner and you can only be 'saved' from this plight by the Catholic Church who will grant you dispensation" or the Protestant churches who bring "salvation" through baptizing you or the Moslem church which declares that you must make a pilgramage to Mecca in order to enter heaven! THESE ASSERTIONS ARE MORE AKIN TO "DISTORTIONS" THAN "FUNDAMENTAL TRUTH", as has been more less clarified in previous paragraphs and will be assiduously detailed throughout this book!!!!

Having had many extended "near death" experiences in the Yogic state of Samadhi, the author has conversed with many "departed souls" from this Earth, who wished they would have had a better understanding of the real nature of God versus the misguided dogma they were taught here on Earth. You can discount the author's statements here as lacking evidentiary force because of one limited perspective. Unfortunately, you CANNOT, or at least should not IGNORE THE NARRATIVES OF MANY OTHER PEOPLE'S "NEAR DEATH" EXPERIENCES which RESOUNDINGLY CORROBORATE THE AUTHOR'S STATEMENTS and lend evidentiary force and credence thereto.

THE FOLLOWING STATEMENTS, IN THE PARAGRAPH BELOW MADE BY THE AUTHOR, ARE NOT FORMULATED WITH ARROGANCE OR SUPERIORITY BUT FROM AN OBJECTIVE PERSPECTIVE OF WHAT WORKS FOR US FOR OUR "GREATER GOOD"—what will provide us with a vastly more satisfying life, not only into eternity but RIGHT NOW!

THE REASON THAT THE FOUR RELIGIONS ABOVE HAVE BEEN EXONERATED, AS WELL AS KRIYA YOGA (which is not a religion but a system of immortal living) IS THAT THE GOAL OF ALL OF THEM IS TO LIBERATE YOU WITH IMMORTALITY AND PERFECTION AS OPPOSED TO LIMITING YOU WITH MALODOROUS DOGMA SUCH AS SIN, SICKNESS, MORTALITY, MEDIOCRITY, DECAY and other ORCHESTRATED UNTRUTHS—standards devoid of Divine inspiration or authorization! IT IS KNOWN, to some insightful people, WITHOUT ANY DOUBT, THAT THOUGHTS OF IMPERFECTION BEGET IMPERFECTION AND THOUGHTS OF PERFECTION LIKEWISE BEGET PERFECTION, AS CREATED IN THE SUBCONSCIOUS OR "MORTAL MIND", which is your perosnal, "personal computer" that not only stores information but WHICH REPLICATES AND CREATES EVENTS AND EXPERIENCES IN OUR LIVES!

This is concept is contrary to the way a magnet works where the opposite magnetic poles attract each other and like magnetic poles repel each other! EVERYTHING THE SUBCONSCIOUS MIND HEARS OR FEELS, IT CREATES OVER AND OVER AGAIN IN YOUR LIFE, because it is a programmable computer which absorbs and dispenses that unto what it has been exposed, via our thoughts and emotions and perceptions!!!!

None of the Christian or Islamic churches, other than Christian Science, have understood why Jesus came to Earth and this has become obfusticated by MAKING ASSUMPTIONS based on an INCOMPLETE PERSPECTIVE of ALL OF THE AVAILABLE RELIGIOUS and SCIENTIFIC EVIDENCE which will be discussed in detail in this book! ASSUMPTIONS AND PERSONAL OPINION ARE NOT EVIDENTIARY FACT BUT MORE AKIN to FANTASY AND HERESAY AND YET WE HAVE BEEN TAUGHT TO ACCEPT THIS AS "IRREFUTALBE TRUTH"! People who feel that science has no place in religion are those people who would rather enshrine "blind belief" in place of the actual facts and the truth related thereto!!!! With such a "mindset", success in life is rather fleeting, if it even occurs anytime, within a SUBSET OF FAULTY KNOWLEDGE!

JESUS' MISSION ON EARTH IS WELL EXPLAINED IN "SCIENCE AND HEALTH WITH KEY TO THE SCRIPTURES", BY MARY BAKER EDDY. This narrative of SCIENTIFIC CHRISTIANITY is sadly missing from the almost all of the Christian churces and yet without it our persepctive of Jesus is so one sided and "thin" as to make us unperceptive to Jesus' purpose. These insights are included in excluded Gospels from the New Testament such as the "Gospel of Thomas". Herein, THOMAS CLEARLY STATES THAT "BELIEF WITHOUT UNDERSTANDING IS OF LITTLE VALUE." And yet the Christian and Islamic churches have essentially told us that we must "believe" and "not to question this belief". AS CERTITUDE, JESUS NEVER TAUGHT THIS DOCTRINE OF "BLIND FAITH". If you read "THE ARAMAIC BIBLE" by Dr. George Lamsa (the author also believes that Dr. Rocco Erico may have also completed or is close to finishing his transalation of the same book), you will find a vastly MORE ACCURATE New Testament which more resmebles Jesus' true message to us!!!!

So the question then is WHY WOULD WE BELIEVE THE CURRENT CHRISTIAN and the ISLAMIC DOGMA, which is based on AN INCOMPLETE PERSPECTIVE, as is well documented in the book, "The Book Your Church Doesn't Want You to Read", by Leedom and Muroy? Is it because alot of other people believe likewise? A MAJORITY OPINION IS NOT NECESSARILY THE EQUIVALENT OF FACTUAL REALITY!!!! AS A MATTER OF FACT, the author can say with certainty, THAT THE MAJORITY RARELY, IF EVER, ARE KNOWLEDGEABLE REGARDING ANYTHING? If they were, the republican democracy in the USA, created by our "founding fathers", would operate at a vastly elevated level from what it does now, which is closer to a socialist democracy or a socialist, communist state that is being pushed into financial insolvency!!!! IT WILL BE CONTENDED, AND IN FACT CAN BE PROVEN ANECDOTALLY FROM SELF

EVIDENT OBSERVATION, THAT AT THIS POINT IN TIME THE "MAJORITY" MAKES INHERENTLY MEDIOCRE DECISIONS, basically because they are swayed by a constant barrage of propoganda from religions, governments, the Illuminati cult and corporations!!!!

Now, it should becoming obvious, to some discerning individuals, that most CHRISTIAN and ISLAMIC and JEWISH THEOLOGIANS AND SCHOLARS HAVE FAILED TO COMPREHEND, UNLIKE MARY BAKER EDDY, THE PERFECT CREATION in the Bible and Torah that is described in the first chapter of Genesis and the beginning of the second chapter where it is recorded: "And God saw his CREATION AND BEHOLD IT WAS VERY GOOD". **PLEASE NOTE IT DOES NOT SAY "PRETTY GOOD"** or that "some things were good and other things not so much".

Additionally, it is basically suspends belief that the theologians and biblical scholars have ignored what Jesus was recorded as saying in the New Testament where he proclaims: "GREATER WORKS THAN THESE SHALL YE DO ALSO"? Note, this statement does not say or infer that you are a "flawed, hapless sinner" but just the opposite thereof because NARY A "FLAWED SINNER" WOULD BE CAPABLE OF PERFORMING JESUS' DIRECTIVE!!!! But the "PERFECT MAN" created by a "perfect God" WOULD BE IMMINENTLY QUALIFIED TO FOLLOW IN JESUS' "FOOTSTEPS" and even exceed his magnificence!!!! In "Science and Health With Key to the Scriptures", Mary Baker Eddy puts it bluntly when she states that God does not ask us to do more than we can accomplish. If this is correct, then following this doctrine of "ACHIEVING GREATER WORKS" CAN BE PERFORMED BY US!!!! And IT WOULD MEAN WE ARE NOT HERE WITHOUT A MEANS OF ASSISTANCE AND DIRECTION FROM OUR CREATOR!

There are some historical researchers and extraterretial investigators who would contend that the story of "Adam and Eve" is about ET personages who came to Earth and displeased their leader, a demi-god, who decided to wipe out "rogue elements" here, who invoked the wrath of their leader, and were exterminated in the flood which was related in the story of Noah!!!! CERTAINLY, THESE BEINGS WHO WERE ELIMINATED IN THE FLOOD, DID NOT REPRESENT or reflect THE PERFECT CREATION DISSEMINATED IN THE VERY BEGINNING OF GENESIS!!!! In a sense, they became "disconnected" from their Creator and hence lowered themselves into a degenerated state of consicousness!

Now the only way we can revere the Master Jesus the Christ is by SUPASSING HIS "WORKS" and FOLLOWING THIS BEHEST, which he revealed to us. OTHERWISE, WE HAVE MISSED CHRIST'S FUNDAMENTAL MESSAGE. Jesus did come here to save us but it was FROM OUR OWN GLARING IGNORANCE OF OUR "REAL NATURE" AND NOT FROM THE FIRES OF HELL! HE WAS GROSSLY MISUNDERSTOOD BY INSIGHTLESS DISCIPLES, BIBLICAL TRANSLATORS AND THEOLOGIANS OF HIS REAL MESSAGE—THE PERFECT MAN, NOT JUST LIMITED TO JESUS HIMSELF, and only understood by Mary Baker Eddy within the Christian perspective and by "The 72 Names of God" in the Kabbalistic Jewish traditions, EVEN THOUGH THE LATTER DOES NOT SEEM TO SPECIFICALLY RELATE TO JESUS!

And yet it does relate to the perfect nature of man AND THERE IS A GREAT POSSIBILITY, EVEN A PROBABILITY, THAT JESUS WAS WELL INDOCTRINATED IN THE KABBALAH since Jesus most likely was a Rabbincal student! If this seems that too much "stretching" for truth is occuring here, remember, the Rabbi's were astonished at his great understanding of scripture, among other things, at a very young age! This gives perspective to this "Rabbinical" situation, as a logical place of Spiritual and Akashic knowledge—especially as contained in the Kabballah!

The author is fully aware that only Rabbi's at least forty years old were/are suppose to study the Kabbalah. Could have and would have an exception have been made by a Rabbi whose understanding was beyond that of his peers? Akashic insight, would lead the author to believe this was the case.

Yogic Avatars and Hindu Vedic priests have claimed that Jesus was initiated into the highest aspects of Hinduism. This would infer and include the science of Yoga! Other texts indicate he may also have been intitated by the Eyptian priests in their esoteric practices! All of this would have happened during "the lost years" of a three year time span where there is no Biblical input as to what Jesus was contemplating and where he was located geographically!

MAYBE THE TRANSLATORS AND THEOLOGIANS KNEW THE REAL MESSAGE OF JESUS AND YET THEY KNEW IF IT WAS REVEALED TO US, THEY COULD NO LONGER CONTROL US THROUGH GUILT, DOUBT AND FEAR? Regardless, Christians and Moslems and Jews may have been sent out to chase tales and their tails, as it were, through circulating logic and "manufactured truths". A circle is a beautiful form but in logic it is obfusticating because there is no point of a definable and ultimate conclusion or Truth, because it has no beginning and no end!!!! Things just keep circulating and obstructing discernable reality and perpetuating confusion! DYT (do you think) that this might be our plight? This is well documented "The Book Your Church Doesn't Want You to Read" by Tim C. Leedom and Maria Muroy which was mentioned several paragraphs previously!

THERE IS NO AGENDA HERE TO CRUCIFY OR DENIGRATE CHRISTIANS OR MOSLEMS OR JEWS. As a matter of fact, the author has great admiration for the devotion and discipline many Moslems, Jews and Christians, Buddhists, Hindus and Yogis exhibit in their religious practices. THIS IS COMMENDABLE BEYOND THE COMPOSITION OF ANY AND ALL WORDS! THE AUTHOR'S MISSION IS TO ATTEMPT TO LOVE ALL OF GOD'S CREATIONS, as was formulated by Paul Foster Case in "The Patterns On the Trestleboard . . . ." and was uttered from the Master Jesus' own mouth when he said, "Love one another! The Jewish scholar, Hilillel, also talked about this same concept.

Also, REALIZE THAT THE AUTHOR IS NOT CLAIMING ANY INHERENT SUPERIORITY TO ANY CHRISTIAN, MOSLEM, JEW OR ANY OTHER RELIGIOUS ADHERENT! He, likewise, was sent out chasing "tales and his tail". But within the overall perspective, the author has been blessed to have had so many insights into how Jesus' teachings have been distorted and hidden, he must speak out even though he WILL UPSET SOME PEOPLE with the hope that he CAN AID IN UPLIFTING OTHER PEOPLE who are open to a different perspective and course of action BECAUSE WHAT THEY HAVE BEEN TAUGHT JUST DOES NOT WORK FOR THEM!!!! IT IS TIME FOR HUMANITY TO "CHART A NEW COURSE" SO THAT MISFORMULATED INFORMATION AND CONCEPTS CAN BE LEFT BEHIND! Please allow yourself to consider a new perspective of Jesus" teachings as a beneficial course of action for yourself! LET THIS BE REPEATED. PLEASE ALLOW YOURSELF TO CONDISER A NEW PERSPECTIVE OF JESUS' TEACHINGS AS A BENEFICIAL COURSE OF ACTION FOR YOURSELF!!!!

The DIFFERENCE BETWEEN BEING AN "INHERENT SINNER" and THE PERFECT CREATION OF GOD IS THAT THE LATTER ALLOWS US TO LIVE OUR LIFE RADIANTLY and WITH ABUNDANCE without the nagging thoughts of "Am I going to hell?" And "Am I worthy to be accepted by my God?" And "Is God Angry with me?" THERE IS A HUGE CHASM BETWEEN THESE OPPOSSING VIEWS of inherent "sin" and inherent perfection!!!! What has really happened, in the inherent sinner situation, is THAT THE CREATOR HAS BEEN IMBUED WITH CAPRICIOUS HUMAN EMOTIONS WHICH THEN PORTRAY GOD ACTUALLY NOT AS THE DIVINE AND LOVING GOD!!!! The Capricious, angry God has us in a state of imprisonment whereas the DIVINE GOD, THE LOVING GOD, HAS LEFT US WITHOUT SHACKLES and we are able to reflect our

Creator's perfection AND LIVE OUR LIVES BY THIS TEMPLATE OR PATTERN!!!!

It could be better for us not to walk around like Dr. Pangloss, in "Candide", saying, "This is the best of all possible worlds", when we have imprisoned ourselves in a dungeon that the Creator never intended us to live within and yet that is where many churches have left us! Quite likely, DEMI-GODS OF EXTRATERRESTIAL ORIGIN HAVE BEEN CONFUSED WITH THE ULTIMATE, ONE AND ONLY CREATOR (or Creator of Creator's). These demi-gods where known as a fact to be quite tempestuous at times, as is revealed in the Zecharia Sitchin's books, "The Bible" and Greek and Norse mythology, among other sources.

SO, THE ILLUMINATI-CULT AND MOST ORGANIZED RELIGIONS HAVE CHOSEN TO FORSAKE THEIR SEARCH FOR THEIR OWN PERFECTION AND DIVINITY WHICH IS RELATED THERETO. It is always interesting yet bizarre to see how people and organizations, which cannot control themselves and are debased by their very actions, feel that it is imperative that they control everybody else who might not even be debased in their person! THIS IS CERTAINLY A BLANTANT EXAMPLE OF CO-DEPENDENCY! All disfuctional "controllers, please learn to control yourselves first before you try to control us! And since you apparently cannot do so AS YOUR DEBASED AND DEPRAVED ACTIONS PROVE, YOUR EFFORTS TO CONTROL US MUST BE SUMMARILY DISMISSED AS BLANTANT HYPOCRISY and uncomposted chicken manure which is very malodorous if not worse!!

The author knows of stench of uncomposted chicken manure from his personal experience in organic horticulture and agriculture, and the odor is unforgetably offensive until it is completely composted wherein it becomes highly beneficial to plants! AND THROUGH THE SEARCH FOR OUR PERFECTION AND THE ENSUING ENLIGHTENMENT, as it were, WE CAN TAKE THE MALODOROUS CHICKEN MANURE AND

TRANSFORM IT INTO A HIGHER FORM AND A BENEFICIAL NUTRIFYER OF LIFE!!!!

THE FOLLOWING INFORMATION IS PROVIDED SO AS TO INFORM YOU AS OPPOSED TO SCARING YOU OR DEPRESSING YOU BECASUE FOR ANY PROBLEM OR DILEMMA LISTED, THERE ARE SOLUTIONS THERETO!!!! The more you read in this book, the more you will perceive the veracity of this statement! **AND THESE SOLUTIONS, PROVIDED BY OUR CREATOR, ARE POWERFULLY COMPLETE AND ALWAYS ARE EFFECTIVE**

Virtually every government on our planet is dispensing malodorous flatulance and serving it to its citizens as the absolute, positive perfumed truth, when the diametric opposite is the case. Just one example would be the "Greenhouse Gas" theory of "global warming" (a scientific fiction so that a "carbon tax" can be levied on the global population). Another would be the need for "free trade" to create economic property for the population at large (it is self evident, except the most non-observant people, that this is a blatant fallacy as the wages of ordinary workers declines). Still another would be that airliners and jet fuel caused the collapse of The Trade Towers (physically, structurally and chemically impossible)! Yet another would be that the "Federal Reserve Bank" is truly a functioning part of the USA government. Check the seal that the bank uses as opposed to the official seal of the USA! Also, check and see where this bank has been incorporated! While you are at it, check and see where the Internal Revenue Service is incorporated? When you see that it is the Northern Mariana Islands, are you wondering why it is not Washington, D.C. OR WHY IT NEEDS TO EVEN BE INCORPORATED? This has the odor of a can of sardines, and putrid ones at that!!!!

From these things discussed and many other things a trend reveals itself and that TREND HAS NO RELATIONSHIP WITH THE TRUTH— NOT EVEN IN THE REMOTEST OF FASHIONS unless you are in a drug induced stupor and unfortunately a large part of our population is misinfluenced and mispercepted about events because the effects of drugs and alcohol have created a perceptual confusion! This book will help to re-educate people—to reveal ARITCLES OF TRUTH TO WHICH WE SHOULD HAVE BEEN EXPOSED in school and church! Our most glaring need is to realign ourselves with our Creator and the author will reveal this because he is compelled by higher spiritual sources to do so, regardless of the consequences!

The Illuminati cult is associated and intertwined with the United Nations, the Bilberg Group, the Trilateral Commission, the Council on Foreign Relations, some of the Christian churces, the Federal Reserve Bank, the Internal Revenue Service, The Bank of England, Wall Street banks and investment houses such as Goldman Sachs, Harvard University, Yale University, Cambridge University, Rhodes Scholars, the British Royal family, The Royal Dutch Family, The Rothchild's, The Rockefeller's, The Dupont's, The Morgan's, The Mellon's, The Schwab's and The Ford's among many others.

These are factual assertions even though many of them may not "sit well" with you because you thought your government was "watching out" for you. Their first allegiance is to the elistist oligarchs, known as the Illuminati Cult. The people and groups listed above ARE ELITIST, OLIGARCHIAL CULTS. THIS NOT A CONSPIRACY THEORY BUT RATHER A CONSPIRACY REALITY! JUST ABOUT EVERYTHING YOU HAVE LEARNED ABOUT HISTORY OR FROM YOUR RELIGIONS, WITH FEW EXCEPTIONS, IS BLATANTLY FALSE AND IN CONTRAVENTION TO YOUR BEST INTERESTS! Are you having problems "disgesting" this? The author of this book certainly did when he first learned of this! Do not despair, however, because "digestive relief" will be provided in this book.

THE AUTHOR DOES NOT WANT TO OVERWHELM YOU BUT RATHER CIRCUMSCIRBE OUR PLIGHT!! So please keep this in mind as the following is laid out before you! **OUR LIBERATION**

FROM THESE SITUATIONS IS WITHIN OUR GRASP AND ACCOMPLISHMENT, as will be explained throughout this book!

Some people and groups who CONSIDER YOU THEIR GOYUM (slaves/animals) AND INFERIOR TO THEMSELVES!!!! PLEASE BE AWARE THAT THERE ARE VERY "BLACK HIDDEN ELEMENTS" IN THE MASONIC ORDER, THE CHRISTIAN CHURCHES AND FACTIONS IN ISRAEL AND GREAT BRITAIN AND FRANCE AND THE NETHERLANDS AND YES, THE USA and more!!! These "Black Elements" use deception and propoganda and stealth to conceal themselves AND THEY ARE MOST ADEPT AT DOING SO, since they have done such for centuries and possibly even millenia! THE PROPOGANDA THEY USE MAKE ADOLPH HTILER LOOK LIKE AN AMATEUR IN COMPARISON AND THIS IS UNFORTUNATELY NOT AN OVERSTATEMENT BUT MORE AKIN TO AN UNDERESTIMATION! We are subtlely being bombarded with this misinformation on a daily basis, both consciously and subliminally!

Rather than attacking a fact of a purported "conspriacy theory", these "black elements" will attack the character of the person presenting a conspiracy fact, casting aspersions as to their character and sanity! Essentially, they are relegating people of "conspiracy fact" to the position of a "lunatic, fringe element ". How is this possible, since we have freedom of speech and freedom of the press?

Well, we really do not have a free and diverse press because of the draconian measures of the purported "Patriot Act", the idiotic notion of "hate crimes" and the fact that mainstream media control has been obtained, directly and indirectly, by the Illuminati cult through "shell" and/or "front" companies. Why did the media believe, without critcal investigation, the fantasies foisted upon us regarding Randy Weaver, of Ruby Ridge, Idaho, being a radical, "fringe", militia element who was dangerous to Americans? Why was there not a critical analysis by the media of the government claims that the "Branch Dividians" and Randy Weaver, in Waco, Texas, were self-immolated since there were requisition orders for flame throwing tanks from Fort Sill, Oklahoma, which were transferred to Waco, Texas?

Why was there not a critical media investigation into the "bombing" of the Murrah Building in Okalhoma City, Oklahoma when is it a known fact, apparently conviently ignored, that an Ammonium Nitrate fertilzer-fuel oil bomb CERTAINLY CANNOT DESTROY A BUILDING FROM THE OUTSIDE OF A STRUCTURE, as it was placed? And why were the two seimic tremors, recorded by a seimigraph, attributed to this event, also "cavalierly" ignored? Why did the press fail to critically look at why Tower Seven, of the Trade Tower complex, collapsed without even being "rammed" by a plane? Why did the press fail to mention that it is physically impossible to melt the "high tech" steel beams with jet fuel in the first two Trade Towers that collapsed?

FOR A LOT OF PEOPLE, THESE ARE RATHER STARTLING OMMISSIONS THAT SHOULD HAVE, AT THE VERY LEAST, BEEN CRITICALLY EXAMINED AND REPORTED BY THE PRESS? The only conceivable conclusion, in regard to our free press, as it were, is MIA (missing in action [actually, missing by inaction])!!!! One of the few media sources that has covered all of these stories and more, is the "American Free Press"! AND IF YOU WANT TO KNOW THE TRUTH ABOUT OUR GOVERNEMENTS, then you will need to avail yourself to this newspaper!

PLEASE NOTE THAT THE AUTHOR IS NOT ASSERTING THAT ALL PEOPLE INVOLVED IN THE PARAGRAPHS ABOVE, REGARDING THE LISTED "COMPROMISED" GROUPS, ARE "BLACK ELEMENTS"!!! That would be factually incorrect. The author assiduously adheres to a standard of truth and excellence. But what is factual is that "black elements" use highly moral groups to promote their "devious dealings" and they remain "CLOAKED" and UNDETECTED therein!!!! THUS THEY ARE FREE TO SPREAD

THEIR NEFARIOUS AGENDA, WHICH IS YOU ARE A "FLAWED SINNER" (this is too ironic to even swallow considering the source from which it emanates), THAT THERE IS NOT ENOUGH ABUNDANCE AND PROSPERITY FOR ALL OF HUMANITY (the irony of this is even harder to accept when you have an "elite few" hoarding everything) and you basically MUST ACCEPT THIS AS YOUR PLIGHT!!!!

THEREFORE, YOU MUST NOT "BLINDLY BELIEVE" EVERYTHING YOU HEAR INCLUDING THOSE THINGS EXPLAINED IN THIS BOOK!!!! You need to cultivate a FUNCTION OF DISCERNMENT, whereby you CRITICALLY DISSECT INFORMATION, ARGUMENTS, PROPOSALS and TREATISES THAT ARE PRESENTED TO YOU!!!!EVEN MORE IMPORTANT, CONSIDER THE SOURCE OF THE INFORMATION AND THE POSSIBLE MOTIVES AND BIAS REGARDING DISSEMINATED MESSAGES AND PROCLAMATIONS!!!! Some sources and countries profess that they are our friends and allies.The proof of their statements can only be EVALUATED WITHIN THE CONTEXT OF ALL OF THEIR ACTIONS! So many of these countries and sources are "talking the talk but not walking the walk".

DO NOT DESPAIR, BECAUSE THE INCREASED HYPERDIMENSIONAL ENERGIES BOMBARDING OUR PLANET NOW WILL EVENTUALLY MAKE IT IMPOSSIBLE FOR ALL BUT THE "PURE IN HEART" AND OF "PURE MOTIVE" TO EXIST ON PLANET EARTH!!!! We are actually now, able to discern those who are not "pure of heart" and would deceive us! **STRENGTHENING OF THE MORPHOGENIC FIELD OF THETA CONSCIOUSNESS IS WHAT WILL ALLOW THIS TO TRANSPIRE!**

THIS IS NOT A BOOK ABOUT DESPAIR BUT RATHER THE EXACT OPPOSITE!!!! THE CREATOR HAS AN ESTABLISHED RELATIONSHIP WITH US THAT ALLOWS US TO FLOURISH IN ANY SITUATION, NO MATTER HOW HOPELESS IT MAY

APPEAR!!!! In the end, a "futile situation" is only an appearance, not reality, NO MATTER HOW INTENSE and MORE AKIN TO A MIRAGE IF YOU KNOW AND UNDERSTAND WHY!

The Illuminati-cult controls directly or indirectly the word banking system, petroleum, pharmeceuticals and food production, and all mainstream media (basically the "whole enchillada"). In essense, organized religion is complicit in this web of the Illumniati with the possible exception of the Moslems (because of their intense dislike of Western Civilization), Hindus, Buddhists, Christian Scientists and Kaballistic Jews. And when we become factually accurate, even these religions have become somewhat tainted, deliberately or not!

The world banking system issues fiat currency, which is money that is backed by nothing of inherent value such as Gold or Silver. Essentially it is "VAPOR CURRENCY" technically known as "fractional currency" or "fiat". This includes Federal Reserve Notes which are not federal at all but issued by a private bank. If you doubt such, research "The Secrets of the Federal Reserve" by Eustace Mullins. Pre-prepare yourself to learn the starkly revealing truths that are inside of this book!

Then if you borrow this vapor currency from a bank they charge you interest—interest on something created from nothing. Basically TEHNC ("The Emperor has no clothes"), as it were! This monetary scheme is effectively usurious, patently unethical, fraudulent and stated as such in "The Torah" and "The Bible"! CERTAINLY, THIS IS A PONZI SCHEME OF ALMOST UNCOMPREHENSIBLE PROPORTIONS WHICH MAKES BERNIE MADOFF LOOK INEPT AND INSIGNIFICANT, by comparison! And now we can really view just how disfunctional such currency is as Greece, Italy, Spain, Portugal, Ireland, Great Britain, Japan and yes, the USA are in various stages of the process of FINANCIAL MELTDOWN! Essentially, every country on the planet could face this scenario very shortly!

INEVITABLY, ANY CURRENCY THAT IS NOT BACKED BY SOMETHING PERCEIVED AS HAVING INHERENT VALUE, WILL CRASH—the only question is when it will occur! For a better overall perspective of economic function, refer to "The Objectivist Journal", edited by Craig Biddle, "The American Free Press" and "The Barnes Review"!

We are charged exorbitant rates for gasoline and other energy products and told this is necessary because there is a shortage of crude oil because the author guesses not enough Dinosaurs died to make adequate amounts of petroleum (another big myth). The real truth is that crude oil is created through an abiotic process not dependent on Dinosaurs and THERE IS MORE THAN ENOUGH OIL FOR AT LEAST ONE HUNDRED YEARS IN THE USA ALONE. But even worse than this is that we could completely eliminate the need for crude oil, which is higly polluting, and have all of our power needs supplied cheaply and cleanly by hydrogen fuel cells, cold fusion and "Tesla technology" and even something as lowly as clean burning alcohol! THIS CAN BE ACHIEVED NOW—NOT HOPEFULLY IN THE FUTURE! But this upsets the vested interests in petroleum by the Illuminati cult, most notably BP, Royal Dutch Shell, Standard Oil and Exxon-Mobil so it is stifled and/or crushed and/or propagandized as impractical, technologically impossible and too expensive! Malodorous flatulence? The stench of this pervades all of these mistruths!

Most pharmceutical drugs have some to a lot of toxicity and are an iatrogenic nightmare (many detrimental side effects). If you find this statement incredulous, check the "Physicians Desk Refereence" and CHECK ANY DRUG THEREIN AND THE TRUTH OF THIS STATEMENT WILL BECOME SELF EVIDENT. Additionally, the VACCINES which you are told must be injected into your children or yourselves HAVE INDUSTRIAL TOXINS, FORMALDEHYDE and THIRMICIL (MERCURY). NONE OF THESE ARE NUTRITIONALLY NECESSARY OR OPTIMAL NUTRIENTS, at least the last time the author researched this topic—actually quite the contrary! Again, if you have doubts or resistance to this, you can quickly Google such information from the Internet or access back issues of "The American Free Press"!

It cannot be denied that there seems to be a "time and a place" for Allopathic drugs but we might be better served having pharmacists formulate herbal remedies and homeopathic medicines. As for vaccines, at least in the way they are produced now, the sooner they are abolished, the better will our health will be unless you consider, as just one example, that Autism is a beneficial thing to live with!

Conversly, ER surgeons do an amazing job of refabricating people with truamatic injuries! Viewing the allopathic medical system that we have in place, it appears it purpose is foster sickness and disease through conscious and subconscious assertions that your body and mind will deteriorate/degnerate but "we can cure you with our medicines and surgeries". This is disingeneous and diabolical considering that our demise or disintegration of our body is a state of consciousness that is being created in our minds through constant reinforcement by "medical experts" and advertisements for medicine from pharmeceutical companies that will "cure us"! The author can only say that this is NVL (not very likely)!!!! As you read this book, you will se why!

Through "The Codex Ailementarus", the Illuminati is trying to outlaw herbal and homeopathic medicines throughout the world in favor to their iatrogenic nightmare medicines (this is actually occurring in Europe right now!) This is undoubtedly the worst way to heal maladies. THESE ALLOPATHIC DRUGS ARE EFFECTIVE ONLY BECAUSE OF THE MASS BELIEF THAT THEY ARE BENEFICIAL! Again, Dr. Newton is not trying to have them abolished since all people should have access to the medicines they desire. Just be sure you are aware of all of the consequences related to ALLOPATHIC DRUGS BECAUSE THEY ARE GENERALLY TOXIC AND OFTENTIMES AT A LOW DOSAGE! This can be quickly gleaned from "The Physicians Desk Reference". YOU WILL BE AMAZED AT WHAT YOU FIND THEREIN! There are usually ten or more side effects related to almost any listed drug! What makes the side effect is some poison or toxin to which the body is reacting because essential buffering compounds have to be removed in order to patent an allopathic drug, which is the synthesis of only one component from a total mix of ingredients!

So the GOAL OF THE ILLUMINATI CULT, through their direct or indirect control of the pharmeceutical companies, IS TO CONVINCE US WE ARE SICK AND DEGENERATING, even with subliminal pictures in the drug advertisements. Then they SELL US THEIR TOXIC MEDICINES for OBSCENE EXPENSIVE PRICES!!!! This is truly a disingenious fraudulent scheme! Why do the mainstream media ignore this? Well, they make a lot of money airing drug commercials and,by the way, THE ILLUMINATI CULT CONTROLS THE MAINSTREAM MEDIA!!!!

Just one rather glaring example of DRUG FRAUD or misuse is that cholesterol lowering drugs can and do trigger dementia, Parkinson's disease and Alzheimer's disease!!!! Considering the alternatives, the author would prefer high cholesterol to mental degernation under any and all circumstances!!!! So you get rid of one supposed problem, that of high colesterol and in exchange you will be given least three other problems. Does this sound like a zero sum game? Eventually, Dr. Newton is certain that it will be shown that high colesterol will be known as a very little problem health problem or no problem at all!!!! When this will be accepted, the author cannot say with a certainy but that it will occur is just a matter of human discovery until this becomes a self evident reality—BUT ONLY AFTER THE DRUG COMPANIES HAVE MADE OBSCENE PROFITS FROM THEIR SCIENTIFICALLY FRAUDULENT MEDICINES!!!! Another example of drug fraud is discussed in Chapter Two regarding Cancer and Oncology protocols. To the uninformed, this will be starkly revealing!

Through Monsanto's Pioneer Seeds, the Illuninati cult has decided to re-engineer foods genetically even though the Creator already created them perfectly. In the process of recreating these foods, so that they could be sprayed with Monsanto's Roundup herbicide to kill weeds without killing vegetables and grains, the seeds were genetically modified and they are patented. The problem with this is that you cannot save seeds from your harvest to use for your succeeding crop for the next planting because of patent infringement. So if you switch to genetically modified (G.M.) seeds, you must buy them from Pioneer seeds every year. Can you say MONOPOLY? Does DIABOLICAL apply? PVL (probably very likely)!!!!

This happened in much of Africa when the seeds were offered in many areas for a very cheap price but within a period of several years the seeds increased about tenfold in price, as has been reported in "The American Free Press"! Additionally, G.M. foods have NEVER BEEN TESTED ON HUMANS to profile their effect on us. Currently Soy, Corn, Alfalfa, Rice and other grains have been modified. Soy, touted as a healtful food is nothing such but rather assaults the Thyroid gland and produces too much estrogen which feminizes men and causes cancer in women and even men!

Also, the Illuminati cult constantly foments wars and, civil wars to make obscene amounts of money selling armaments and things related thereto. You may querry, Dr. Newton, you must be kidding—how do you know this? Well the author knows this because "The American Free Press" closely monitors the diabolical Illuminati cult and they just discovered, through confidential contacts, that they were calling for a large war in the Middle East at their June 2011 meeting in Switzerland. It is also known there is a xenophobic desire to attack Iran because it is "dangerous". The irony/hypocrisy with this is that the Illuminati cult is vastly more dangerous than any purported "enemy" which they identify as "radical fringe" or "dangerous terrorists"!

Additionally, they instigated the wars in Iraq, Afganistan and Libya with propoganda and "reputed facts" that had no relation to even a delusional reality let alone a real factuality. Sadam Hussein did not have a nuclear program of any significance nor did he have any significant amounts of biological and nerve gas agents and those he did have he received from the USA, through the efforts of Donald Rumsfeld. Beyond this, Afganistan has never been conquered in our recorded history. Alexander the Great, the British military at its zenith and the Russian military machine at its apex ALL WERE SUMMARILY DEFEATED IGNONOMOUSLY IN AFGANISTAN! And there were very few Al Queda operatives in Afghanistan but there are many in Pakistan!

In addition to this, the Illuminati cult is heavily invovlved in munitions and the production of war munitions. This is why they are always fomenting wars and civil wars. WHAT BETTER WAY TO SELL YOUR WEAPONS THROUGHOUT THE WORLD THAN BY INSTIGATING CONFLICTS? DYT (Do you think)? It seems the Illuminati is oblivious to the karmic consequences of their actions!

The Illuninati cult in conjunction with the world's governments and many organized religions are GREEDY, DISINFORMATIVE, CO-DEPENDENT and DO NOT CARE ABOUT YOU EVEN THOUGH THEY VEHEMENTLY CLAIM OTHERWISE. If these religions did have our best interests foremost, would we not be living in an actual "Paradise" as our Creator intended, irrespective of the actions of Adam and Eve, as John Milton described in "Paradise Lost"? Or at the least, would we not have a more even distribution of wealth throughout this country and throughout the world?

Whatever you are told by your government or the Illuminati cult or their tentacle organizations and groups listed above or our organized religions (Christian Science, Kabbalistic Judaism, Buddhism, and Hinduism being the exceptions), the DIAMETRIC OPPOSITE IS TRUE! These governments operate sophisticated propaganda machines that would make Adolph Hitler even envious. Once you come to this realization, you can throw off the shackles they use to bind us through illusions and distortions! PLEASE NOTE, as was stated previously, THAT THEY NEVER REFUTE A POSITION OF SO CALLED "CONPIRACY THEORIES"—RATHER THEY ATTEMPT TO ATTACK AND DISCREDIT AND DIMINISH THE PEOPLE PRESENTING THESE "THEORIES" WHICH MORE OFTEN THAN NOT ARE CONSPIRACY REALITY! So why let disingenious people bambuzole us over and over again with specious arguments? Being swayed by gross untruths, gossip and inuendo play nicely into the "hands" of the Illuminati cult. So knowing this allows us to extricate ourselves from being bamboozuled by their propoganda, which admittedly, is almost incessant!

JESUS SAID THAT IF YOU SEEK THE TRUTH, THAT IT WILL MAKE YOU FREE! Every Christian Scientist knows this statement as should you. In Kabbalistic Judaism, within "The 72 Names of God" from the book of Exodus 14, verses 19-21 the following names would correspond with those of Jesus: #23 which is "Mem Daled Hey" (sharing the Wisdom); #26 which is "Hey Aleph Aleph" (order from chaos); #37 which is "Aleph Nun Yod" (seeing the big picture); and #59 which is Hey Resh Chet" (connecting to the Light [which is God]).

The Illuminati, the governments and the organized religions have fooled us into believing they are God or Godlike. HOWEVER, THEIR ACTIONS BESPEAK OTHERWISE. In "Thirmunduram", by Kriya Yoga Siddha and MahaAvatar known as Thirumoolar, he states, "There is but one God and Nandi is his name." Nandi in Yoga and Hinduism is associated our God and Creator. Nowhere does it say that the Illuminati, the world's governments or organized religion are God even though they present themselves as such through their words, actions, unconstitutional laws ("The Patriot Act") and arbitrary/freedom robbing decrees such as Presidential Executive Orders (War Powers Acts)!

Dr. Newton will descend from his "soap box"/pulpit now and tell you that you CAN DISSOLVE THE "SHACKLES" OF THE POWERFUL ELITE be they private (the Illuminati cult) or governmental or eccleseastical/theological. THE AUTHOR IS NOT TRYING TO SCARE OR DEPRESS YOU BUT RATHER TO DESCRIBE OUR PREDICAMENT AND A WAY IN WHICH WE EXTRICATE OURSELVES AND RECLAIM OUR PERFECT STATE OF CONSCIOUSNESS known as "ALEPH KAF ALEPH", the seventh name of God from the Kabbalistic "72 Names of God". While you may consider that the Creator's perfect creation is a delusional figment of the author's imagination, it is proveable from ancient extraterretial information, the Bible and Torah (much of which could have been related by demi-god/extra-terrestials), The Vedas, Kriya Yoga and physics, quantum physics and mechanics and plasma physics and particle physics. These things indicate that the author is far from being incorrect or hallucinating.

Actually, **IT IS MORE THAN POSSIBLE THAT SOMEONE ACCUSED OF DELUSIONS OR HALUCINATION CAN BE FOR MORE BASED IN VERIFIABLE TRUTH THAN THE DISFUNCTIONAL AND DIABOLICAL NOTIONS OF MOST RELIGIONS, GOVERNMENTS AND THE PRIVATE SHADOW GOVERNMENT (ILLUMINATI CULT)!!!!**

Dr. Newton knows, from personal experience when he first encountered this information of betrayal on all levels on our planet, Earth, that it is very unsettling to be told that your government, religion and puppet/shadow government (Illuminati cult) HAVE BETRAYED YOU! Again, Jesus told us THAT IF WE SOUGHT THE TRUTH, IT WOULD MAKE US FREE! It will be said once again, every Christian Scientist knows this statement and for good reason as it gives you the STANDARD FOR LIVING YOUR LIFE! We must pull our heads from our ostrich holes before it is too late and we are destroyed by our unwitting and/or willing ignorance!! By this course of action, we will bring things back to their intended perfect state!!!!

ALL IT REQUIRES IS AN UNMASKING OF THE CULPRITS (Illuminatu cult, unenlightened religions, co-dependent governments), A REPROGRAMMING OF YOUR SUBCONSCIOUS MIND (our personal, personal computer) that results in ESTABLISHING OUR CONSCIOUSNESS AT THE LEVEL OF THETA. SO LET US BEGIN THAT PROCESS OF EXTRICATING OURSELVES FROM THE MOUNTAIN OF MANURE WHICH HAS SPEWED FORTH FROM THE MOUTHS OF THE ABOVE MENTIONED OFFENDERS!! Actually, this process has already begun, although it may not be evident at this time. TIWTDC (This is way to damn cool) BECAUSE RELIEF IS ON THE WAY!!!!

In the "Emerald Tablets" of Hermes Trimigestis he implores us to LIFT OURSELVES FROM A STATE OF OBSCURITY. IF WE DO THIS OUR FREEDOM WILL BEGIN! Otherwise, our enslavement will continue. In Dr. Newton's first book, "Pathways to God", he stated that if you take one step toward God, God will take a hundred steps toward you!" Kriya Yoga Siddha, Thirumoolar says in "Thirumandiram" the following, in regard to this concept:

"22. Seek Him, He Seeks You
The Lord of Maya-world that has its rise in the mind,
He, knows yet all our thoughts but we do not think of Him;
Some be who groan, 'God is not favourable to me;'
But, sure, God seeks those who seek their soul to save."

In "The Book of Tokens" in the "Meditation on Tsaddi", Paul Foster Case give us the following about God which is paraphrased by Dr. Newton because of "reservations" by B.O.T.A. about allowing this to be copied but you can check the exact translation online:

Men believe that they are seeking God,
But God is actually looking for them.
God is the seeker of seeker's,

And when he finds us,
All our questioning is ended.
The fish takes the hook,
Believing that there is food to find,
But actually, the fisherman will have the fish as his meal.

PLEASE READ THE LITERAL TRANSLATION OF THIS BY 'GOGGLING' "THE BOOK OF TOKENS" AND THE "MEDITATION ON TSADDI".

Mary Baker Eddy in "Science and Health With Key to the Scriptures" says something similar when she states in her chapter on prayer that GOD ALREADY KNOWS WHAT WE NEED BEFORE WE ASK! Thirumoolar says essentially the same thing as Dr. Newton but more eloquently and many millenia before his first book, "Pathways to God". Mary Baker Eddy and Paul Foster Case are also more eloquent than the author and were so many decades before. LET THIS, THEN, BE SO! GET READY TO SOAR AS THIS BOOK WILL SURELY ALLOW YOU TO DO! You have "purchased" a ticket to ThetaLand, the land of your Creator and it is the best "ride" in the "amusement park" of life! Enjoy the "trip", as it were!

About the Author of this Book

Dr. Robert Newton, J.D., N.D., born on October 31, 1946, was obsessed about the nature of God since about 1951. Having been exposed to the Baptist Church in his earliest years, he found nothing that would "quench" his "thirst" in his pursuit of God. Instead, he just learned about so-called "guilty sinners" who needed to avoid hell! He later attended a Mehodist Church and some of his "thirst" God knowledge was quenched. However, in 1962, a lifelong friend of his mother, Reba Lawler, suggested that he attend a Christian Science Sunday School in Pomona, California. Immediately, upon his attendance there, his "thirst" of knowledge for God was quenched like never before with help from his teacher, John Alfred Clark, who was like a surrogate father to him. Dr. Newton experienced many spiritual/metaphysical healings of himself and was amazed by the power of Christian Science and the radical truths contained in "Science and Health with Key to the Scriptures", by Mary Baker Eddy. Until this time, he had never read such an amazing treatise, which relates the Science of Christianity

Dr. Newton grew up in Pomona, California, in this incarnation and graduated with honors from Garey High School in 1964. He lettered in most sports except football. He achieved the rank of Eagle Scout in 1961. He attended Mt. San Antonio Community College for two years and graduated from California State University at Fullerton in 1968 and was on the Dean's list. His degree was a B.A. in Speech and English with specialized courses in semantics, linguistics, syllogistic logic, rhetoric, creative writing and propoganda. He was a member of the intercollegiate debate team at CSUF.

Dr. Newton attended Western State College of Law and graduated from American College of Law in 1975 with a Juris Doctorate degree. He worked at the "Legal Aid Society of Orange County" for about a year. He served in the California National Guard from 1969 to 1975 and was discharged honorably. He worked as a Christian Science healer (not a journal lsited practitioner) until 1982. Dr. Newton received his California Landscape Contractor's license in 1975, and was designing and installing landscapes beginning in 1972. He won several awards for landscape design and installation from California Landscape Contractor's Association (CLCA) from 1975-1984. He was also an officer for two years in CLCA.

Dr. Newton spent a lot of time surfing, riding dirt motorcycles and skiing. In 1982, he was "T-boned" by another dirt motrocycle rider which severly injured his head, throat and basically his entire body. He went to a psychic who perceived that he was in a very bad motorcycle accident. She told him that he should be in a hospital because he was severly injured. Instead of a hospital, Dr. Newton employed his knowledge of Christian Science to heal himself with the aid of a Christian Science practitioner within several days!

However, after this accident which shook him up even more emotionally than physically, Dr. Newton began to explore metaphysical disciplines other than Christian Science. He studied various psychic and Theosophical disciplines at Psynetics. He studied and practiced Buddhism for several years.

In 1982 Dr. Newton studied at the "Tibetan Foundation" based on the books of Alice Bailey, a noted person from the discipline of Theosophy. In the Tibetan Foundation, he took many classes in the metaphysical sciences and he became a "Certified Channel" of the psychic dimensions/realms. Dr. Newton "channeled"/connected with entities from other dimensions in public in Southern and Central California.

Also in 1982, Dr. Newton undertook training in Tai Chi Chuan and became very proficient in attracting and dispensing large amounts (Chi/ Prana/life force/ electromagnetic energy). This was utilized in energizing and healing himself and other people. From Tai Chi Chuan, Dr. Newton started to actually feel the presence of the Creator through the energy dispensed from this discipline.

In 1984, Dr. Newton went to Egypt with Robert (Chuck) and Mary Schwartz and Robert Mueller, et. al., and had an intense "out of body" experience meditating inside the sarcophogus in the "King's Chamber" of the "Great Pyramid of Cheops". He actually entered a deep state of Samadhi, although he knew nothing of Samadhi from this incarnation. Doc also was spontaneiously experiencing past lifetimes while walking through the "Temple of Luxor" where he apparently was a priest at least several times. He was able to perceive and identify parts of the temple which did not exist any longer but were verified as existing from various Egyptian texts. The Prana/Chi/life force Dr. Newton felt most strongly in Egypt was inside the Pyramid of Cheops in the King's Chamber and in the temples in Luxor.

In 1987 Dr. Newton went to the Yucatan Peninsula for the "Harmonic Convergence" as detailed in Jose Arguelles books. There he mediatated in the various temples and pyramids of the Mayas in Chichen Itza, Playa Azul, Palenque and Uxmal, finding the most Prana in the Pyramid of the Sun in Palenque.

In 1988, Dr. Newton moved to Virginia and operated an organic farm as well as landscape design and installation company. He engaged in studies with the International Hermetic Order of Ascelpiads and its Heirophant, Dr. David DeLorea. He attained the level of third degree of the Ascelpiads and opened an Asklepion Temple in Rixeyville, Virginia. At the Asklepion, Doc taught classes in healing in conformance with the teachings of Asclepias, the greatest of Greek and European healers in his ancient time. The classes invovled healing with herbs, with lucid daydreaming and subliminal message tapes.

Classes were also taught in Quartz crystal and gemstone energetics and Pyramid dynamics. These classes were directed at increasing Chi/Prana/life force in order to reach higher levels of consciousness/spirituality and to facilitate physical and emotional healing. Other classes focused on dowsing to measure human "energy fields" and locating geomantic features such as magnetic leylines and electromagnetic vortexes. In these vortexes, class participants experienced higher levels of energy, "oneness" with their Creator and physical healings.

After exposure to the works of Roy Burdett and the book, "Treat Yourself: by Dr. Jack Prince, Dr. Newton also began teaching classes in magnetic healing in conjuction with the Voll Accupuncture System. These classes were taught at the Askelpion and along the East Coast USA.

While with the Asclepiads, Dr. Newton corresponded with Dr. Henry Smialek, who among other things, exposed him the "Gayatri Mantra", which was taught to Henry by Sri Satchi Sai Baba, a Hindu MahaAvatar. After reciting thousands of repetitions of the "Gayatri Mantra", Doc was beginning to understand the chapter on prayer in "Science and Health with Key to the Scriptures" by Mary Baker Eddy. Basically, Mrs. Eddy exhorts us to "pray without ceasing" and that is what a mantra allows you to do, even as you are working, throughout the day!

In 1990, Dr. Newton wrote his book, "Pathways to God". This book dealt with crystal and pyramid energetics as a way to actually feel the "energies of God" and validate the existence of our Creator. The book also deals with mantras, toning, Tai Chi and other techniques which validate the ACTUAL EXISTENCE OF GOD.

In 1991, Dr. Newton received his doctorate in Naturopathic Medicine (Natural Medicine) from Clayton School of Natural Healing. The modalities involved in his studies included Herbology, Homeopathy, Reflexology, Accupressure, Massage, and Nutrition.

Also in 1991, Dr. Newton moved back to Southern California and studied "Sound Signature" technology with Sharry Edwards and became a certified practitioner therof. This is a healing system using sound waves from the Diatonic Scale but at the subwhoofer level. At about the same time, Dr. Newton began to study the field of "Sympathetic Vibratory Physics" based on the ground breaking work of James Keeley, a musician, who used sound to heal and to create "perpetual motion" machines.

In 1992, Dr. Newton was studying with Dr. Jesse Partridege about new techniques in magnetic healing and natural health therapies. Also at about the same, Doc was studying Dr. Samuel West's book, "The Golden Seven Plus One", invovlving Lymphology and Manual Lymph Drainage based on a system of removing blocked blood lymph to heal and detoxify the body.

In 1994, Dr. Newton was initiated into Kriya Yoga by Yogi Marshall Govindan Satchidanada. This involved Asanas (stretching exercises), Kriya Dhyana meditation and Kriya Kundalini Pranayam (a structured, energizing breathing protocol). He also completed second and third level Kriya Yoga initiation and received many initiated Sanskrit mantras (repetitive prayers). At the third level initiation Doc learned the breathless practice of Samadhi and more initiated Sanskrit mantras.

In 2001, Dr. Newton was initiated into the first level Reiki healing technique and experimented with this healing protocol. In 2002, Doc was exposed to a truly monumental text, "The True History and Religion of India" by Swami Saraswati. This book traced the civilized origins of India back to 1.9 billion years on an unborken line due to its favorable geographic position on the Earth. This book was based upon ancient Indian scripture, includes "The Vedas" and "The Upanishads".

In 2006, Dr. Newton heard Richard Hoagland in several seminars speak about the 12-21-2012 cosmic cycle and was fascinated by Hoagland's exhaustive documentation at the Whole Conscious Expo in Los Angeles. In

2008, Doc was again impressed by Hoagland's very detailed explanations of 2012, the Apollo Mission to the Moon and what was brought back therefrom, and additional discoveries of civilization on Mars and our Moon.

In 2008, Dr. Newton received a certificate in "Theta Healing" based on the work of Vianna Stibal. He has found that this technique greatly accerates all types of healing work and spiritual mind programming systems. Theta techniques also make the concepts from "The Secret" much more effective!

Authors and persons and books who have influenced Dr. Newton include Bruce Cathie's "The Bridge to Infinity", various writings of Rudloph Steiner and Nikola Tesla as well as Neem Karoli Baba, Sri Satchi Sai Baba, Paramahansa Yogananda of "The Self Realization Fellowship", Sri Aurobindo, Babaji Nagaraj (the acknowledged leader of Kriya Yoga), Yogi Marshall Govindan Satchiananda of "Babaji's Kriya Yoga", Dr. J.J. Hurtak, author of "The Keys of Enoch" and Mary Baker Eddy founder of Christian Science and writer of "Science and Health with Key to the Scriptures". Also, Dr. Newton has been strongly influenced by "The Yoga Sutras", by Patanjali, "The Bhagavad Gita", "The Vedas" and the "The Upanashads", "Thirumanduam", by Thirumoolar, "The Emerald Tablets" of Hermes Trismegistus, and various "Builders of the Adytum" teachings, including "The Patterns of the Trestleboard: The Truth About Self".

Dr. Newton has also found value in the book, "The Secret" which is infinitly more effective when combined with "Theta Programming" and "Theta Concsiousness Programming". Also, he highly recommends the "AIM" program of healing fequencies discovered by Dr. Steven Lewis. This works with a radionics protocol.

In 2010, Dr. Newton was certified in "Light Speed Learning" taught by Thomas and Jane Morton. This involves ABSORBING INFORMATION FROM BOOKS, ETC. at the SUBCONSCIOUS LEVEL OF

LEARNING. This light speed technique allows you to absorb the contents of a book in several minutes.

In 2011, Doc began teaching classes about the physics of the light body and Theta consciousness and completed this book. His activities include surfing, snowboarding, jet skiing, wake boarding, riding dirt motorcycles, hiking, golfing, performing tremdendous amounts of Kriya Kundalini Pranayam and spending large spans of time in Samadhi, even during daily acitivies.

Aknowledgements

(giving thanks for those who taught, nutured and shared with the author):

The author expresses gratitude to most of his teachers throughout his educational history and to the other people listed in this book!

Miss Anne Juhl was my ninth grade English and history teacher. She demanded excellence and taught me the concepts of English composition and Greek and Roman mythology which I have found is not really myth but more akin to actuality!

John Clark was like a surrogate father to me. He was my Christian Science Sunday School teacher and taught me the basics and advanced concepts of the science of Christianity. He really added stability and spiritual structure in my life when I was very vulnerable and confused as a teenager! I could NEVER THANK YOU ENOUGH! YOU WERE ALWAYS "THERE" FOR ME! You are a very advanced spiritual being! Without you I could have fallen off of an "emotional cliff"! This is a certitude beyond any doubt!

Reba Lawler was my mother's best friend for many years, an advanced being as can be observed by the way she lives her life and a ChristianScientist on a level of understanding where few reside and undboutedly "lives from her heart" AND FOR THIS SHE BLOWS ME AWAY! Tremendous amounts of light radiate from her body! By her "works" and her "light" I know her! She was instrumental in my being "linked" to John Clark, listed just above.

Alfred Noyes, my high school social studies teacher, taught me to "think outside of the box" and encourage my pursuit thereof! I did not always agree with you but in retrospect, you knew more about things at that time than I did!

Dr. Harry Heyboyer taught me to be discriminating about the rampant revisionist history (fantasy history) in our history books.

Dr. Pitkin taught me the concepts of advanced English composition at California State University at Fullerton, California (CSUF). He was very determined to make me a better writer and he surely eventually succeded.

Dr. George Enell was one of my rhetoric teachers at CSUF and was instrumental in making me a better public speaker and really stretched me intellectually. You could never slide "half baked" ideas by Dr. Enell! He certainly was a great orator, as he had full command of the English language!

Dr. Young my oral interpretation teacher at CSUF made me a better presenter of literature and drama and challenged me to think "outside of the box".He challenged me to strive for excellence!

John Klein was one of my bosses in the grocery industry. He was not well educated. However, he knew how to work and think efficiently and demanded that I learn the same. His approach to work was creative and definitely beyond his peers—actually he did not have any peers in the grocery industry in that he always took underperforming grocery stores and made them profitable—without exception, which proves anecdotally that you do not need to be highly educated "schoolwise" to have great "mental powers" and insight!

Robert "Chuck" Schwartz was my first meditation teacher and instructor in metaphysics, crystal and gemstone energetics and Eygptology. I really learned a higher level of understanding about the symbolic nature of Egyptian Hieroglyphics from him! Our trip to Egypt was really a "trip" as it were!

Robert Mueller gave the author many insights into spirituality and sexuality and is a "deep tissue" massage therapist, par excellance! He was also the first person to relate to me the existence of the so-called "Iluminati".

Major Virgil (Postie) Armstrong taught me about extraterrestial beings and the many levels of reality which exist concurrently in the same space! He really stretched my belief system at that time and I am glad he did! He also detected the divinity within myself which other poeple were too terrified to consider! Thank you cubed, for your belief in me!!!!!!!!!

Dr. Paul Spin was an USAF psychologist who I met in the "Tibetan Foundation". He also added content to my metaphyscial understanding and to my knowledge of the Creator. Dr. Spin "pissed off" a lot of people because they were terrified by his understanding of things which other people could not perceive or believe or look at!

Dr. David DeLoria, Hierophant of the Ancient Order of Asclepiads, strectched my understanding of many things and conferred upon me the "Third order of the Ascelpiads". Your directing me to buy the books on Asclepias and Appollonius was a prescient move on your part. I learned a lot of "truth" and it made me freer and more informed!

Dr. Henry Smialek, is a wholistic dentist and fellow Asclepiad, who introduced me to the "mother of all mantras", "The Gayatri Mantra" as desiminated by Satguru and MahaAvatar Sri Satchi Sai Baba. He helped me understand pyramid energetics more fully and I really enjoyed his counsel!

Yogi Marshall Govindan Satchianada, The Kriya Yogi who heads "Babaji's Kriya Yoga", taught me Kriya Yoga levels I-III and taught me well in Kriya

Asanas, Kriya Dhyana Meditation, Kriya Kundalini Pranayam, Samadhii, and taught me many powerful Sanskrit mantras. The knowledge and practices you conveyed to me are priceless and invaluable! He can be reached at "Babaji's Kriya Yoga. net" via the internet.

Charlette Newton Smith was my first and is my third wife. With very little formal education, she is not only extremely intelligent but has an understanding of the spiritual realms equalled by very few individuals. She is a Kriya Yoga Yogini not only conversant in this discipline but an assiduous practitioner thereof. She emanated from the Angelic realms and is woefully underappreciated for which humanity should surely be ashamed!

Parvatti, AKA Pamela Thomas, a Kriya Yoga Yogini, being in your presence made the assimilation of Kriya Yoga more easily facilitated and in blessed me! She has prescient astrological insights!

Patrice Rybicki was my girlfriend between my first and second marriages. Truly a person who operates fundamentally "from her heart" and also in touch with the Angelic beings! She gave me feedback on my first book, "Pathways to God".

Linda Joy Rose, author of "Your Mind:The Users Manual", which gave the author insights and perspective about hypnosis.

My deceased father, Charles Marvin Newton, was basically "braindead" to the spiritual dimensions. He did, however, instill an intense "work ethic" in me as well as demanding excellence in all of my pursuits and nurturing tenacity in me! He was also an inventor and a senior computer billing programmer.

My Mother, Nadine Newton Feldheim, prodded me into excellence and was a tenacious defender of me and my abilities. She exposed me to the realms of art, music and dance. She encouraged me to explore many things!

Cindy Cardenas was instrumental in exposing me to the "72 Names of God" from Exodus," The Emerald Tablets" of Hermes Trismegistus and "ThePatterns on the Trestleboard: The Truth About Self", by Paul foster Case. These things have really embellished my book and my classes! I am much indebted to you! You made this book vastly easier to write and have given it a greater "depth" than I would have ever anticipated!

Thomas and Jane Morton taught Doc "Light Speed Learning", the ability to absorb books and information at the Theta level of subconsiousness. There are few better people on this Earth and you would be blessed to meet and study with them as I did. They truly understand the "big picture" which I will be revealing to you in the following pages. Also, after taking their "Light Speed Learning" seminar I was in a state of perpetual bliss/euphoria for an entire month! Thank you also for helping me to realize that there are really are "Akashic records" of past and present events and knowledge. You made the composing of this book immensely easier! They are available at "Light Speed Learning.com"

Mary Baker Eddy, the most amazing and accomplished person and healer, man or woman, who has existed on Earth in the last 2000 years. Her quest for the truth about Christianity and the science therein was relentless and highly detailed. She is the author of "Science and Health With Key to the Scriptures" and the founder of the First Church of Christ Scientist in Boston, Massachusetts. She is the seminal person in the field of Christian scientific metaphysics! She raised people from the "dead"! By her great works and writings, we know her. READ HER BOOK!!!! Certainly her book made this book possible!

Amachi, or Ama "hands down" the most loving presence I have everencountered on Earth, extremely charitable and also a great healer. Truly the greatest Indian "holy woman"/Avatar but she would never admit to such! Her childhood was the worst imaginable and yet she never resented this and transcended her situation! By her works you know her greatness and you feel it in her presence!

Satchi Sai Baba, a loving and charitable Maha Avatar and SatGuru, was responsible in disseminating "The Gayatri Mantra" (a very powerful prayer), manifested objects from the atomic field and will soon return to us in his mission to make us better people! Truly the greatest Indian "holy man" but he would never admit to such either! By his works he is known to multi-millions of people around the world!

Siddha Babaji Nagaraj, Satguru and MahaAvatar, is the active head of Kriya yoga on Earth, attained Soruba Samadhii almost two thousand years ago—yes 2000 years ago. He has been in the same body for about 2000 years! He works relentlessly on the "inner planes" (spiritual dimensions) to lift humanity into their template of perfection! He works constantly to bring Kriya Yoga consciousness to humanity! His devotion to uplifting humanity to its perfect state cannot be underestimated and from our perspective, impossible to comprehend!

Sri Yogi S.A.A. Ramaiah, taught the author's teacher, Marshall Govindan Satchidananda, the whole discipline of Kriya Kundalini Yoga. Yogi Ramaiah was directly instructed by Babaji Nagaraj, who is entrusted with dispensing the knowledge of Kriya Yoga throughout the world!

Siddha Thirumoolar, Kriya Yoga Satguru and MahaAvatar is the author of "Thirmanduram" which is a classic Yogic and Hindu text at the highest level and a "remote" teacher of the author!

Siddha Patanjali, Kriya Yoga Satguru and MahaAvatar, is the author of "The Yoga Sutras" which were an essential text in the creation of this book!

Krishna or Krishn is the Son of Vishnu involved in "The Mahabarata" and the subject of "The Bhagavad Gita" which are both classic Yogic and Hindu texts beyond the highest level and he is a recent "remote" teacher of the author!

Goswami Kriyananda, author of "The Spiritual Science of Kriya Yoga", has been very useful in giving the author information and perspective for this book!

Nogababa, an enligthend being, has been in the same body for over 700 years living at over 16000 feet of elevation! This is a feat of immense proportions in and of itself! Most people cannot even be at this elevation without Oxygen supplementation, let alone live continually at this altitude!

ArchAngel Michael is an aspect of the Sun and provides protection for all who invoke his name!!!!

Dr. Samuel West, wrote the "Golden Seven Plus One", about "manual lymph drainage" and using Prana (light) to heal. Truly, I learned to heal borken bones using your light technique. You are truly under-recognized and under-appreciated, but certainly not by the author of this book!

Paul Foster Case, whose revelation of the BUILDER OF THE ADYTUM materials available from the same, has blessed us with the compilation of "The Patterns on the Trestleboard: the Truth About Self". Also, he reintroduced humanity to "The Emerald Tablets of Hermes Trismegistus" and has blessed us greatly by doing so. You are so amazing—I would have really enjoyed studying with you! Truly you are an extremely evolved soul! You will be enriched by studying his group's materials!

Zecharia Sitchin for intensive research about the extra-terrestrial tablets found in Sumer (an ancient city in Iraq) detailed in his books. This is just one of the sources that reveal to us that space aliens have interacted with us in a major way and have affected events that have transpired on our planet such as the magnificant ancient architectural buildings and temples and pyramids. Sitchin is the source that writes about "Planet 'X'" AKA known as "Mardock" AKA "Nibiru".

The Kabbalah Center for bringing the "72 Names of God" to the attention of the general public. How greatly we have been blessed by the Berg family for upraising our consciousness! These names are truly the "hidden jewel" of the Bible/Torah and are without equal therein! Your life would be enriched by studying their publications! The author is aware that there seem to be some financial irregularities within this group and the he does not condone such. Nevertheless, the information in the names of God are an invaluable source from which we re-establish our perfect world!

Hermes Trismigestis, an Avatar—a teacher among teachers—An extraterrestial who revealed to us "The Emerald Tablet of Hermes Trismegistus". He greatly aided in the building of the vaunted classic Greek culture. He was likewise instrumental building the classic Egyptian culture at its zenith. He was known as Thoth in Egypt and my teacher on Eyptology, Robert (Chuck) Schwartz, used to always extol his contribution to the Eyptian spiritual traditions! Dr. Hurtak, in "The Keys of Enoch", points out that Hermes and Thoth are also known as Enoch.

Enoch has given us a path to the "light body" as revealed in the "Keys of Enoch', by Dr. Hurtak and for that we have been blessed!

Asclepius, son of Apollo (generally considered mythological but more than likely an elightened extraterretrial being), was a legendary herbal healer who became a lucid daydreaming healer working at the Theta/Divine level of consciousness. Dr. Newton never thought he would follow directly in your footsteps! How interesting the way a life can change!

Julio Rivas, a Christian Science Practitioner, par excelance and who can explain Christian Science and God and God's qualities with a clarity unmatched by anyone that the author knows. Mr. Rivas has an aura above his head that can extend to two to three feet or rivaling that in the various pictures of Jesus the Christ. He is a spiritual healer at the highest level and the most evolved Christian I have ever encountered! He appears to be living in the Spiritual "Light Body" more than a physical body.

Mary Jane Heitzman, Christian Science Practitioner, you have been an awesome healer for decades and have pulled my wife back from the portal of death at least twice. We do not agree about everything—I know you will find this book problematic—but I respect your works!

Vianna Stibal is, a Registered Nurse, who was diagnosed with "uncurable" cancer and who had the practice of "Theta Healing" revealed to her. Truly she has blessed humanity through this revelation and has aided in the creation of this book.

Louise L. Hay wrote the book, "You Can Health Your Body", has aided me greatly by cataloguing the emotional causes of sickness, disease and problems we encounter. This was really necessary for me to experience because I was really in denial as how I was creating various kinds of sicknesses in my life. Thank you so much for your research and insight. You are very underappreciated by the general public! READ HER BOOK! Your book made this book possible, without a doubt! You are the pioneer in the field of "emotional healing"!!

Dr. J.J. Hurtak, is the author of the "Keys of Enoch", which is a revolutionary book involving the Kabballah, Spiritual Sciences, Physics and extraterrestrial beings. PROBABLY THE HARDEST BOOK TO READ THAT YOU WILL EVER ENCOUNTER BUT MORE THAN WORTH THE EFFORT! Certainly, Dr. Hurtak's book made this book possible!

Dr. Wayne Dyer has worked tirelessly to show people that their potential is unlimited! You have given me a better perspective on spiritual matters and life in general which are really one and the same thing!

Bruce Cathie, is the author of "The Bridge to Infinity" and "Beyond the Bridge to Infinity". These are stellar books involving Geomancy, Physics and Quantum Physics and Mechanics and the Spiritual Sciences. A MUST READ FOR ALL SEEKERSOF TRUTH WHO WISH TO "PUSH THE BOUDNARIES".! When I read your books it really validated many things I had been feeling!

Robert Temple, author of "The Sirius Mystery", has done tireless research regarding extra-terrestial interaction on Earth, from 5000 years ago. Truly, Temple has a must read book, as are the books of Sitchin!

Jane Roberts is the author of the "Seth" books including "Seth Speaks" and "The Nature of Personal Reality". She was truly a channel for knowledge and understanding, unlike many of today's "pop psychics". You should read at least one of her books to expand your consciousness!

Sir Issac Newton, was a great mathematician and scientist and biblical scholar who had great insight into action of particles, which we now know as atoms, even though he did not have an atomic collider or a Helium ion microscope! He must have accessed the "Akashic Records" to receive his insights!

Ervin Laszlo, who wrote and edited the book, "The Akashic Experience", you have helped in expected and unexpected ways in writing this book through your great understanding of the "Akashic Field"! A MUST READ BOOK!

Leo F. Ludzia, who srote the book, "Life Force", thank you for your insights on this subject, as it was useful in the composition of this book!

Roy Burdett, generously shared his knowledge of magnetic accupuncture with the author!

Dr. Jack Prince wrote the book "Treat Yourself" which also educated the author in magnetic accupuncture!

David Wilcock, author of "Source Field Investigation", truly a consciousness altering book based upon scientific principles.

Rudolph Steiner was more than conversant in education, Theosophy, science and the arts. Your insights prove that you are a "Renaissance Man" and had a great knowledge of Metaphysics!

Nikola Tesla, a scientist and thinker still vastly beyond his peers! This man truly understood Prana and how to harness it, unlike anybody else!

Albert Einstein had scientific insights that have enlightened us and his spiritual insights were powerfully simple!

John Keely, a musician and scientist, understood the power of music unlike any other human and who used this knowledge to create perpetual motion machines!

Dr. Frederick Bell was a NASA scientist who wrote the "Death of Ignorance" and it is certainly well worth your reading this text. Also, Dr. Bell is responsible for the company known as "Paradyne", which has created various Pyramid energy devices and technologies, that aid in entraining Alpha and Theta consciousness, allowing the the transcendence into other dimensions of existence.

Jeffrey Hoagland, creator of the company "Metaforms", has created useful Pyramid devices that also facilitate Alpha and Theta consciousness.

Max Planck, a "Manhattan Project" physicist, had an uncanny knowledge of the "atomic field" and gave perspective to the author regarding this!

Jay Lakhani, is a physicist who has acutally critically looked at the data accumulated in the various fields of physics and actually perceives the spirit/energy creation of the world and ourselves!!!! HE HAS ACQUIRED A "BREAKTHROUGH" PERSPECTIVE OF PHYSICS!

SatGuru Sivaya Subramuniyaswami, AKA Gurudeva, established the Kauai Hindu Monastery and "Hinduism Today", a true Avatar who can easily explain our inherent perfection. The author is most indebted to you for your clear insights into Divinity!!!!

Tim C. Leedom and Maria Murray, wrote the book, "The Book Your Church Doesn't Want You to Read" and was a useful source for the author.

Dr. Rocco Erico, co-pastor of the "Church of Daily Living, who has wirtten an English tranlation of "The Aramaic Bible"; Aramaic was the Hebrew Dialect of Jesus. YOU ALSO NEED TO READ THIS BOOK!!!!

Dr. George Lamsa wrote the first translation into English of "The Aramaic Bible".

Reverund Richard Hill, of the "Church of daily Living", exposed the author to "The Keys of Enoch" and has a lot of knowledge regarding the spiritual realms.

Peter Caddy is the founder of "The Findhorn Garden" which is about organic gardening and using beings from the fourth dimension so as to maximize farming harvests!

Michaelle Small Wright is the author of the "Perelandra Workbook" which expands upon the information in "The Findhorn Garden"!

Dr. John Bradenbury, a plasma physicist, has given the author insight into vortexial physics!

Richard de Wolf, gave the author information on the "Four Corners" intergallactic vortex!

William Haney relayed to the author information and insight into "anointing oils" and other things related thereto!

Mitch Battros has given the author information regarding the Earth-Sun connection and has written a book entitled, "The Earth-Sun Connection" and a website, "Earthchangesmedia.com".

Wiley Brooks describies HOW NOT TO ACHIEVE THE STATE OF BREATHAIRIANISM!

Jack Davis and Jasmuheen for describing HOW YOU MIGHT ACTUALLY ARRIVE IN A BREATHAIRIAN STATE OF BEING!!!!

"The American Free Press is the only national newspaper that reports the news which is ignored/ "blacked out" by the mainstream media. It's coverage encompasses all subjects!

Ken Keyes, author of "The Hundredth Monkey", is a book that should be read by all of humanity! It explains how morphogenic fields (mass thoughts), affect consciousness and our perception of "reality".

George Orwell, author of "Animal Farm", well described the Socialist/ Communist miasma infecting the world's governments!

Aldous Huxley, author of "Brave New World" and "1984", which similarly to Orwell, describes our enslavement into Socialism/Communisum

Dr. Robert Becker, is the author of "The Body Electric" and used electrical currents to regenerate salamander limbs! This books proves the spiritual nature of us humans!

Dinsbaugh, a healing pioneer, has detailed his revelation of color therapy healing!

Steven Lewis, a Chiropracter, created the AIM program of radionic healing which is very effective!

Swami Bohinatha and The Kauai Hindu Monaster have shown the author the power of purity of their thoughts and the invaluable information that they dispense throughout our planet!

Swami Saraswati created "The True History and Religion of India" and this has aided the author in having an overall history of this world and Hinduism.

Dr. Michael Jensen has shared valuable insights with author about the noetic effects of sin from his website

Valery Kondratov, has written several revolutionary treatises regarding the recurrent forms of atomic creation and pyramid energetics. She has demonstrated, rather conclusively, that there is a controlling intelligence/presence on the atomic level of creation, from whence emanates all forms manifested on our planet and throughout the Universe! Your research really confirms the investigations of the author, who is deeply indebted to you!

Dr. Hugh Ross is an Astrophysicist who has basically also proven that there is factor of "atomic intelligence" that allows life to exist here on Earth. His work regards the extremely narrow parameters within which life manifests and again, the author is grateful for your research and insights!

Dr. Hubert Yockey wrote the book, "Information Theory, Evolution and the Origin of Life" which details how our DNA is a "base pairs" binary computer code. This work, likewise, shows there is an intelligent presence as a creational force on our planet!

Louis Contant, in the 1800's, figured that there were forces beyond the "material realm" without any scientific instrumentation

Physicist Alain Aspect proved that atoms can "communicate" with each other at a distance of many trillions of miles!!!!

George Noory is the host of the "Coast to Coast" radio show. Thank you so much for having the guests on your show. They made tge writing of this book so much easier and complete!

William Henry has studed the Gnostic texts from Israel and has come to many of the same conclusions as the author which are revealed in, "The Secret of Sion".

Nora Gedgaudas has studied the negative effects of vaccines, among many other things.

Andrew Basiago has given the author information regarding "DARPA" and "The Pegasus Project"

DR. NEWTON IS INDEBTED TO ALL OF THE PEOPLE LISTED ABOVE AND ENRICHED BY THEIR UNDERSTANDING AND INSIGHTS (or lack thereof in one case)!!!! Anyone who helped the author and was omitted, please know it is not intentional!

CHAPTER ONE

WHERE IS GOD AND WHAT IS THE NATURE OF GOD AND HOW DOES THIS RELATE TO YOU/US? HOW DO WE KNOW GOD EVEN EXISTS?

Virtually all of the World's religions assert that God is everywhere. Some disciplines such as Pantheism and Hinduism state that God is in everything, which can be actually be proven through the research of physics, quantum physics and mechanics. Scientifically, this appears to be true but no one has explained how this is possible. The ANTHROPOMORPHIC GOD (God in a body) would be PRECLUDED FROM BEING EVERYWHERE— limited by the confines of a material shape. The author seems to remember Mary Baker Eddy expounding this concept in "Science and Health with Key to the Scriptures". The concept of God being everywhere is easily achieved, however, if GOD is SPIRIT or an ATOMIC FIELD from which all objects in the Universe are comprised!

In "THE BHAGAVAD GITA", translated by Avatar Parmahansa Yogananda, on page 369 it states that "CREATIVE COSMIC CREATION" is COMPRISED OF LIGHT AND YAGNA, which is FIRE AND LIGHT, and AUM which is SONIC (VIBRATIONAL) PERFECTION. Amazingly enough, THIS CONTEXT COULD BE USED TO DESCRIBE ATOMS. What a fortuitous coincidence! DYT? These ATOMS are comprised of ELECTROMAGNETIC PARTICLES (with the qualities just described above) and NO DENSE MATTER HAS BEEN FOUND IN THEM, EVEN IN THE GREATEST OF ATOMIC COLLIDERS, located in Hadron, Switzerland. The author has heard a report that Hadron Collider scientists have captured "anti-matter" for less than a minute. Dr. Newton's question to them would be, "How can

1

you find "anti-matter" when you have not even found matter?" Did you actually find Spirit/energy? What would be your measure of comparison? Additionally, WHY DO YOU EVEN HAVE TO PRESUME THAT MATTER IS (this will be discussed comprehensively in future chapters, especially Chapter Five)?

It would be nice to have Sir Issac Newton's perspective on this! One thing about Sir Issac Newton we know is that he was a great mathemetician and his book about mathematics, "Principia", is regarded as the greatest such treatise of all time! Mathematics has often been claimed to be "pure science" and it is since there is no room for opinion and that would have been the frame of reference from which he would approach all things! We also know that he did extensive experimentation in the field of Physics. And part of this work dealt with optics wherein Newton posited that LIGHT is "STREAMS OF MINUTE PARTICLES". This certainly seems to DESCRIBE the functioning of PHOTONIC particles and ATOMS, even though that concept did not exist at time of Newton's incarnation!

The ATOMIC FIELD, being omnipresent and an aggregate of all atoms, is INTER-RELATED TO ITSELF through a type of SENTIENCE and/or TELEPATHY. This has actually been measured in a controlled experiment where atoms which were agitated likewise affected other atoms many kilometers away! In fact, in 1982 Physicist Alain Aspect proved that **ATOMS CAN COMMUNICATE WITH EACH OTHER AT LEAST WITHIN 10 TRILLION MILES!!!!** The same process occurs when a laser is aimed at an object wherein the atoms and photons emitted from the laser will affect other atoms and photons at a tremendous distance there from.

This atomic field is the BASIC BUILDING BLOCK OF CREATION which allows it to be in and PERMEATE EVERYTHING since it is an ELECTROMAGNETIC PRESENCE which weaves its way through the ENTIRE UNIVERSE in different forms and permutations and is an INHERENT PART of Einstein's "UNIFIED FIELD THEORY" and is the substance of Gravity! Additionally, these atoms can release tremendous amounts of energy as in an atomic explosion. HOW MAGNIFICENT AND DIVINE THESE ATOMS TRULY ARE! It is also known that bacteria exhibit these same characteristics of sentience and/or telephaty. It could be concluded that this is just "a coincidence" but this is unlikely because this also applies to fungii and viruses!!!! This is clearly explained in Ken Keyes' book, "The Hundredth Monkey", as applied to bacteria.

The electric qualities of these atoms are carried in the neutrons, protons and electrons and subparticles such as neutrinos, anti-neutrinos, anti-protons, muons, photons, psi particles, leptons and quarks and charm quarks. The properties of these are electromagnetism (except for the neutrinos), light and vibration. You may notice that DENSE MATTER has not been included in these descriptions and for good reason—it DOES NOT EXIST and if it did exist, it would be inferior, subject to dimunition, decay and disintegration—basically as valuable as piffle! These disintegrating properties do not occur with atoms. The ACTUAL PROPERTIES of the ATOM appear INDESCRUCTIBLE although their form can be mutated and manipulated for different purposes. In "The Yoga Sutras", by Kriya Yoga Siddha, Satguru and MahaAvatar Patanjali, it discusses "GUNAS" which are described as COSMIC ENERGIES of "LIGHT, MOTION and MASS". This would certainly appear to be describing atoms, WHICH INCLUDE ALL OF THESE PROPERTIES!

Also, in VEDIC COSMOLOGY, from "The Vedas" which are ancient Hindu texts, ten thousand years or more old (actually more like millions of years old but ten thousand years is more the the "accepted date), it is stated that there is a "SPIRITUAL ELEMENT IN ALL MATTER." Since it has been revealed that SPIRIT is ELECTROMAGNETIC ENERGY, Prana or Chi, which are INDESTRUCTIBLE, THIS IS ANOTHER INDICATION THAT SPIRIT, PRANA, CHI, ATOMS, ARE THE REAL BUILDING BLOCKS OF ALL CREATION AND NOT

DETERIORATING MATTER as most everybody has been deluded and/ or misinstructed into believing and thinking!

In his book "The Fabric of the Universe", Dennis Postle talks about how particle physicists have found only energy and no matter in their search for the existence of the same. And this is what the Taoists were claiming more than 1500 years ago! How did they know this before the particle physicists? Obvioiusly, their knowledge of particle physics or the operation of creation predates that of our scientists! DYT?

Now you may counter that we and our universe certainly appear to be material and that we and our universe are constantly degrading and that we bleed when we are cut by something. BUT APPEARANCE IS NOT NECESSARILY REALITY, as physicists delve deeper into this concept, even though you could make such a case through syllogistic logic. However logical this would be, it is inaccurate if the premises are not valid and they are not in this case. A MIRAGE LOOKS VERY REAL AT A DISTANCE AND WHEN YOU YOU GET CLOSE TO IT, IT DISAPPEARS. In a sense, TEHNC (the Emporer has no clothes), as it were!

The aggregate of human consciousness (mass consciousness) is what makes matter appear real and in Chapter Five this will be discussed in more depth. So it is with the Illuminati, their corporations and the world's governments and religions. The illusion is that they have your best interests in mind when "oh contrar" is the reality! Check out the message on the "Georgia Headstones" and you might see what Dr. Newton means. Just make sure you can really handle the Truth before you search for it!

Dr. Newton is astonished that after MANY DISSECTIONS AND SUBDISSECTIONS AND SUB-SUBDISSECTIONS OF ATOMS IN WHICH DENSE MATTER HAS NOT BEEN DISCOVERED, PHYSCISTS HAVE NOT FOCUSED ON THE ELECTROMAGNETIC ENERGY THAT EMANATES FROM THE ATOMS. The particle physicist's quest is akin to the futile search of "Don Quixote", where Don

Quixote went out searching for perfection all over the planet when it in fact already resided inside himself!!!! This too will be further explicated in Chapter Five

In "The Emerald Tablets" of Hermes Trismegistus, Hermes implores us to remove our consciousness from a state of "obscurity" in order to perceive the perfection wrought by our Creator! He also says that when we take the power of God and integrate it into our Earth, the PERFECTION THEREOF WILL BE REVEALED. This book will aid you to that end! YOU WILL BE GIVEN TECHNIQUES AND DISCIPLINES THAT WILL ALLOW THIS TO BE MANFIESTED IN YOUR LIFE—GUARANTEED—IF YOU DO THIS WITH INTENT AND A DEDICATED RESOLVE! Any effort less than this will be futile and will produce insignificant results! For this task, A FOCUSED, REGULAR EFFORT WILL BRING BOUNTIFUL RESULTS!!!!

In "Science and Health with Key to the Scriptures", Mary Baker Eddy devotes much space as to the ILLUSORY NATURE OF MATTER AND IMPERFECTION and basically states that since "GOD IS SPIRIT" (energy is Dr. Newton's explanation) and perfect, therefore man and GOD'S CREATION must likewise mimic/REFLECT THESE PROPERTIES. It should be duly noted that Mrs. Eddy discovered this and the science of Christianity just as modern physics was in its infancy. Also, she believed that the world was not affected by "atomic force" and that was because that the early physicists considered the atom to be a material presence which now can be proven as false! UNFORTUNATELY, MANY OF TODAYS PHYSICISTS STILL BELIEVE THAT THE ATOM HAS DENSE MATTER OF SOME TYPE AND YET ALL OF THEIR RESEARCH INDICATES OTHERWISE! Maybe they could WTHU (wake the hell up)? To go through the uncomfortable feeling of this process would eventually be liberating for them resulting in a coherent understanding of God's creation of the Universe! Or they could keep chasing their tales/tails as is occurring right now, as it were!!

IT IS INHERENTLY UNSCIENTIFIC TO ASSUME THINGS, ESPECIALLY WHEN THERE IS NO EVIDENCE TO SUPPORT THESE ASSUMPTIONS! This is the quandry of the physicists of today! This is also the predicament of almost all politicians who almost inevitably take positions and make decisions from a position of misinformation/malinformation and with an incomplete and/or distorted factual basis!

The author must tell you and will prove to you in subsequent chapters that you bleed and your "body" deteriorates because you have created such in your conscious and subconscious (your personal computer-brain) thoughts and stored information in your DNA (personal computer chips)! If you truly see youself as PERFECT AND COMPRISED OF SPIRIT, energy, God, through REPROGRAMMING OF YOUR SUBCONSCIOUS/MORTAL MIND, YOU WILL BEGIN TO REFLECT GOD'S PERFECTION as Mary Baker Eddy proclaimed in "Science and Health with Key to the Scriptures"!!!! The first thing that will happen in this reprogramming process, is that more light will emante from your body. A second thing that will occur is that your health will vastly improve. A third thing that will occur is that there will be more prosperity in your life

MRS. EDDY LIKEWISE PROVED THE VERACITY OF HER STATEMENTS and the statements just made by the author, in "Science and Health . . . .", IN A NUMEROUS FASHION BY DEMONSTRATING THEM IN HER LIFE THROUGH HEALING THE SICK AND RAISING THE DEAD. And considering the medocrity by which she was surrounded, this is not an insignificant feat! So basically MRS. EDDY PROVED ANECDOTALLY THE ACCURACY and TRUTH OF HER REVELATIONS TO US!!!! From a state of having no money, she literally created the worldwide Christian Science movement and not by taking large sums of money from "rich" people. Mrs. Eddy apparently knew how coalse the atoms into larger forms, although she would not agree with the author, regarding this conclusion.

So, from all of the preceding statements in this chapter we can declare that IF ATOMS (micro creation) ARE PERFECT AND GOD IS CONTAINED IN THIS ATOMIC FIELD, then it is reasonable to conclude that man and the EARTH AND THE UNIVERSE (macro creation) must inevitably EMANATE and REFLECT this SAME PERFECTION. In "The Emerald Tablets" of Hermes Trismegistus, Hermes, of extraterrestial origin, states that WHICH IS ABOVE IS THAT WHICH IS BELOW and, vice versa, THAT WHICH IS BELOW IS THAT WHICH IS ABOVE and that knowing this is what allows us to PERFORM MIRACLES. Also it states that GOD IS PERFECT and and CONSUMES THE WHOLE WORLD and PENETRATES EVEN SO-CALLED DENSE MATTER!!!! Additionally, we know that the electrical bonds which allow the atoms to coalse into molecules work within a parameter of three one hundredths of one percent. And it is this precision which allows the larger forms, such as ourselves to exist. This is discussed in detail in Dr. Hugh Ross, a physicist, in "Origin of the Universe: New Scientific Evidence for the Existence of God"

Such knowledge could have allowed Hermes, as he was known in Greece and Thoth, as he was known in Egypt, and Enoch as he was known to the Kabbalist's, to levitate multi-ton stones into place for the building of Temples and Pyramids. Even today, in Tibet, Tibetan monks can levitate multi-ton rocks up the side of a cliff, as described in "The Bridge to Infinity" by Bruce Cathie! Although this is somewhat digressional, the author is obsessed about applying theory to reality, as has will be displayed here and throughout this book!

Max Planck, one of the brilliant scientists involved with "The Manhattan Project" which created the atomic bomb said: "All matter originates and exists only by virtue of a force which holds the atom together. We must assume behind this force is the existence of a conscious and intelligent mind. This mind is the matrix of matter." This is a substancial validation and complimentary of what was said above by the great Hermes Trismegustis and Hermes knew this thousand's of years before Max Planck! We could take what Planck is saying and conclude everything EMANATES FROM THE MIND OF THE CREATOR WHO MADE ATOMS and ATOMS COMPRISE LARGER FORMS (so called matter) which we perceive through our consciousness. And DIVINE INTELLIGENCE, IN ITS OMNIPOTENCE, CREATES THE TEMPLATES THAT COMPRISE THESE FORMS.

Another explanation of this, as was discussed several paragraphs earlier, and actually scientifically accurate, would be that the "**SMALL FORM**" (**individual atoms**) **coagulate/coalesce/bond** into to larger and more complex things or the "**LARGE FORM**" (**aggregated atoms/molecules/ multiples of molecules**) such as ourselves and other things and objects on our Earth!

"The 72 Names of God" reveal to us us that the phrase "Aleph Kaf Aleph" helps us to restore things to their perfect state, implying that perfection has existed as the normal state of being and creation! This is contained in Exodus 14, verses 19-21 AND IS IN HEBREW AND WAS NEVER TRANSLATED INTO ENGLISH because biblical scholars did not understand the symbolic meaning of the words—only the literal meaing listed in the Torah/Old Testament. Be aware that the names could have come from extra—terrestial "Gods" known as Yaweh or Jehoval or Elohim who could descended from the planet Nibiru, AKA as Mardock or Planet "X" and even Sirius, The Pleiades and Andromeda. Some of this is discussed in detail in Zecharia Sitchin's in many books which are well worth reading and adsorbing such as "When Time Began: The First New Age"! Equally as informative on this subject is Robert Temple's book, "The Sirius Mystery"!

Most of the eleven statements in "The Patterns onf the Trestleboard: The Truth About Self" by Paul Foster Case would not be possible without a VAST ATOMIC FIELD DEVOID OF MATTER (as Mary Baker Eddy stated regarding the illusional nature of matter), energy (as Physics and Quantum Physics and Mechanics and Plasma and Particle Physics prove EVEN THOUGH THE DATA THEREFROM HAS BEEN IMPROPERLY INTERPRETED), Prana (Yoga contends), Chi (as Toasists proclaim), light, vibration (quantum physics explanation)! And these statements truly portray a World where God, the CREATOR, IS IN CONTROL and ACTIVELY AIDS US IN BEING SUCCESSFUL beyond our wildest dreams WHEN WE LEARN HOW TO COUPLE OURSELVES INTO A UNION WITH THE CREATOR. The process of Yoga allows us to initiate this process and "Yug" in Sanskrit literally means union (this will be explained in detail in Chapter Three)! So, how fortuitous for us that we have Yoga at our disposal and for our use!

"THE PATTERNS ON THE TRESTLEBOARD . . . ." REVEAL TO US A "TEMPLATE OF GOD'S CREATION" and can essentially be distilled into the following tenets: We live in a POWERFUL FIELD OF ENERGY, in a UNIVERSE that is ETERNALLY CREATED AND SUSTAINED, which provides us with UNFAILING WISDOM, which GUIDES US TO BEING LIBERATED, which PROVIDES US WITH ALL OUR NEEDS BEING MET (mundane and esoteric) FROM "LIMITLESS SUBSTANCE", where JUSTICE PREVAILS IN OUR LIVES, where ALL CREATION IS BEAUTIFUL from the smallest to the largest things, where UNFAILING WIDSOM leads us to a STATE OF LIBERATION (FREEDOM), which occurs in a FORCEFIELD OF "LIMITLESS LIGHT", where LIFE IS ETERNAL and where SPIRIT/ENERGY/PRANA/CHI INFUSES OUR BODIES! This is chock full of METAPHYSICAL (beyond physicality) CONCEPTS which are germain to this book! You can procure the literal translation of "The Patterns on the Trestleboard: The Truth about Self" from The "BUILDERS OF THE ADYTUM" (B.O.T.A.).

Basically, it has been revealed here that many great thinkers/perceivers of reality are seeing the same pattern of creation as discussed in this book! In a B.O.T.A. lesson on "The Life-Power", by Paul Foster Case, it talks about South Sea Islanders and their word "mana" which is a mental force and energy which permeates all creation. It is also attributed to Louis

Constant, a French occultist, in 1869, that there is a FORCE WHICH IS DISPERSED THROUGHOUT THE UNIVERSE that is VASTLY MORE POWERFUL THAN STEAM. Constant referred to this as the "GREAT WORK" which PRODUCES LIGHT, FLUIDITY, has the PROPERTIES OF CONSTANT VIBRATION AND properties of ELECTROMAGNETISM which is described as "ASTRAL LIGHT". All of this is fundamentally revealing the actions of atoms and photons, individually, and as atomic force which is atoms collectively. And all of this was revealed to Constant through the study of ancient esoteric symbols instead of instrumentation and experimentation! THIS WOULD INDICATE THAT THE ESOTERIC SCIENCES CAN BE AS INSIGHTFUL AS CONVENTIONAL SCIENCE, which is a significant revelation, in and of itself!!!! How amazing are the insights of Case and Constant!

The author wants to take you into the "PROMISED LAND" and the OASIS (OverArching Spiritually Integrated Sciences [AKA Esoteric Sciences]) and this place is METAPHYSICAL (beyond physicality and matter). This "PROMISED LAND" is the REALM of ATOMS and ATOMIC FORCE and is known "LIFE FORCE", PRANA, CHI and SPIRIT, among others. Study the proclamations of Paul Foster Case, learn and memorize them and you will begin to be aware of MANY BLESSINGS COMING INTO YOUR LIFE and not just figuratively but manifested actually (the Case proclamation, "The Patterns on the Trestleboard: The Truth About Self" and "The Emerald Tablet" of Hermes Trismegustis are available from the "Builder's of the Adytum", as was mentioned previously in regard to the "Patterns . . . ."). This ioccurs because the TRUTH OF THE CREATOR IS A MAGNET FOR ATTRACTING POSITIVE THINGS INTO OUR LIVES! Since so few people actually know of these Truths, positive things often elude them! This becomes starkly self evident when you contemplate these statements!!!!

TRULY, THEN WE HAVE BEEN BLESSED BY THE CREATOR and that is exactly the nature of God—to bless us!. Why this is the author cannot explain but that it is true, is an "axiom of creation"! REMEMBER, OUR THOUGHTS WILL LITERALLY CREATE OUR LIFE! WE NEEED TO LIBERATE OURSELES! "TUNING INTO OUR GOD" WILL MAKE OURSELES MORE CREATIVE AND BETTER PROBLEM SOLVERS! IF WE WANT TO CHANGE OUR REALITY/OUR LIVES, WE MUST CHANGE THE FREQUENCY (wave length) OF OUR THOUGHTS TO THE LEVEL OF THETA! It will be revealed, in subsequent paragraphs and chapters, starting in Chapter Three, how this can ACTUALLY BE CREATED BY US! THIS MUCH WILL BE STATED ABOUT THETA, AND THE RESULTING HIGHER CONSCIOUSNESS THAT EMANTES THEREFROM, IS THAT IT LITERALLY CREATES AN ACCELERATED CONDITION OF ENLIGHTENMENT, as it were, BOTH in the so-called "PHSYSICAL" AND SPIRITUAL DIMENSIONS!!!! This is an alchemical transformation both figuratively and literally!

TTATOD (Time to awaken to our Divinity)!

The only thing which prevents this are conscious and more importantly, subconscious thoughts, BASICALLY FEAR, AND THE FREQUENCIES OF OUR THOUGHTS WHICH CREATE THIS CONDITION OF FEAR AND THE LACK OF FEELING WE ARE NOT WORTHY TO BE DIVINE! Daniel Gardner talks about this in depth in "The Science of Fear". The antidote to this syndrome of fear is "Mem Nun Daled" (overcoming our fears) from "The 72 Names of God" from Exodus. Louise L. Hay speaks extremely cogently about this in "You Can Heal Your Life", WHERE FEAR COMES UP REPEATEDLY AS A CAUSATIONAL FACTOR IN SICKNESS AND DISEASE, AS DOES FRUSTRATION AND ANGER AND DEPRESSION!! These emotions can be distilled essentially to fear about "this, that and the other"!!

Through kinesological muscle testing, it can be dramatically revealed how we are weaker physically when we are in the state of fear or any other negative emotional state! Conversely, when we are happy and smile and say "positive things", we are significantly stronger! These results will appear and repeat, consistently, without exception!

There is a prevalent belief that we cannot and do not deserve everything, that basically we are "unworthy"! "SAMESH ALEPH DALED" from The 72 Names of God" DENOTES "THE POWER OF PROSPERITY" and it "yours for the taking". When you live in THETA CONSCIOUSNESS, which will be discussed in depth from Chapter Three onward, OUR THOUGHTS TRANSCEND AND SUPERCEDE FEAR AND DOUBT! You know THINGS WILL ALWAYS "WORK OUT". FEAR IS "FACTORLESS IN OUR LIVES!!!!

AND THIS FRAMEWORK of "GOOD THOUGHTS" EVOKES and MANIFESTS "GOOD EVENTS" IN OUR LIFE! Yes, it sounds simple, it is simple and it SIMPLY WORKS when you enter a STATE OF POSITIVITY or thinking positively, A NATURAL RESULT HAVING YOUR CONSCIOUSNESS ANCHORED IN THETA/DIVINE MIND/ SUPERCONSCIOUSNESS/COSMIC CONSCIOUSNESS!!!! In a real sense, the potential exists to extract ourselves from seemingly negative, no-win situations! THE POTENTIATING FACTOR OF "EXALTATION" COMES FROM A THETA FREQUENCY "MINDSET"!

There is a saying, most likely promulgated by the Illuminati cult, "That you can't have it all". THIS STATMENT WAS MEANT TO ENSLAVE YOU! Actually what the author has just revealed to you indicates otherwise, that WHEN FEAR AND DOUBT DISAPPEAR, PROSPERITY AND ABUNDANCE NATURALLY FOLLOW AND CANNOT BE PREVENTED ANYMORE THAN THE RISING WATERS OF A MASSIVE FLOOD. The Illuminati cult, many religions and most all governments would PREFER THAT YOU LIVE IN FEAR and IGNORANCE, SO THAT YOU ARE UNAWARE OF THE TRUTHS discussed in this book. The author has seen the validity of fear being vanquished from consciousness in his own life! Once he CHANGED THE PROGRAMMING of his SUBCONSCIOUS MIND (the fear frequencies) AND THE DOUBTS RELATED THERETO! The author has seen other people apply these concepts with the same results!

Gurudeva, sums up the real nature of us humans when he says in "The Kauai's Hindu Monastery" newletter of July 2011: "We are immortal souls living and growing in the great school of earthly experience in which we have lived many lives. Vedic rishis have given us courage by uttering the simple truth, 'God is the Life of our life.' A great sage carried it further by saying there is one thing God cannot do: God cannot separate Himself from us. This is because God is our life! God is the life in the birds. God is the life in the fish, God is the life in the animals. Becoming aware of this Life energy in all that lives is becoming aware of God's loving presence within us.

We are the undying consciousness and energy flowing through all things. Deep inside we are perfect this very moment, and we have only to discover and live up to this perfection to be whole. Our energy and God's energy are the same, ever coming out of the void. We are all beautiful children of God. Each day we should try to see the life energy in trees, birds, animals and people. When we do, we are seeing God Siva in action. Aum Namah Sivaya"

So, these statements reveal THAT WE HUMANS ARE MORE AKIN TO DIVINITY THAN FLAWED HUMANOIDS! BUT WE CAN ONLY BE THESE DIVINE BEINGS IF WE FIRST KNOW AND PERCEIVE THIS SO THAT WE CAN ACTUALLY ". . . . LIVE UP TO OUR PERFECTION SO WE CAN BE THIS . . . ."!!!! AT THE MOST FUNDAMENTAL REALITY, IT IS IMPOSSIBLE FOR US TO BE ANY THING OTHER THAN "DIVINE" since we are as inseparable from God as light is from the Sun and water is from a stream, a lake or the Ocean!

From the Patterns on the Trestleboard ALL OF OUR NEEDS ARE MET (number 4). And if WE BELIEVE OR THINK DIFFERENTLY,

13

WE MANIFEST LACK AND LIMITATION! But if we know the truth of number four, if we repeat this often and program into our subconscious at the level of Theta consciousness, we begin to BECOME A PROSPERITY MAGNET whereby wealth can come to us in ways and from sources we never previously considered or even knew about. If we try to create the specific circumstances and means by which prosperity can come to us, WE MIGHT NOT PERCEIVE IMPENDING PROSPERITY when such is literally in front of our faces because we are looking for wealth, elsewhere! This is thoroughly discussed in the book, "The Secret".

Also, many Hindus and Yogis have manifested prosperity in their lives by repeating the Sanskrit mantras for Ganesh (or Ganesha) and Lakshmi which are aspects of Shiva (God). It is most likely the VIBRATIONAL PERFECTION OF THESE SANSKRIT MANTRAS THAT ALIGN US WITH OUR CREATOR AND CAUSE PROSPERITY TO GRAVITATE TO US!!!! Also, as a critical element of receiving continued abundance in our life, WE MUST CONTINUALLY GIVE THANKS FOR WHAT WE ALREADY HAVE. Mary Baker Eddy was very emphatic about this PROCESS OF GRATITUDE and it is well documented in the book, "The Secret".

So the above paragraph is part of the nature of the Creator—GREAT ABUNDANCE—NEVER RATIONED BY LIMITED RESOURCES. LIMITATION NEVER—I REPEAT NEVER CAME OR COMES FROM GOD—ONLY FROM THOSE PEOPLE WHO WANT TO DENIGRATE OR REPLACE GOD—WITH THEIR VASTLY INFERIOR MODEL OF LIMITATION and MALODOROUS EXCREMENT! The powerful servant of God, Mary Baker Eddy, proved this irrefutably when she built the First Church of Christ Scientist in Boston, Massachusetts in the middle of World War One. Mrs. Eddy was widely derided as being deranged and/or completely "unrealistic" for even considering such an undertaking since virtually all of the world's resources and manpower was funnelled into the "war effort", OR SO IT WAS BELIEVED!

How did Mrs. Eddy create this church under impossible circumstances? Mrs. EDDY'S CONSCIOUSNESS WAS FIRMLY ENSCOUNCED IN THETA/GOD CONSCIOUSNESS and she LIVED IN THE REALM OF SPIRIT (energy) and knew that there was NO MATTER and that God blesses us with UNLIMITED ABUNDANCE! This unlimited supply of things becomes manifested within the realm of Spirit which then relegates matter to a nonrelevant factor! Mrs. Eddy saw the church as already created before it actually was and her STEADFAST CONCENTRATION and DETERMINATION BROUGHT IT INTO FRUITION! We, ourselves, can do exactly what Mrs. Eddy did and she herself told us much the same in "Science and Health With Key to the Scriptures".!

Dr. Newton knows a journal listed Christian Science Practitioner in Los Angeles, Julio Rivas, who heals people "by the bushell" because HE ONLY PERCEIVES A PERFECT, SPIRITUAL GOD who loves his people so much that he would never create them imperfectly or from caprious, decaying, deteriorating matter. Mr Rivas' aura (the Prana/ etheric energy depicted in virtually every picture of Jesus) surrounding his body and head is at "Christlike" proportions akin to that of a Maha Avatar which Jesus and the Yoga Siddhas are (by their "light" and "works" you will know them)! Although this is not directly related to abundance, it is tangentially enough so as to make a prescient point. HEALING AND PERFECT HEALTH AS WELL AS ABUNDANCE IS NOT RATIONED BY OUR CREATOR, although it may be rationed by your health insurance or HMO, as it were! There are a great many other Christian Science Practitioner/ healers, thousands actually, throughout the World, who likewise do many great healing works like Mr. Rivas! They are listed in "The Christian Science Journal".

Dr. Newton will prove that there is an "UNLIMITED PERFECTION" in our Universe, throughout this book, through a preponderance of evidence!

15

We will learn about Kriya Yoga techniques, among other things, which can TRANSFORM US into our ALREADY EXISTING DIVINITY. And the great Kriya Yoga Siddhas, such as Patanjali, as explicated in "The Yoga Sutras", knew thousands of years ago that Man is made in the image of God. Gee, this kind of sounds similar to what Hermes Trismegustis said thousands of years ago. And what "The 72 Names of God" from Exodus said thousands of years ago. And what Jesus demonstrated and exhorted us to do ("Greater works than those shall ye do also.") thousands of years ago. And what Mary Baker Eddy said one hundred and thiry five years ago! And what Paul Foster Case said decades ago. DO YOU SEE THE SYNOCHRONICITY (a recurring pattern) HERE?

Please do not dismiss the PREPONDERANCE OF EVIDENCE just presented and ESTABLISHED! IF WE PERCEIVE THIS, IT WILL FORCE US TO AWAKEN TO OUR INHERENT PERFECTION AND WE WILL BE TRULY BLESSED! Never has the need to be blessed been more necessary than right now! And this is ACHIEVABLE RIGHT NOW! And in Chapter Three, onward, WE WILL "GET DOWN TO IT"!!!!

TTATOD (Time to awaken to our Divinity)!

So what has been established in this chapter and will be even more so explained in Chapter Five, is THAT MATTER DOES NOT EXIST SCIENTIFICALLY AND THEOLOGICALLY AND IN COSMOGENY OR COSMOGRAPHY! BUT JUST SUPPOSE, for the purpose of discussion and examination, THAT MATTER DOES IN FACT EXIST! Would not you want to transcend this state of inherent and continual sickness, disease and death? Fortunately for us THIS IS POSSIBLE THROUGH KRIYA KUNDALINI YOGA, TAI CHI, THE "BACKFLOW MEDITATION", "THETA PROGRAMMING", "THETA CONSCIOUSNESS PROGRAMMING" and "CHRISTIAN SCIENCE TREATMENT" which INFUSE our bodies with ELECTROMAGNETIC ENERGY, also known as "LIFE FORCE",

PRANA, CHI, SPIRIT, LIGHT and SONIC PERFECTION and in the process, somehow "tame" and/or eliminate our "negative emotions"!!!! And these disciplines will be thoroughly discussed in Chapter Three! BUT PLEASE READ CHAPTER TWO, FIRST, AS IT IS GERMAIN TO THE FRAMEWORK OF THE ENTIRE BOOK!!!!

Also, and this is of extreme importance to note—THIS CANNOT BE EMPHASIZED ENOUGH—**IF YOU ARE LIVING YOUR LIFE UNDER THE INFLUENCE OF ALCOHOL OR DRUGS** (and yes, this includes "medical Cannabis") **YOU WILL ONLY HAVE FLEETING GLIMPSES AND PERCEPTION OF WHAT YOUR CREATOR IS CAPABLE OF PROVIDING FOR YOU, if any at all**. And this is a best case scenario! As long as you LIVE IN THE STUPOR THAT THESE SUBSTANCES ELICIT IN YOU, YOU WILL KEEP DRIVING YOUR CAR OFF OF A CLIFF, as it were. If your quest is "essential truth" and knowledge which leads to Divinity and th!e establishment of your **DIVINE ESSENCE, IS BETTER FACILITATED WITHOUT DRUGS AND ALCOHOL!!!!**

Dr. Newton does not care to judge whether you are "right or "wrong" in your choice of substance usage and/or abuse. Dr. Wayne Dyer, a man the author respects as much for his demeanor and actions as well as his words, says that his spiritual teacher, who the author remembers as Ram Dass, told him that he would never reach his full potential on Earth if he imbibed in alcohol and drugs (a. & d.). Dr. Newton has only seen one or two possible exceptions to this statement and it is Dr. Timothy Leary and Dr. John Lily, of LSD fame, and this is might not even be completely accurate, although both of them seemed to exhibit aspects of Divinity, especially Dr. Leary, who the author met before he passed away from the Earth plane, as it were!!

The amount of people which seem to be afflicted with this "substance abuse" syndrome is of monumental proportions and almost beyond comprehension! If we need a daily glass of wine or bottle of beer to relax in the evening, almost inevitably this leads to two doses daily of the same and can quickly multiply wherein you we in a situation of abuse (intoxication). IN FACT, IT IS WELL KNOWN THAT THE MORE WE IMBIBE IN THESE THINGS (a & d), THE MORE WE WILL NEED AND WE WILL EVENTUALLY GET TO A POINT OF WHERE THE NICE FEELING OF OUR "HIGH" WILL EVENTUALLY DISAPPEAR. So then we will need substancial amounts of (a. & d.) just to feel like a normal "non-substance abuse" state of consciousness because of dopamine and endorphin depletion and "blowing holes" in our etheric energy field (Spirit, Prana, Chi, life force)!

THE REASON PEOPLE CRAVE ALCOHOL AND DRUGS IS THAT THEY ARE PULLED/INFLUENCED SUBCONSCIOUSLY TO CRAVE THE ALPHA/THETA CONSCIOUSNESS! And since alcohol and drugs offer a TEMPORARY PORTAL THERETO, they NATURALLY ATTRACT us to THESE SUBSTANCES. The information in this book gives us a NATURAL PORTAL TO THE EUPHORIA OF THETA CONSCIOUSNESS!!!!

The dilemna of alcohol abuse is only excaserbated by the "media". Whenever someone has a problem or is trying to relax in a T.V. show or movie, what is the one thing they invariably do? They have a drink and usually another and another! The amount of mental clarity that you have following such imbibing is akin to very little or absolutely none because your computer/brain is malfunctioning, if it is active at all! ALCOHOL AND DRUGS WILL SKEW THE OPERATING SYSTEM IN OUR COMPUTER-BRAIN and the HARDWIRE LINK THAT IT HAS TO OUR CREATOR!!!! This lack of mental clarity is dicernable from anecdotal observation and from human brainwave studies!

Cannabis is little different because there is almost no one who can use it occassionally although most users thereof delusionally claim to be using it only "recreationally" when the reality is that it is used to help achieve a better state of "life functioning". Whether better "life functioning" results is highly questionable since the more we use, the more the subconscious craves the inhalation or ingestion thereof. Cannabis creates cognitive misfunction and malfunction and some studies have indicated that it can cause genetic damage at the level of RNA and DNA (your personal computer chips). The medical Marajuana phenomenon is, in too many cases, just an excuse to "recreationally" abuse/overuse Cannabis. As the author will cover in this book, it is possible to create and/or repair DNA, BUT WHY "SCREW IT UP" in the first place!

Additionally, anything medically approved as a Cannabis healing protocol, can be treated better with other herbal supplements and alternative healing modalities! One example is using the herb, Petasites, which is a more effective pain killer than Cannabis or Vicodin. You have never heard of Petasites? Might that be because it costs pennies versus multiple of dollars to procure?

While Dr. Newton does not favor restrictions/laws on the use of (a. & d.) substances, he is extremely dismayed by the proliferation of Cannabis useage and alcohol consumption because of the many deleterious effects there from. The author knows there have been SCIENTIFIC BREAKTHROUGHS by AMAZONIAN INDIANS from their LIMITED/CONTROLLED DRUG USAGE and that many people including Dr. Timothy Leary, Dr. John Lily, artist Alex Gray and many other artists and musicians have had great revelations and insights from the use LSD. But even Alex Gray, in "The Akashic Experience" by Ervin Lazlo, does not recommend doing what he did!

VERY FEW OF THESE PEOPLE OR GROUPS APPEAR ABLE TO EVEN MARGINALLY REMAIN IN THE STATE OF NON-DRUG INDUCED HIGHER (actually Theta) CONSCIOUSNESS! Why? Could it be the fact that THETA CONSCIOUSNESS WAS ARTIFICIALLY INDUCED? Once we reach adulthood, might it be a better decision to be responsible and remain in a state that we can be guided by your

Creator rather than an alcoholic stupor or a haze of Cannabis or other mind enfebbling drugs? DYT? Do you believe that they can provide you with better guidance than your Creator? IF YOU FOLLOW THE PROTOCOLS AND DISCIPLINES THAT WILL BE COVERED IN THIS TEXT IN UPCOMING CHAPTERS AND PERFORM THEM DAILY—YES, DAILY—YOU WILL POSITION YOURSELF TO BE IN A NATURAL "HIGH"/EUPHORIA!!!! Before you classify this as a delusional notion to be summarily disregarded, YOU MIGHT WANT TO AT LEAST FORCE YOURSELF TO TRY DR. NEWTON'S UNCONVENTIONAL APPROACH TO "REAL CONSCIOUSNESS"! This is actually the Creators approach to "real consciousness" and not the author's!!!!

IF YOU WANT A LIBERATING AND MORE PERPETUAL ALTERNATIVE (and also more cost effective) WAY THAN THE A. & D. SPIRAL OF MALFUNCTIONING and MISFUNCTIONING, THEN PLEASE CONSUME THIS BOOK AS YOUR SUCCESS IN LIFE DEPENDED UPON IT BECAUSE IT WELL MIGHT! Under the CONDITION of A. & D., WE ARE MOSTLY IN A CONDITION WHERE WE CANNOT RECEIVE THE CREATORS "THETA RADIO FREQUENCY" AND UNFORTUNATELY, WE HAVE CUT OURSELF OFF FROM OUR GREATEST ASSET (our God), DIVINE ABILITIES AND DIVINE RIGHTS! When you access THETA CONSCIOUSNESS, NATURALLY, you no longer have any need for a. & d. This is "certain and most true"—no bull excrement! THINK OF THE MONEY YOU WILL SAVE! Think of the expanded consciousness you will have perpetually!!!! DYT?

Now, to answer the question of how the nature of God, the content of this chapter, relates to us, the answer is basic and simple. THE NATURE OF GOD IS THE NATURE OF US AND THAT IS SPIRIT, ENERGY, PRANA, CHI, LIGHT, ELECTROMAGNETISM and SONIC VIBRATION WHICH GIVE US PERFECT HEALTH,

IMMORTALITY AND UNLIMITED ABUNDANCE! And this will be expounded upon from Chapter Three onward!!

But as a teaser, this much has already been revealed. As was said earlier in this chapter, Yogi Paramahansa Yogananda, of the "Self Realization Fellowship" states in his interpretation of "The Bhagavad Gita" on page 369, that there are two components of "intelligent Cosmic Creation". First there is YAGNA or AGNA which is FIRE or LIGHT. And then there is AUM or OM which is the "COSMIC VIBRATION" which Dr. Newton equates to "sonic or vibrational perfection". And this is the basis of creation which includes US!

Also, the answer the second question as to how we know that God exists, it can be easily deduced from the foregoing discussion in this chapter. THERE IS SOMETHING THAT IS CONTROLLING THE ATOMS, whether you want to call it God or Dog or Womba or whatever, and the **RECURRING NINE FORMS OF ATOMIC CREATION as are discussed in Valery P. Kondratov's treatise, "The Geometry of a Uniform Field" and "Fabric of the Universe".** Kondratov reveals how there are **NINE GEOMETRIC FORMS WHICH RECUR WITHIN AND ARE THE BASIS OF ALL LEVELS OF CREATION, in figure 1 of the above treatise! WOULD THE FOREGOING INDICATE A STATE OF RANDOMNESS/CHAOS, WITH NO CONTROLLING FORCE/INTELLIGENCE?** NML (Mathemetically not likely, unless you consider a quadrillion to one more than the remotest of possibilities), for all intensive purposes!

These "nine forms of creation" are correlated with "**NINE ENERGIES OF CREATION". These energies includes the Weak Nuclear, Electrical, Magnetic, Photonic-temporal, Spatial temporal, Phonon-time, Strong Nuclear, Vibration and Gravitational. This is contained in Valery Kondratov's treatise. "THE CONFORMATION OF THE NINE ENERGIES OF EGYPTIAN TRADITION" and these energies are actually listed in the ancient writings of Egypt. Valery Kondratov's**

works are accessible via the internet by Goggling Valery P. Kondratov.
Certainly her work and insights into complicated things are exceptional.
See the diagram that follows for a depiction of the nine Geometric forms
that underlie all manifested creation.

Additionally,discussed previously, as per Dr. Hugh Ross' treatise, "Origin
of the Universe . . . .", we know that **LIFE FORMS CANNOT EXIST
ON EARTH, IF THEY VARY MORE THAN THE PARAMETERS
OF THREE ONE HUNDREDTHS OF ONE PERCENT (3/100's of
1%). This applies to both the ELECTROMAGNETIC FIELD and
THE STRONG NUCLEAR FORCE. If the electrical bonds and the
nuclear bonds between the atoms are too strong, then they cannot
coalse into molecules and bundles of molecules. If the electrical
and nuclear bonds between the atoms are to loose, once again no
molecules can be formed! IF MOLECULES CANNOT BE FORMED,
NEITHER CAN WE NOR THE OBJECTS THAT SURROUND
US!!!! Did this happen by chance/chaos?** Once again, the author must
empatically state, MNL (Mathematically not likely), for all intensive
purposes!

**So, once again, this entire chapter incidcates through a
PREPONDERANCE OF EVIDENCE, THAT THERE IS A
CONTROLLING FORCE/INTELLIGENCE WHICH WE CAN
CALL GOD/CREATOR, for lack of a better term!**

The Nine Geometric Forms of Creation

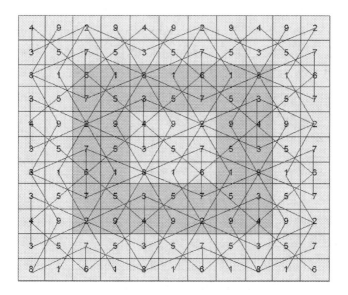

"These 9 geometric forms are the templates and sub-templates of atomic and subatomic creation, of which all things are comprised"

Summarizing:

We know that God is everywhere (**OMNIPRESENT**) such as discussed in all of the world's religions (EVEN THOUGH A LOT OF THEM **IGNORE THE APPLICATION OF THIS**), in the Pantheistic view, from Hermes Trismegistus in "Emerald Tablets, from Paul Foster Case in "The Patterns on the Trestleboard" . . . , from Mary Baker Eddy in "Science and Health With Key to the Scriptures", from the Kabbalistic "72 Names of God" from Exodus, from Taoism and from the oldest of sources Kriya Yoga Siddhas/Satgurus (Maha Avatars) and from Vedic Cosmology!

This obvioiusly controverts the beliefs of most Christians, Moslems, Jews and even some Buddhists and Hindus but we need to be more interested in the true nature of God instead of clinging to "cherised notions" based on "blind faith". The admitted blindness of such belief should dispense with its validity in and of itself! As is stated in "The Gospel of Thomas", belief without understanding is of no value. **BLIND FAITH**/BELIEF **ONLY LEADS TO MORE BLINDNESS** and more **MISUNDERSTANDING** and **MISINFORMATION**! With this as a comparison, the "blind man" might see more than the man with sight!

We know that an anthropomorphic God (God in a body) is impossible if God is everywhere, as virtually every tradition tells us. Conversely, GOD ENSCOUNSED IN A VAST FIELD OF ATOMS IS INHERENTLY EVERYWHERE because atoms proliferate and constitute all creation and are interconnected with each other through some type of sentience! Physics, Quantum Physics and Mechanics validate this concept when you view the data and theories which have been revealed!

Where God is is wherever ATOMS RESIDE which INCLUDES ALL SPACE AND THUS GOD CANNOT BE ANTHROPOMORPHIC!

We know that these atoms are perfect and indestructible, although they may change form, and have a type of sentience/telepathy among themselves.

The nature of God is atoms including Spirit, energy, Prana, Chi, Orgone, electromagnetism, light, vibration among other properties AND THESE ATOMS AGGREGATE AS AN ATOMIC FORCE FIELD!

We know the the small form, which is atoms, aggregates into the large form, which is the "atomic field", which allows objects to be manifested on this or any other dimension!

THE NATURE OF GOD IS TO BLESS US WHICH CAN BE OBSCURED BY OUR SUBCONSCIOUS THOUGHT VIBRATIONS

WHICH CREATE A CONDITON OF FEAR AND DOUBT WHICH BLOCK THESE BLESSINGS FROM OUR CONSCIOUSNESS!

Anything which controverts the perception of perfection is merely ILLUSORY, AKIN TO A MIRAGE!

WE HAVE THE ABILITY TO TAKE THE CONSUMING POWER OF THE CREATOR AND UNLEASH THE EXISTING UNDERLYING PERFECTION ON OUR EARTH, according to Hermes Trismegustis. Mary Baker Eddy, Paul Foster Case, Kriya Yoga Siddha/Avatar Patanjali, Krishna in "The Bhagavad Gita" and "The 72 Names of God" from "Exodus".

We can reprogram/unprogram FEAR VIBRATIONS through our dwelling constantly on the truth of Creation and living in Theta consciousness.

WHEN YOU ARE ENTRAINED IN THETA CONSCIOUSNESS, YOU TRANSCEND DOUBT AND KNOW THAT "THINGS WILL WORK OUT", and you will manifest all of your needs.

PROSPERITY IS YOURS FOR THE TAKING (**Samesh Aleph Daled**) because PROSPERITY AND ABUNDANCE ARE NON-RATIONED PROPERTIES OF GOD!

ALL OF OUR NEEDS ARE MET BY GOD IF WE KNOW AND BELIEVE THIS; OTHERWISE FEAR AND DOUBT PREVENT THIS FROM BEING MANIFESTED IN OUR LIVES, THE RESULT OF MISPROGRAMMING IN OUR SUBSCONSIOUSNESS/BRAIN COMPUTER!.

Mary Baker Eddy, founder of Christian Science, built a huge church when it seemed impossible SIMPLY BECAUSE SHE KNEW THAT THERE ARE NO SHORTAGES IN GOD'S PERFECT CREATION—ONLY UNLIMITED ABUNDANCE!

WHAT IS REALLY BEING DISPENSED HERE IS METAPHYSICS (or the "land" beyond the physical and the material).

Patanjali (Kriya Yoga Siddha), Krishna (an incarnation of Vishnu), Hermes Trismegustis (demi-god), "The 72 Names of God" from Exodus and Jesus (the wayshower) knew thousands of years ago of God's perfect creation as did Mary Baker Eddy and Paul Foster Case in more recent times.

THIS HAUNTINGLY REOCURRING SYNCHRONICITY OF THE PERFECTION OF GOD AND ITS CREATION KEEP REAPPEARING (A mere coincidence? Really? Not likely)!

EVEN IF MATTER DOES EXIST, AND ITS EXISTENCE HAS BEEN SHOWN TO BE ILLUSIVE, WE CAN STILL TRANSCEND FROM THIS STATE OF BEING TO THE OPTIMAL LEVEL OF BEING ELECTROMAGNETIC ENERGY, "LIFE FORCE", PRANA, CHI, SPIRIT, LIGHT and SONIC PERFECTION!

This can be achieved through the DEDICATED PRACTICE OF KRIYA YOGA, TAI CHI, "THE BACKFLOW MEDITATION", "THETA HEALING", "THETA CONSCOUSNESS HEALING" and CHRISTIAN SCIENCE TREATMENT.

WE NEED TO EXTRACT OURSELVES FROM DEPENDENCY ON ALCOHOL AND DRUGS (yes, Cannabis too) SO THAT WE CAN REALIZE OUR DIVINE POTENTIAL; OTHERWISE THEY WILL INTEFERE WITH THE CREATOR'S "THETA RADIO FREQUENCY" AND BLOCK US FROM RECEIVING OUR "DIVINE RIGHTS" and guidance! Theta Consciousness trumps alcohol and drug consciousness! Once we have achieved Theta Consciousness, we know the truth of this statement from our own experience!!!!

Now, to answer the question of how the nature of God relates (the content of this chapter) to you, the answer is basic and simple. THE NATURE

OF GOD IS THE NATURE OF US AND THAT IS SPIRIT—YAGNA which is FIRE and LIGHT and OM and AUM which is "DIVINE VIBRATION" or "sonic perfection"! And from these emanate perfect health and unlimited abundance!

To answer the second question, How do we know that God exists, the whole text of this chapter indicates a controlling force/intelligence, whether you call if God, Dog, Womba or whatever! We know from the detailed work of **Valery P. Kondratov,** that **THAT THERE ARE NINE RECURRING GEOMETRIC FORMS ON THE ATOMIC LEVEL CREATION—** which just happens to be all of creation**!!!!** We also know from the research of **Dr. Hugh Ross, THAT CREATION OCCURS ON THIS PLANET WITHIN THE PARAMETER OF THREE ONE HUNDREDTHS OF ONE PERCENT in regard to the Electormagnetic Field and the Strong Nuclear Force. Thus, randomness/chaos theory is relegated to a state of mathematical impossibility, for virtually all purposes, both mundance and cosmic!!!!**

CHAPTER TWO

HOW DO ALLOPATHIC HEALING (Traditional Medical Healing), HERBAL HEALING, ENERGY HEALING AND SPIRITUAL HEALING OCCUR? WHAT DOES THIS HAVE TO DO WITH THE" LIGHT BODY"?

First Dr. Newton will state, as did Mary Baker Eddy (MBE) in "Science and Health with Key to the Scriptures", that health is the natural state of man! This might sound ludicrous to many people considering the appearance of more and more maladies which seem to be inflicting themselves on mankind. Nevertheless, we have just established that the Creator's creations are perfect and thus this would have to include all people including the vilified Illuminati. It would be impossible to have perfection if man in general or a man in specific was the exception to this rule.

Fortunately or unfortunately, ALL PEOPLE CREATE THEIR SICKNESSES AND PROBLEMS AT THE LEVEL OF THEIR EMOTIONS. The author is well aware of germ and toxin approach to disease! But the EMOTIONAL COMPONENT OF DISEASE IS THE REAL CAUSATIONAL FACTOR and has been more than adequately detailed in Louise L. Hay's book, "You Can Heal Your Life". WHAT WE ARE DEALING WITH HERE IS A MASS PERCEPTUAL BELIEF THAT IT IS IMPOSSIBLE FOR THINGS AND OURSELVES TO BE PERFECT!!!! And this idea has been programmed repeatedly, from the sources listed in the "Prologue", into our subconscious mind-computer!

THE PROFOUNDNESS OF "YOU CAN HEAL YOUR LIFE" IS THE GREAT SIMPLICITY AND CLARITY OF THE DIAGNOSES AND THE REMEDIES contained therein. Dr. Newton remembers vividly what a "real kick in the head" was the realization that he was creating his health or lack thereof through his emotions! And this "kick in the head" ephiphany came exactly from reading Louise Hay's book and therefore it would be probably be a beneficial reading for anyone reading this text!

CHRISTIAN SCIENTISTS AND THETA HEALERS WOULD BE IMMENSELY BENEFITED FROM READING LOUISE HAYS BOOK! From Akashic sources, it has been revealed to the author that OUR THOUGHTS AND EMOTIONS LITERALLY AFFECT and PROGRAM THE BINARY CODE OF OUR "DNA". Also, we know that from an article in "Hinduism Today" that there is a scientific study that indicates TELOMEARSE ACTIVITY, at the end of the strands of DNA, can be AFFECTED BY ACTIVITIES INCLUDING CHANTING and SANSKRIT MANTRAS, by which we can ELIMINATE SICKNESS and DISEASE in the body! This may well INVOLVE REPROGRAMMING THE BINARY PAIRS OF DNA!!!! This will be discussed more thoroughly in upcoming chapters.

The perfect creation is clearly inferred in the first Chapter of Genesis where it states of the God's creation,". . . and behold, it was very good." Hermes Trismegistus, in "The Emerald Tablets" states our "Father" is perfect and consumes our "whole world", referring to our Creator. Mrs. Eddy states in "Science and Health . . ." that God is perfect and "Man is created in the image and likeness of God". Hermes also tells us that ". . . that which is above is that which is below for the performance of the miracles of the one thing". ATOMS, THE "BELOW" COMPONENT, FROM WHICH CREATION IS MANIFESTED, ARE PERFECT, replicated CHARGES of ELECTROMAGNETIC ENERGY. And thus MAN, THE "ABOVE COMPONENT", CONSTITUTED FROM THESE PERFECT ATOMS, IS LIKEWISE A PERFECT MANIFESTATION OF ELECTROMAGNETIC FORCE! This is inevitable if atoms are perfectly acting entities as they certainly appear to be!!!! The author is aware that much of this information is repeated from Chapter One and this is necessary as a background of what is coming next.

AT HIS ESSENCE, THEN, MAN IS NOT SUBJECT TO AILMENTS AND DISEASE AT THE LEVEL OF PERFECTION WHICH PERMEATES HIMSELF AND ALL CREATION! If you have difficulty "swallowing" this, it is recommended that you start at Chapter One again and reread through to this point of this book! THIS IS A CRUCIAL FUNDAMENTAL TENET OF THIS BOOK!!!!

In the case of ALLOPATHIC HEALING, many Pharmalogical medicines seem to heal or lessen the severity of a malady. What occurs is that the energy vibration of the medicine affects the conscious/ subconscious mind of the patient which causes a lessening or alleaviation of the symptoms. However, because Allopathic drugs synthesize the active ingredient from plants and discard the inactive ingredients (buffering compounds) iatrogenesis (side effects) and create this undesirable condition. Caveat to all Earthlings: DO NOT MUTILATE OR CHANGE THAT WHICH IS ALREADY PERFECTLY CREATED BY GOD OR IT WILL RESULT IN IMPERFECT DENIGRATIONS/FAULTY TEMPLATES AND INCOMPLETE HEALING! The Theta-Divine connection has been ignored! THE MASS BELIEF THAT THESE MEDICINES ARE EFFECTIVE IS IN FACT WHAT MAKES THEM SEEM TO CURE! Right now, the "medical establishment" and the pharmecuetical companies are conjuring and creating ailments for which you need treatment and the medicines related thereto and this is achieved via adverstisements that have subliminally affective pictures!!!!

The downright inaneness/idiocy of the "allopathic protocols" for Cancer are self-evident if you view them from a neutral position. Irradiating a body to kill Cancer cells might be a good thing were it not for the toxic effects of radition. Using Chemotherapy to kill Cancer cells would also appear to be beneficial were it not for the fact that it is laced with heavy metals such as PLATINUM and LEAD among others, which decimate bodily organs.

Additionally, it has been revealed in Dr. Leonard Coldwell's book, "The Only Answer To Cancer", that there are the elements of "MUSTARD GAS" in the "CHEMO COCKTAIL"!!!! Chemotherapy has a devastating effect on the Liver AND DOES NOT DISCRIMINATE BETWEEN THE KIILING OF CANCEROUS AND NON-CANCEROUS CELLS of the patient and Radiation, likewise, damages anything to which it is exposed like internal organs and the entire body. Wow, what a wonderful protocol!

Removing cancerous tumors might be a good thing if doing so did not spread Cancer throughout the body. Dr. Newton would plead with oncologists to realize the purpose of a tumor is to collect and localize Cancer cells. Remove the tumor and Cancer spreads. Maybe you might want to cogitate on this revelation and eliminate bodily toxins before you remove the tumor! THERE ARE MANY NATURAL DETOXIFICATION PROTOCOLS, SUCH AS CHELATION and "THE BUDWIG PROTOCOLS, WHICH WILL ELIMINATE TUMORS without surgery! Since the author has seen the effectiveness of these "alternative protocols" with his own eyes on many occassions, this more than some "farfetched", idiotic proclamation! WHAT IS "FARFETCHED" and IDIOTIC IS THE EXISTING ONCOLOGICAL PROTOCOLS!!!! Of this, the author is more certain than his own name!!!!

All of this reveals the utter incompetence of the oncological cancer protocol. Even worse is the fact that this is the only legal way to treat cancer in most of the USA, with exception of maybe two states. So what has been created is a condition where it is illegal to treat Cancer without toxic and damaging protocols. We should be so grateful for our governments protecting us from benign, non-toxic treatments! If you use a Christian Science treatment which is non-medical and the patient dies, parents could be in sticky legal territory because of the draconian medical laws that have been enacted, should a child die! But if the child dies from the normal oncological protocol, the doctor will never be indicted, unlike the parent. Personally, Dr. Newton knows of no governmental body or bureaucracy that can make decisions even as good as himself, let alone better! WELL, ACTUALLY THE CREATOR MAKES SUBSTANCIALLY BETTER DECISIONS THAN THE AUTHOR but the list after God is rather short!!!!

There are many natural Cancer therapies that do not affront the existing systems/organs within the body. They include electrical frequencies from a "Rife" generator (akin to a radionics device), pharmaceutical grade Aloe Vera, 35 % Hydrogen Peroxide (diluted), Ozone, "The John Ellis Water Machine" (it creates H2O2), the combination of low fat cottage cheese and flax seed oil (the Dr. Budwig protocol), the "grape diet" protocol, chelation therapy, "alkaline protocol" (including the "baking soda protocol"), the "Gerson protocol" (involving juice fasting, alkalizing the body Ph [an alkaline battery has much more energy than a nickel-cadmium battery] and coffee enemas), photo-luminesence wherein blood is exposed to an ultra-violet light through a transfusion process, and Chelation. THIS LIST IS NOT EVEN COMPREHENSIVE. ALL OF THESE THINGS AND MORE ARE THAN EFFECTIVE for the intended purpose of treating a Cancerous condition and much more effective and less invasive than the accepted Oncological protocols!

From personal knowledge and experience, Dr. Newton knows that these "a;ternative protocols" are unquestionably effective and cost hundreds of dollars instead of many hundreds of thousands of dollars for the "allopathic Cancer protocol" used by Oncology, notwithstanding the toxins to which you will be exposed and routinely ignored and/or dismissed by many Oncologists! It has been reported in the "American Free Press", numerous times, that neither Chemotherapy nor Radiation actually eliminate Cancer but rather make it go into "hiding" for a period of time until it returns. Additionally, they have reported that YOU ARE MORE LIKELY TO DIE FROM CHEMOTHERAPY AND RADIATION THAN FROM CANCER ITSELF. Should not this be enough to severely doubt these protocols? Most Oncologist's already know this so why isn't this information shared with you?

Could the DISEASE OF GREED be the culprit? PVL (probably very likely)!

Additionally, for cancer treatment, we have the Christian Science protocol and you could be immensely helped and supported by a Christian Science Practitioner in your "treatment". Also, we have the "Theta Healing" and "Theta Consciousness Healing^{TM}" protocols that have definitely produced results in curing Cancer! These will be discussed thoroughly in this chapter under "Spiritual Healing". With these protocols, you are WORKING AT THE LEVEL OF CAUSATION—YOUR EMOTIONs, FEARS, and RESENTMENTS AS OPPOSED TO CHASING AN ENDLESS TRAIL OF THE EFFECTS OF DISEASE. Do you think that treating causation would be superior to chasing symptons?

The same "natural" and "spiritual" protocols would apply to AIDS/HIV. Did you know that this virus was created in a government lab in Beltsville, Maryland and is an offshoot of the Cancer virus? Then it was introduced into Africa via the administration of small pox vaccinations? How benign our governments are? CONSPIRACY REALITY—NOT SOME HALLUCINAGENIC THEORY, as exposed by Tom Bearden, among others, in one of his books! This is just another incidence corroborating Dr. Newton's contention that your government does not have your best interests at heart! You mean they actually have one (a heart)? ACTIONS ALWAYS SPEAK LOUDER THAN WORDS, which are often more akin to flatulance than truth!

With HERBAL MEDICINES, HOMEOPATHIC MEDICINE and FLOWER REMEDIES, these concoctions are in their naturally compounded state of creation. Again, they create a vibrational energetic frequency which causes a shift in consciousness that effectuates a "healing" and almost always without iatrogenesis. The consciousness of the patient is aligned more closely with the DIVINE PARADIGM OF HEALTH BUT STILL NOT OPTIMALLY BECAUSE THERE IS AN INTERLOPING FACTOR BETWEEN OURSELVES AND THE CREATOR! We still have not accessed the Theta-Divine link! But we are closer because we have not interferred with the natural chemistry of the Creator. IT IS A SUBMASS OR MINORITY BELIEF THAT MAKES THESE REMEDIES EFFECTIVE! They are effectuating an emotional shift in consciousness that facilitates the healing!

The modalities of ENERGY HEALING include ACCUPUNCTURE, ACCUPRESSURE, MAGNETIC HEALING and MAGNETIC ACCUPUNCTURE, LASER HEALING and LASER ACCUPUNCTURE, REIKI, QUI GONG and RADIONICS. All of these methods of energy healing rely on the use of PRANA, CHI, ORGONE, ELOPTIC, ELAN VITAL, et. al., also known as LIFE FORCE and/or GOD FORCE. At its essence is ATOMIC FORCE— ELECTROMAGNETISM, LIGHT and VIBRATION. These healing methods are vastly superior to allopathic medicine and superior to herbal, homeopathic and flower remedies. From Dr. Newton's anecdotal experiences he knows this to be ". . . . certain and most true" (Hermes Trismegistus).

ACCUPUNCTURE, ACCUPRESSURE, LASER ACCUPUNCTURE and MAGNETIC ACCUPUNCTURE, REIKI, "The AIM" program and "SOUND SIGNATURE" CATALYZE a higher level of PRANA or CHI in the body through accessing MERIDIANS (energy pathways) which run throughout the body. The author has heard complicated explanations as to how this occurs. But at the essence of this healing is that the increased prana/chi circulating through the body puts the body MORE IN A STATE OF ENERGY/ SPIRIT and LESS IN A STATE OF DENSE MATTER. Accupuncture works because the body is "hardwired" to transmit Prana throughout the body via meridians/nadis/energy channels/nerves/blood vessels!!!!

ALSO, A HIGHER CONSCIOUSNESS IN THE ALPHA/THETA RANGE IS EFFECTED. How the consciousness shift occurs Dr. Newton cannot explain with certainty but that it occurs can be verified through KINESIOLOGY, a muscle testing procedure whereby the effectiveness or ineffectiveness of something is measured. Most likely what occurs is that ATOMS OF THE BODY ARE STIMULATED TO RESONATE AT A HIGHER RATE OF VIBRATION (like a laser), CAUSING THE BODY TO MORE RESEMBLE ITS PERFECT TEMPLATE OF SPIRIT (Electromagnetic energy, Prana, Chi, light and vibrational perfection) and the result is healing!!!! The Theta level is the realm of healing and health because it is the level of Divinity and Superconsciousness! So again, WHAT MAKES THESE MODALITIES WORK IS BRINGING THE BODY INTO COMPLIANCE WITH ITS REAL NATURE/ TEMPLATE WHICH IS SPIRIT/ENERGY!

MAGNETIC HEALING AND LASER HEALING also work in a similar way to the description above and can also access the meridians/nadis/ energy channels. REIKI and QUI GONG also work similar to magnetic and laser healing. RADIONICS focuses electromagnetic frequences to displace disease and sickness. Once again, in these modalities, Prana/Chi is augmented in the body and a theta consciousness shift occurs and healing results as you are in a state of Theta, Divinity and Superconsciousness! REIKI and QUI GONG employ attracting and using Prana/Chi in the hands to energize the body to its natural state of health. The same described atomic stimulation facilitates the "healing process" with these modalities also!

"SOUND SIGNATURE" therapy uses the notes of the Diatonic musical scale at the subwofer level (bass and ultra bass sounds). When employing this protocol the notes of a person's voice is recorded with a Chromatic Tuner. Then you chart the notes as to the number of times they occur during your recording of a voice sequence. From this you will ascertain which notes do not occur or rarely occur in an individuals speech patterns. And then you make a recording of these missing or weak notes at the subwofer level and as a person listens to this, their sickness, disease, malfunction, etc. will be eliminated. What most likely is occurring here is that frequencies are beneficially affecting a releaase of negative emotions which effectuates a cure. A SONIC/VIBRATIONAL PERFECTION IS RESTORED IN THE BODY!

The "AIM" program, developed by Dr. Stephen Lewis also cures maladies with frequencies, oftentimes at a level which cannot be detected with instrumentation. Basically, a radionics or radionic-like device is generating frequencies which are transmitted to a person through their picture which sits on the "plate" of the radionics device. The electro-magnetic radio like waves are once again probably allowing a release of emotional negativity that once again restores the body to its perfect state (Aleph Kaf Aleph).

In the DINSBAUGH PROTOCOLS, colored lights are used to alleviate various maladies.Although there is usually a lag factor in the occurrence of healing, it is in fact effective and the cure is lasting! That this protocol is unknown to doctors and the general public is a testament to the repressive mentality of the FDA.

In the case of SPIRITUAL HEALING (theta energy healing) we are working directly AT THE LEVEL OF THE CREATOR without substances (medicines) to realize/ return the state of health to the patient but we are still dealing with the subconsious (your body's computer). Christian Science healing (which does not recognize the subconsious but this may equate to their term "mortal mind" or "material mind") discounts the symptoms and/or the malady treated and focuses on the template of the "perfect man" or "metaphyscial man". It should be noted that a CHRISTIAN SCIENCE PRACTITIONER MIGHT BE MORE EFFECTIVE AT HEALING YOU THAN YOUR OWN PERSONAL HEALING EFFORTS. This is true because the practitioner is not wrapped up in your veil of fear and our lack of worthiness to be "whole" and healthy! Also, Louise L. Hay in "You Can Heal Your Life" and "Heal Your Body" has well chronicled the emotional component of sickness and disease. And she states that "CRITICISM, ANGER and RESENTMENT" are the cause of most maladies and that is essentially true. The author would add FEAR to this list and OVERCOMING FEAR is the thirty fifth name of God ("Mem Nun Daled"), in the middle of "THE SEVENTY TWO NAMES OF GOD", FROM EXODUS of the Torah!

When these or other emotional causations are removed, health is the inevitable and natural result. THROUGH THETA HEALING AND "THETA CONSCIOUSNESS HEALING"™, EMOTIONS CAN QUICKLY BE REMOVED AT THE LEVEL OF CONSCIOUS AND SUBCONSIOUS THOUGHTS!!!! From experience, Dr. Newton has found this far superior to most other permutated versions of spiritual healing. The more you focus on the SYMPTOMS, the more FEAR GESTATES IN YOUR CONSCIOIUSNESS and SUBCONSCIOUSNESS. WHEN FEAR ABOUNDS HEALING DOES NOT OCCUR—NADA, NUNCA (nothing, never)! When we focus on "Mem Nun Daled" we can mollify our fears from this one of the "72 Names of God".

It is profoundly significant that Asclepias, the greatest herbal healer in Greece, Europe and Asia at a time before Jesus, realized that he would accomplish greater healings through facilitating a state of lucid daydreamming in his patients. And his results exceeded his expectations! The lucid daydreaming state is at least at the level of Alpha brainwave/ consciousness and can often achieve Theta brainwave/ consciousness. This THETA consciousness (A STATE OF DIVINITY, SUPERCONSCIOUSNESS AND EUPHORIA/ BLISS) is in CONJUCTION and ALIGNED with the ATOMIC FIELD and DIVINE CONSCIOUSNESS! And that is what makes the Theta "state" so POWERFULLY TRANSFORMATIVE! It could well be true that you we enter ANOTHER DIMENSION of reality or a PARALLEL REALITY at the threshhold of THETA CONSCIOUSNESS!

CHRISTIAN SCIENCE HEALING occurs at this Theta level even though Mrs. Eddy never stated this concept. She did state, however, that the act of prayer (affirming the power of God to heal) and doing so WITHOUT FEAR OR DOUBT does consistently result in healing effects which restores man to his/her existing "perfect state". Mrs. Eddy often referred to man's necessity to align itself with the "DIVINE MIND" and herein lies the THETA STATE OF BEINGNESS. Possibly even WILLING YOURSELF INTO THE BELIEF OF PERFECTION CAN ACTIVATE THE THETA CONSCIOUSNESS with extreme concentration and fearless belief! THERE IS RESEARCH WHICH SHOWS THAT TELOMEARSE ACTIVITY IN THE BRAIN FROM CHANTING AND PRAYER WILL EFFECTUATE HEALING. This will be covered more fully in a later chapter.

IN THETA CONSCIOUSNESS WE ARE ALIGNED/CONNECTED VIA THE ATOMIC FIELD WITH DIVINITY AND HEALING NECESSARILY FOLLOWS AS WE PERCEIVE THE PERFECT AND TRUE CONCEPTS OF CREATION!!!! You will not likely find this printed anywhere else except Vianna Stibal's book, but this sprang into consciousness while Dr. Newton was in a verifiable state of Theta! BY CHANGING AND RAISING OUR CONSCIOUSNESS TO THE REALM OF THETA WE CAN GRADUALLY AND WITH EXPERIENCE, QUIDKLY CHANGE/IMPROVE OUR HEALTH and BANISH DISEASE FROM THE BODY!

"THETA HEALING" is a healing/programming protocol that was revealed to Vianna Stibal after she was diagnosed with uncurable cancer. She healed herself through this system and the nice thing about it is that it is more protocolized than Christian Science treatment. In the class on "Theta Healing" which Dr. Newton received, he was not told how to achieve the Theta level but rather given a way to know if we resided in Theta consciousness. That leaves is in an uncertain predicament which the author would rather not deal with!

"THETA CONSCIOUSNESS HEALING™" is an extension of "Theta Healing" which has been created by Dr. Newton. It is not necessarily better than "Theta Healing" but it is more detailed and gives specific indicators that allow you to absolutely know that you are at Theta level when you are using this system of healing. Dr. Newton's Theta Healing class was not taught by Vianna but rather by a teacher authorized by her. He found it a most glaring ommission that this was not included. For Dr. Newton, he already knew Theta consciousness techniques but the rest of his class was "short changed" because they did not. This is a powerful spiritual healing modality but the author won't be revealing this proprietary system in this book because it is copyrighted and/or proprietary. An alternative system that has been unveiled to the author will be revealed in upcoming chapters, which is "THETA CONSCIOUSNESS HEALING™".

WHAT MAKES SPIRITUAL HEALING SO AMAZINGLY EFFECTIVE IS ITS DIRECT LINK WITH THE CREATOR, DIVINITY, SUPERCONSCIOUSNESS—THETA CONSCIOUSNESS —WHERE WE ARE OPERATING AT THE LEVEL OF THE CREATOR'S PERFECTION! Since the ATOMS ARE ALL THAT COMPRISE OUR BODIES, and PERFECTLY FUNCTIONING ATOMS to wit, the only thing that can ever make us SICK is our NEGATIVE EMOTIONS/FEARS and the thoughts attached to them and your lack of worthiness to be Divine. And if you keep your consciousness at the THETA LEVEL, your NEGATIVE EMOTIONS/ FEARS BASICALLY DO NOT EXIST and, oops, SICKNESS and DISEASE DISAPPEAR! Not only is this simplistic, it actually occurs, as a certitude! A person who is HAPPY and HAS A POSITIVE ATTITUDE and PERSPECTIVE WILL CONSISTENTLY TEST STRONGER IN KINESOLOGICAL "MUSCLE TESTING" THAN A SAD, ANGRY, NEGATIVELY ASPECTED PERSON!!!! In tests that Dr. Newton has observed, THERE APPEARS TO BE A DIRECT LINK TO HEALTH AS RELATED TO THE DISPLAY OF EMOTIONAL EXPRESSIONS!

IT IS IMPORTANT FOR "THETA HEALERS", "THETA CONSCIOUSNESS HEALING™" and EVEN CHRISTIAN SCIENCE HEALERS TO BE AWARE THAT EMOTIONAL PATTERNS THAT WE HOLD CAN BE TRACED BACK TO OUR RELATIVES AND

ANCESTORS. Vianna Stibal, who created the "Theta Healing" protocols, believes that this goes backward to seven generations. Dr. Newton, from Akashic input and Kinesological validation, is feeling that there is no limit at seven generations and that such effect goes back as far as it exists and/ or existed within your relatives and ancestors. THE CAVEAT HERE IS THAT WE CAN EXPERIENCE SICKNESS, ANGER, FEAR RESENTMENT AND A LACK OF ABUNDANCE FROM ASPECTS WHICH WE HAVE NOT DIRECTLY CREATED OURSELVES. Fortunately for us, we can easily remove these things through Theta Reprogramming protocols, which will be detailed in Chapter Four!!!!

So to answer the question of the title of this chapter, WHICH RELATES TO THE "LIGHT BODY" or "body of energy", ENERGY HEALING AND SPIRITUAL/THETA HEALING MODALITIES ARE ABLE TO AID IN CATALYZING A NON-MATERIAL BODY WHEREAS ALLOPATHIC MEDICINE WILL NEVER, EVER ACHIEVE SUCH! Because if such was possible for allopaths to do this, their patients would HAVE THE POTENTIAL OF AN IMMORTAL BODY IN THIS LIFETIME! Para ellos, no es possible para este pasar (for them, this is not possible to occur)!!! WITH CHRISTIAN SCIENCE HEALING AND THE TWO THETA HEALING PROTOCOLS, THE IMMORTALITY OF THE BODY IS MORE THAN JUST A REMOTE POSSIBILITY AND IS ACTUALLY ACHIEVEABLE!!!!

In the "Death of Death", by Siddha, Satguru and MahaAvatar Babaji Nagaraj, it is plainly stated that when all other means of healing are ineffective, repeating the name of the Lord (as in a mantra or rosary), for two hours in the morning and two hours in the evening, for a total of forty eight days will cure any malady or disease as a certainty. Also he states that repeating his mantra, "Om Kriya Babaji Nama Aum", as directed above, will heal with similar results. The author feels this would also work with other exalted religious figures such as Jesus, the Christ!!!! Although Babaji Nagaraj does not mention this specifically, THE SAME PROTOCOL WOULD WORK TO RAISE THE DEAD AND TO

EFFECTUATE "PHYSICAL BODY" IMMORTALITY AKA THE "LIGHT BODY"!!!!

IN REVIEW:

Healing with ALLOPATHIC MEDECINES can be an iatrogenic (side effects) nightmare, FILLED WITH UNDESIRABLE SIDE EFFECTS. Plant remedies have been actually chemically altered BY REMOVING BUFFERING COMPONENTS! THEY ARE EFFECTIVE ONLY BECAUSE OFF THE MASS BELIEF THAT THEY HEAL!

The existing allopathic Cancer protocol using radiation and chemotherapy is toxic and damages the body and the surgical removal of tumors actually spreads Cancer because a tumor's purpose is to gather toxins/diseased cells in one place.

Herbal, Homeopathic and flower remedies are undisturbed plant remedies more in line with the paradigms established by the Creator and usually have no side effects! As a remedy with more purity, it is a more Divine and effective cure! THESE REMEDIES WORK BECAUSE OF THE SUBMASS BELIEF THAT THEY CURE! They are effectuating an emotional shift in consciousness which allows healing to manifest!

Energy healing, including accupuncture, accupressure, Reiki, Qui Gong, Dinsbaugh Protocols, "Sound Signature" and the "AIM" program and Radionics catalyze more prana/chi/energy in the body RAISING IT TO A HIGHER SPIRITUAL DIMENSION (higher energy) and less material thus eliciting a state of Theta/Divine consciousness (which is the natural metaphysical state of man, anyway)! By balancing the body's energy fields, a shift in emotional concsciousness allows healing to occur!

Spiritual healing, theta modalities of healing, (Christian Science, lucid daydreaming, "Theta Healing", "Theta Consciousness Healing"™) are of ultimate value and in ALIGNMENT WITH THE CREATOR!

Theta/Divine consciousness raises the energy of the body to its true state of perfection (again, the natural state of man)! THE ONLY THING WHICH CAN PREVENT THIS TYPE OF HEALING IS FEAR AND A LACK OF WORTHINESS TO BE DIVINE!

POSITIVE EMOTIONS ALWAYS ELICIT HEALTH WHEREAS NEGATIVE EMOTIONS ARE THE CAUSATIONAL FACTORS IN SICKNESS AND DISEASE! This is consistently verefied by Kineosological "muscle testing".

Medicines heal by effectuating a vibrational energy which causes an emotional shift of consciousness in the patient. Herbal medicines are more closely aligned with the creator since they have not been changed from their natural state of creation! The herbs are a higher healing modality!

In Energy Healing, Prana/Chi is augmented, theta/divine/super consciousness ensues and healing results! More Prana is infused into the body which lifts it to its natural state of perfection. This is still a higher method of healing!

Spiritual healing occurs by eliciting Theta consciousness which directly aligns us with Divine Consciousness and the vibrations of this energy, Spirit, Prana, Chi, etc., restores us to our perfect state (Aleph Kaf Aleph)!!!! These spiritual modalities are the optimum and ultimate modalities of of healing!

Christian Science Healing, "Theta Healing" and "Theta Consciousness Healing" are three very powerful spiritual healing modalities!

So in answering the question of how this relates to the "light body", the answer is that ENERGY HEALING AND SPIRITUAL/THETA HEALING CAN CATALYZE THE "LIGHT BODY" (etheric energy body) WHEREAS ALLOPATHIC MEDICINE WILL NEVER,

EVER ACHIEVE THIS! If it were effectual in taking the body to the transformational state of Light, then patients treated in this manner would not have a propensity to die!

In "The Death of Death", by Babaji Nagaraj, there is a protocol of healing maladies and disease by repeating the name of God. The same could well apply to raising the dead and "physical body" immortality!

CHAPTER THREE

THE LEVELS OF CONSCIOUSNESS AND HOW TO ACHIEVE THETA/GOD CONSCIOUSNESS AND THE "LIGHT BODY"/"SPIRITUAL BODY".!

So if you want to be with God, attuned to the frequency of your Creator, you need to be in Theta consciousness. Let us consider why this is so. Beta consciousness is the basest (not basis) level of thought. It considered "left brained" and is more chaotic than calm, more random than focused. This is a "brain frequencey at eleven hertz or higher. Thomas Morton of "Light Speed Learning" calls it "very annoying" and to someone like him who resides essentially in Theta consciousness it is just that!

Dr. Newton's Kriya Yoga teacher, Marsahall Govindan Satchidanada calls it the "monkey mind" as did his teacher, Yogi Ramiah. The author calls it "jibber jabber", a phrase from Mr. "T" of the "A-Team" television series in reference to the utterances of the character, Murdoch. An individual in Beta is so focused on "base needs" and "life's necessities" that the "BRAIN FREQUENCY/CONSCIOUSNESS" IS NOT "TUNED" into GOD or DIVINITY. The bi-polar mind is akin to the "monkey mind" alternating between the depressed Beta frequencies and the more liberating Alpha consciousness. If there is no liberation from Beta via Alpha, the bi-polar mind will often become suicidal! Sometimes, psychotropic drugs can temporarily pull the bi-polar mind from Beta to a more beneficial Alpha consciousness but these drugs will never permanently enscounse consciousness in Alpha, and the side-effects there from are substancial!

When you are highly irritated or frustrated or depressed or resentful or fearful, you are trapped in Beta consciousness. And you are really trapped and/or blocked from experiencing the greatness and abundance which the Creator wants you to experience and to live in bliss and euphoria. This is the plight of the vast majority of humanity! So how do we change our "station" from the "Beta frequency" and tune it into the Alpha/Theta consciousness?

The receiver in our consciousness begins to receive "THE GOD FREQUENCY" as it tunes into "ALPHA FREQUENCIES". These are achieved in MEDITATION, sometimes prayer, creative ACTIVITIES such as art and music (either creating or listening or appreciating such) and sometimes in sporting activities. EXTREME SPORTING activities such as surfing (including wind), wake boarding, snowboarding, skiing (water and snow), dirt motorcycle riding, sky diving and base jumping. Alpha is achieved during distance running. Having done most of these activities, Dr. Newton can attest to the "Alpha and Theta effect" achieved. At Alpha consciousness, SPIRITUAL HEALING can occur, better PROBLEM SOLVING is achieved, more HAPPINESS and SATISFACTION are perceived and MORE CREATIVITY is experienced and SPORTS PERFORMANCES are ENHANCED!

But TRUE DIVINITY EXISTS at the LEVEL OF THETA and DELTA CONSCIOUSNESS. As discussed in the last chapter, this is where SPIRITUAL HEALING OCCURS! This is where SOLUTIONS are ROUTINELY DISCOVERED to UNSOLVABLE PROBLEMS! This is where CREATIVITY SPILLS FORTH UNRESTRAINED! This is where things are INVENTED. This is where ATHLETIC PERFORMANCE REACHES "SUPERHUMAN" LEVELS! Guess what? When you INCARNATED on Earth you were ALREADY "TUNED" INTO THIS FREQUENCY. So what the hell happened? Well, we were born in Theta Divinity but unfortunately, by the time we are five or six years old our "schooling" begins to "pound" the Theta consciousness out of us. Beta thoughts and logic become the supreme standards! SO WE WERE REPROGRAMMED TO OUR OWN DETRIMENT, over the long run!

It appears that we need an educational model that leaves this intact, such as that espoused by the brilliant Rudolph Steiner, whose concepts have been adopted by Waldorf and Montessori schools. However, the Illuninati-cabal-cult would not like that BECAUSE THERE WOULD NOT BE ENOUGH COMPLIANT SLAVES TO DO THE MENIAL JOBS TO KEEP THINGS "RUNNING" so that the super elite/Illuminati cult can live comfortably and then some! Although this may initially sound paranoic to some people, when this is seen in from a wholistic perspective, you can see that this statement is less paranoic and actually more correctly insightful!

But HOW IS THIS THETA/DIVINITY RECREATED IN OUR CONSCIOIUSNESS? It can happen at the level of MEDITATION which is achieved at about HALF AN HOUR TO AN HOURS LENGTH, ESPECIALLY WITH KRIYA DHYANA MEDITATION, from Kriya Yoga. It definitely happens after three rounds of KRIYA KUNDALINI PRANAYAM at an extended breathing cadence and other related Pranayam Mudras (positions) which are from Kriya Kundalini Yoga. It strongly happens during SAMADHII from Kriya Kundalini Yoga. It intensely occurs during a KUNDALINI "AWAKENING". It happens during an extended session of the TAI CHI STANDING MEDITATION or the TAI CHI FORM at about one half to one hours length! It happens during "The BACKFLOW MEDITATION" of extended duration. It happens during EXTENDED SESSIONS OF SANSKRIT MANTRAS such as "THE GAYATRI MANTRA", "THE MRITYONJAYA MANTRA", "THE BABAJI MANTRA", and "THE RAM (or Rama) MANTRA".

It happens during an INTENSE MUSICAL PERFORMANCE. It happens during REPETITIVE CHANTING. It happens during TONING. It happens during VERY EXTENDED DISTANCE RUNNING! It happens during EXTREMELY INTENSE SESSIONS OF EXTREME SPORTS, which is what makes these activites so addictive because you feel "so damn good".! It happens in GOLF WHEN YOU HIT AN "UNBELIEVABLE" SHOT! It happens during an INTENSE SESSION OF DANCING! it happens after an EXTENDED and INTENSE SEXUAL ENCOUNTER where you LITERALLY MELD WITH YOUR PARTNER!

Dr. Newton has experienced most of these things so he has anecdotal validating evidence of these experiences! And we really need to experience these things to know the effectivenss thereof. The more we practice these protocols the more time you will be residing in Theta Divinity until it basically becomes "automatic" and more or less a full time condition in our everyday life. THIS IS WHEN YOU ARE "GUIDED FROM ABOVE" BY OUR CREATOR!!!! And this is when we are in AN ACCELERATED CONSCIOUSNESS OF ENLIGHTENMENT, as it were!!!!

So let us look at each of these disciplines/protocols:

KRIYA DHYANA MEDITATION is a series of six different meditations for each day of the week. On the seventh day, all six of the separate techniques are combined into one meditation and at the end, you ask Kriya Siddha Yogi and Satguru Babaji Nagaraj a question to which he usually reponds. This is a great Theta consciousness technique but is rather complicated and needs to be taught by Dr. Newton's Kriya Yogi Marshall Govindan Satchianada or one of his authorized teachers who can be reached via the net at Babaji's Kriya Yoga. Net or by Dr. Newton, in his classes/seminars.

KRIYA KUNDALINI PRANAYAM was taught to Dr. Newton, in this incarnation, by Yogi Marshall Govindan Satchianada, founder of Babaji's Kriya Yoga. In reality, the author had obviously learned this in another incarnation or incarnations because he was basically already performing it (about a decade previous to his formal training) but he was not aware that it was a very advanced breathing cadence and technique. The author also spontaneously went into Samadhii after learning the second protocol in Pranayam breathing in his class with Govindan so he was obviously previously adept at this too. "Prana" means "life force" and "Yam" means "control of" and that is just what occurs once you commence serious practice of Pranayam!

KRIYA KUNDALINI YOGA consists of these componnets but is not necessarily limited to only these:

First is **KRIYA YOGA ASANAS,** which are powerful stretching exercises that improve the the functioning of the body overall and the spinal cord or "spinal channel" which is literally revitalized and highly energized with Prana (electromagnetic energy). These Asanas prepare you for the rest of the Kriya Yoga protocols.

Second is **KRIYA DHYANA MEDITATION,** which helps focus your mind (possibly like a laser beam) and helps to quell the "Monkey Mind"/"Jibber Jabber" of Beta consciousness and transforms you into Alpha and Theta consciousness.

Third is **KRIYA KUNDALINI PRANAYAM,** which is an extremely powerful breathing protocol, unlike any other in Yoga, Hinduism and Buddhism or any other religion or discipline. It too includes six different components, each of which is practiced on a different day of the week. On the seventh day all six of the components are performed simultaneously. It powerfully entrains a state of Theta during an extended practice each day.

Fourth is **SAMADHI,** which you will, in many cases, morph into once you are extremely proficient in Pranayam. It is a BREATHLESS STATE OF CONSCIOUPSNESS!

Fifth is **KUNDALINI AWAKENING,** which can happen in several ways but is most reliably accomplished by mastering Pranayam and Samadhi.

Sixth is the repetition of **SANSKRIT MANTRAS.**

Seventh is **BHAKTI** and **JANA** Yoga.

The first three of these and the sixth are to be performed daily. The fourth can be performed, whenever, but is most easily accessed after at least 3 rounds of Pranayam with a thirty to forty second cadence for each completed breath.

As ws mentioned earlier in this book, the word Yoga comes from the Sanskrit word YUG which means union. A union is something which joins things together and so in a figurative and literal sense, as it were, YOGA IS UNIFYING OR **REJOINING WITH OUR CREATOR**! BOTH KRIYA **DHYANA** MEDITATION and KRIYA KUNDALINI **PRANAYAM** NEED TO BE TAUGHT TO YOU BY AN EXPERIENCED, COMPETENT TEACHER such as Dr. Newton's Yogi Govindan Satchidanada or one of his authorized teachers contactable via the net at Babajis Kriya Yoga.net or through one of Dr. Newton's seminars. In the case of PRANAYAM, IF PERFROMED CORRECTLY, THE BENEFITS CAN BE UNLIMITED. If PERFOMRED INCORRECTLY YOU CAN CAUSE HARM TO YOUR HEART AND BODY AND YOUR EMOTIONAL EQUILIBRIUM—NO BULL SHIITE! If this happened to Paul Foster Case, an acknowledged spiritual adept, it can happen to you likewise! Please learn from the mistakes of other beings, rather than falling into the same "pit" as those who went before you.

Someone as clearly spiritually evolved as the "adept", Paul Foster Case, stated in his wirtings that he was emotionally and physically damaged by practicing Pranayam without supervision. It was intended by the author to reveal the complete protocols for Pranayam but after considerable deliberation regarding this and actually writing the paragraphs about the protocol to explicate this, he has changed his intention. He knows from experience with his students that it is vital to have continual support to master the Pranayam protocols.

To perform Pranayam, you should be in the "Lotus" position, seated on the floor with your legs crossed either in full or half Lotus if you can perform this, otherwise just "cross legged". Also, it can be performed sitting in a chair but in a forward position without your back resting against the upright part of the chair, otherwise you will become too relaxed and will be prone to enter the state of slumber. You would be better served by the Lotus position because you blood pressure will be lower. Your spine needs to aligned as straight as possible so the Prana/life force can enter your body with less resistance.

PRANAYAM ALLOWS YOU TO TAKE THE PRANA IN YOUR BREATH AND CONVERT IT INTO A QUASI-SOLID STATE OF LIGHT OR ENERGY WHICH IS AN ASPECT OF SPIRIT AND, OVER TIME, CONVERTS YOUR BODY INTO ITS INTENDED PERFECT FORM, so states Goswami Kriyananda in "The Spiritual science of Kriya Yoga"! Yogiraj Gurunath Siddhanath says on his internet website that the spinal breathing of Pranayam creates an "magnetic oxidation" that causes Prana to be directed into the Spine and in so doing helps us to regain our Divine essense.

Avatar and Yogi Parmahansa Yogananda, in his English translation of the "Bhagavad Gita" says that the Prana inhaled through the Pranayam breath and carried within the spinal column "magnetizes" (energizes) and bathes body cells with light and this is actually more nourishing than food. And so this is the beginning of an eventual state of non-decay and immortality in the body. All of these perspectives on Pranayam listed above, have validity as verified from the author's experience and other Kirya Yogi's and Yogini's with which he has conversed!

This process of energizing the body with Prana may be gradual but IF YOU ARE COMMITTED AND DISCIPLINED IN YOUR PRACTICE OF PRANAYAM, OCCUR IT WILL AND THE MORE YOU PRACTICE, THE SOONER IT OCCURS! Again Prana means life force energy and yam means control; both of these are Sanskrit words. So, PRANAYAM allows you to CONTROL/DIRECT ELECTROMAGNETIC ENERGY OF THE PRANA AND BEGINS TO ANCHOR YOUR CONSCIOIUSNESS IN THETA DIVINITY, specifically because of the specific protocols invovled therein. You more fully control your life through optimum health, unlimited abundance and fulfilling relationships! Your body will become lighter, as it were, as can be verified through a CHANGE IN YOUR AURIC/ETHERIC FIELD (the electromagnetic energy which surrounds your body) which can be measured with dowsing rods, an electrometer and a magnonmeter.

The basic Pranayam breathing is done with your mouth closed and all air is inhaled and exhaled through your nose and not the mouth. This breathing process is repeated a total 16 times which comprises one round. You will need to perform the "Kecharee Mudra" as it enables you to breathe in the unbalanced Pranayam breath. Without this key mudra, you will not be able to do a proper Pranayam breath. If you practice regularly and with dedication, you can reach a level where you can do Pranayam at a rate of two breaths per minute or less! This is part of what will put you in Theta conscioiusness. The other part of the Theta activation is a process known as "Eka Nylai". For some people this will be uncomfortable but mastering this is more than worth the effort because of the Theta/Divine/Superconsciousness pathway it provides to "Cosmic Consciouness" and your immortal "light body"!

Some incompetent plagarizer(s) have purpored to publish the Pranayam protocol of Yogi Govindan Satchidananda and Yogi Ramiah online. However, these people or person, apparently unattendant to acuracy and precision, have not revealed the Kecharee Mudra and without such YOU WILL NEVER PERFORM PRANAYAM CORRECTLY AND RECEIVE THE BOUNTIOUS BLESSINGS THAT ARE ATTACHED THERETO! Also, they are misinformed as to the nature and color of Bindu. Certainly this is a major mistake. Even a bigger mistake is when you cannot plagerize within a framework of accuracy! Please be advised against listening to or following people who are not fanatic about being extremely accurate, especially as it relates to Pranayam. Following such people will inevitably lead you to the infamouns "Shiite Creek". You would be better served by reading "Babaji's Kriya Yoga: Deepening Your Practice", by Jan Ahlund and Marshall Govindan Satchidanada.

AGAIN YOU ARE CAUTIONED ABOUT PERFORMING THIS BREATHING PROTOCOL IF YOU HAVE HEART OR BLOOD PRESSURE PROBLEMS OR ARE PREGNANT OR HAVE SCARLET FEVER! AND IN FACT, YOU WILL NOT GET ALOT OF BENEFIT FROM WHAT HAS BEEN REVEALED UNTIL YOU ADD THE OTHER COMPONENTS OF PRANAYAM. So go learn it from an experienced teacher as Paul Foster Case would exhort you to do!

Pranayam should be practiced before sunrise or when you first arise from your sleep session. The early morning energy is more conducive to practicing Pranayam. Additionally, it is undoubtedly the most important thing you can do. So if you make it your first "task", you will be certain to accomplish this practice which will "set the table" for your day. THIS MUST TAKE PRIORITY OVER THE INTERNET, TEXTING, FACE BOOK AND OTHER RELATED JIBBER JABBER. You should work up to three rounds of Pranayam in the morning and one to three rounds at night or you could do four to seven rounds in the morning like the author AFTER AT LEAST SEVERAL YEARS OF EXPERIENCE! BUT DON'T FORCE THIS PROCESS OR YOU COULD DAMAGE YOUR HEART—LET IT EVOLVE NATURALLY. There is not a Pranayam Olympics that Dr. Newton is aware of!

ANYONE WITH HEART OR BLOOD PRESSURE ISSUES SHOULD BE WARNED AGAINST PRACTICING PRANAYAM BECAUSE THE INITIAL PRACTICE THEREOF CAN BE STRESSFUL, BOTH PHYSICALLY AND EMOTIONALLY

Humanity, on this Earth, has reached a critical junction in its survival where it may be imperative that as many people as possible get this information and PRACTICE and MASTER IT. WHEN CIVILIZATION BREAKS DOWN FROM NATURAL DISASTERS AND "OTHER FORCES" AND THE EXISTING MEDICAL ESTABLISHMENT IS OVERWHELMED BY PATIENTS, **PEOPLE WILL NEED ALTERNATIVE AND SUPERIOR WAYS TO HEAL THEMSELVES!!!!** IN A FLOOD, A BOAT WITHOUT LEAKS HAS CONSIDERABLY MORE VALUE AND USEFULNESS THAN A SHIP WITH LEAKS?! **If you are not adept in the Pranayam breath, your "boat" has leaks, most likely in your auric/pranic field of bodily energy!**

Pranayam and Samadhi combined with "Theta Healing", "Theta Consciousness Healing"™, and Christian Science healing will be a blessing to humanity and very possibly an imperative modality that allows survival of humanity! THAT THIS WILL BE VERY RELEVANT WITHIN A YEAR OR SO IS HIGHLY LIKELY!

IF PRANAYAM IS NOT PRACTICED PRECISELY, SUCCESS WILL BE MINIMAL OR LESS! PLEASE READ THE PRECEDING SENTENCE AGAIN. IF PRACTICED WITH PRECISION AND DEDICATION, THE RESULTS ARE SUBTLELY IMMENSE AND THE BENEFITS THEREFROM ARE BENEFICIAL IN OBVIOUS AND SUBTLE WAYS! The author apologizes if you feel that he has been overly redundant on the above discussed points. Please accept the fact that what is being conveyed is extremely important and that when PRANAYAM is PERFORMED CORRECTLY, there will be INCREASED OXYGEN SATURATION in the body as can be measured with a pulse oximeter. Additionally, the ETHERIC OR AURIC FIELDS around and in the body (electro-magnetic) will be greatly enhanced which can be verified with dowsing rods! It is boosting your Pranic energy so that you are "TUNED INTO DIVINITY" as well as the Eka Nylai that transports you to Theta/Divine/Superconsciousness and all the attendant benefits drived therefrom. SO THERE ARE HEALTH AND SPIRITUAL REWARDS WHEN YOU ASSIDUOUSLY PRACTICE PRANAYAM.

Dr. Newton's Kriya Kundalini Pranayam teacher, Govindan, always would tell us that he could tell if we had been practicing Pranayam by looking at our auras and that is a true statement! Equally as true, is that KRIYA YOGA ESTABLISHES "A STATE OF FREEDOM" which is anchored in a practitioner's consciousness when regularly practiced with dedication for a long period of time. This comes to us from "The Yoga Sutras" by MahaAvatar and Satguru Siddha, Patanjali. Paul Foster Case, in "The Life Power" B.O.D.A. lesson refers to Swami Vivekananda who reveals that EVERYTHING IN OUR LIFE BECOMES REALIZED BECAUSE OF PRANA. From this, we can easily surmise that Pranayam is the portal by which we learn to control Prana and all of the forces of nature. This thus GIVES THE MASTER OF PRANAYAM COMPLETE CONTROL OF HIS SURROUNDINGS and the use of SUPERSENSORY PERCEPTION or all PSYCHIC ABILITIES. So the author would inevitably conclude that you need to learn Pranayam, immediately if not sooner, if you are physcially able to do so!!!!

However, in place of Kriya Kundalini Pranayam, until you are taught such, you can practice "**THE BACKFLOW MEDITATION**", taught to Dr. Newton by Reverund and Eyptologist, Robert (Chuck) Schwartz. You do this by performing a slow, deep, rhtymic, diaphragmatic breath with the inhalation being the same length as the exhalation. When you are inhaling, pull and see or feel your breath or a column of light moving down your spine through the back top of your head and passing through the Medula Oblangata at the middle back of your cranium and then passing all the way down your spine. The eyes are turned upward to aid in shifting your consciousness to the spinal and Medula Oblongata areas, as opposed to the normal process where light is brought down through the middle of the body. Repeat this process with each cyclic breath. This is extemely energizing as the Pranic force (life force of the Creator) is optimally progressing not only down the spine but through part of the Crown Chakra (the energy portal on the top of your head), the Medula oblongata (which for some reason has not been considered a significant energy portal but nevertheless is) and the Base Chakra, located at your tailbone.

A Map To Healing

Backflow Meditation

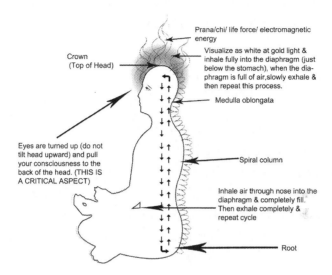

Prana/chi/ life force/ electromagnetic energy

Visualize as white at gold light & inhale fully into the diaphragm (just below the stomach), when the diaphragm is full of air, slowly exhale & then repeat this process.

Crown
(Top of Head)

Medulla oblongata

Eyes are turned up (do not tilt head upward) and pull your consciousness to the back of the head. (THIS IS A CRITICAL ASPECT)

Spiral column

Inhale air through nose into the diaphragm & completely fill. Then exhale completely & repeat cycle

Root

Diagram # 2a : Side view

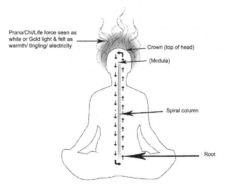

Prana/Chi/Life force seen as white or Gold light & felt as warmth/ tingling/ electricity

Crown (top of head)

{Medula}

Spiral column

Root

Backview of the Backflow Meditation

Use a base meditation posture sitting cross legged on the ground or sit in a chair. See & breathe a column of light and feel the electricity of the Electromagnetic Energy (Prana/Chi/Life Force) causing down into the crown & bending back to the Medula Oblongata down the back of the neck & spinal column & end at the tail bone and then see the energy circulating back up & then down in a continuous cycle.

You will get a "spacey"/trance like feeling from this & that includes a dimensional/consciousness shift into Alpha and Theta consciousness. This is a close replication of how this was taught by Robert(Chuck) Charles Schwrit PULLING YOUR CONSCIOUSNESS TO THE BACK OF YOUR HEAD IS OF CRITICAL IMPORTANCE.

Diagram # 2b

Not only is the "Backflow" process energizing as was just mentioned, many people will feel electricity transiting their spinal and cranial regions and you will enter Theta Divinity! How this exactly occurs has not been discovered but that it occurs has been demonstrated repeatedly. So you can use this in place of Pranayam in the Theta Consciousness healing protocol! You can also use the Tai Chi "Standing Meditation" technique which will be discussed in a few paragraphs

SAMADHI, where you enter a state of bliss/euphoria where breathing naturally stops and the heart stops beating, can be easily achieved by performing three rounds (48 repetitions) of Pranayam at a two breaths per minute (or less) cadence. Again, YOU NEED AN EXPERIENCED TEACHER FOR THIS PROCESS for this VERY ALTERED STATE OF CONSCIOUSNESS or Dr. Newton to teach it to you in his seminars. You will achieve a deep Theta consciousness and/or Divinity and/or super— consciousness in Samadhii that could well "blow you away"!

What essentially occurs during Samadhi is the Prana (God's life force) is sustaining the body without breathing or blood circulation. You will achieve a very deep level of Theta Consciousness! DO NOT TRY THIS WITHOUT SUPERVISION AT FIRST AND IF YOU HAVE HEART AND BLOOD PRESSURE PROBLEMS OR OTHER HEALTH ISSUES! In this state of Samadhi, Theta Consciousness Healing is facitated at a faster rate and with more effectiveness BECAUSE YOU HAVE A STRONGER LINK TO OUR CREATOR!!!! It is important that when we "leave" Samadhi, and the "sleep cycle", THAT WE BRING BACK INFORMATION AND INSIGHTS DERIVED THESE "ALTERED" DIMENSIONS AND INTEGRATE IT INTO OUR LIVES IN THIS DIMENSION!!!! Conversely, the "you" that exists in the dimension you visited in Samadhi and/or the sleep cycle NEEDS TO DO THE SAME!!!!

In a **KUNDALINI AWAKENING**, one way to actuate this is through the intense and devoted practice of Kriya Kundalini Pranayam and/or through

Samadhii. Dr. Newton first entered this intense Kundalini consciousness guided by Dr. Paul Spin, who helped him to reach rather radical realizations about God, even confronting God about things he was unhappy with vis a vis the Creator. Other Kundalini encounters he had occurred when he was laying down on magnetic beds/pads; one of these magnetic pads had an external electrical source to intensify its effect.

YOU NEED TO BE FOREWARNED THAT A KUNDALINI AWAKENING WILL BE THE MOST INTENSE AND DISORIENTING EXPERIENCE YOU HAVE EVER HAD. Dr. Newton has read/heard experiences from "triping" on LSD and although somewhat similar this does not seem comparable! Let the author explicate. First, this experience does not come on "nice and easy" but rather "hard and intense". Secondly, your head will feel like it is literally on fire yet you will not be burned literally—but maybe figuratively. Thirdly, you will lose your equilibrium and will be not only physically but mentally disoriented because you have never experienced anything as remotely intense and Divine!!!! But concurrently with these side effects you will lose touch with your supposed "materiality/physicality" and you will be in such an intense state of Divinity that you will feel your "oneness" with the Creator as discussed by Patanjali in "The Yoga Sutras" and you will be in the most intensive state of euphoria/bliss imaginable! This has been correlated by Gopi Krishna's book about his Kundalini experiences.

YOU HAVE BASICALLY MOVED INTO A HIGHER SPIRITUAL/ENERGY DIMENSION IN AN EXTREMELY INTENSE MANNER, WHERE FEW PEOPLE HAVE GONE BEFORE! The author strongly recommends the Kundalini experience BUT ONLY IF YOU ARE ONLY BASICALLY WITHOUT FEAR AND WITH EXPERIENCED SUPERVISION AND THOUSANDS OF "ROUNDS" OF KRIYA KUNDALINI PRANAYAM!!!!

TAI CHI is probably from Kriya Yoga Siddha, Boganathar, who was one of Siddha Babji Nagaraj's teachers. There is no direct proof of this of which the author is aware but it is well known among the Kriya Yoga Siddhas that Boganathur spent considerable time in China during its very early history and he was more than likely the most spiritually evolved person there, at that point in time. The known site of the beginning of Tai Chi is China. It is Dr. Newton's belief that having been an Avatar of Kriya Yoga, Siddha Boganathar created Tai Chi to fit in with the belief systems and traditions of China.

Irrespective of Dr. Newton's understanding, Tai Chi is more or less a Chinese Kriya Yoga! This is deducible from the fact that they both deal with Prana (Spirit, energy) although the Chinese call Prana, Chi. They are one and the same, being an intense electro-magnetic field generated by atoms which is directed and controlled by the Creator! The Tai Chi "Standing Meditation" is performed by standing with your knees bent and your shoulders sloped forward and being as relaxed as possible.

From this erect state you breath completely into your diaphram (just above the stomach) and you visualize either golden or white light coming down from the Creator passing through the top of your head and going down to the "Dantien" (just above your stomach). You exhale completely and then repeat the process of the complete inhalation and as you repeat this you see a ball of light increasing in size and intensity with each breath.

You also see the golden or white light going down through your legs down to your feet and anchoring yourself into the Earth. From the ball of light you see this energy radiating out to all the extremeties of your body. As you do this you should feel a warming and/or tingling and/or electricity in your hands, head and possibly your feet. If you visualize yourself in a pool of water up to your chest, you will be able to lift your arms in a straight position in front of your chest without using any muscle powerin a relaxed state (see diagram following), "The Standing Meditation should be performed facing northward in the Northern Hemisphere!

Tai Chi "Standing Meditation"

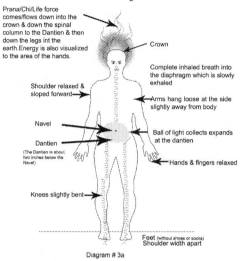

Prana/Chi/Life force comes/flows down into the crown & down the spinal column to the Dantien & then down the legs int the earth. Energy is also visualized to the area of the hands.

Crown

Complete inhaled breath into the diaphragm which is slowly exhaled

Shoulder relaxed & sloped forward

Arms hang loose at the side slightly away from body

Navel

Ball of light collects expands at the dantien

Dantien

(The Dantien is about two inches below the Navel)

Hands & fingers relaxed

Knees slightly bent

Feet (without shoes or socks) Shoulder width apart

Diagram # 3a

E.M. energy & (Prana/Ch/life force) is visualized and breathed diaphragmati-cally as white or gold light that is pulled down into the crown(TOH) & down the spiral column to the dantien(just below the navel), where a ball of light is cre-ated which expands with each inhaled breath. The energy/light is directed down the legs into the earth & grounds you thereto . As the light accumulates, you visualize and breathe it o the exhaled breath throughout the body, includ-ing the hands. This will energize the body enough for the next parts of the Standing Meditation

Raising the arms sans muscles (floating arms)

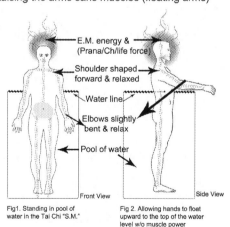

E.M. energy & (Prana/Ch/life force)

Shoulder shaped forward & relaxed

Water line

Elbows slightly bent & relax

Pool of water

Front View

Side View

Fig1. Standing in pool of water in the Tai Chi "S.M."

Fig 2. Allowing hands to float upward to the top of the water level w/o muscle power

Diagram # 3b

You do not actually have to stand in a pool of water. H/E, visualizing such will help your first attempts in using Chi to lift your arms sans muscles. This position can be sustained for a long period of time.

If you turn your hands toward each other from the raised arm position and see one hand with a negative charge and the other hand with a positive charge, your hands will be pulled close together with no muscle power. Just as the hands are about to touch, turn the charges in your hand to the same charge and your hands will be pushed apart. If you repeat this process multiple times, you will begin to feel a "ball" with a tingling or electrical current between your hands (see diagram below).

Tai Chi "Standing Meditation"

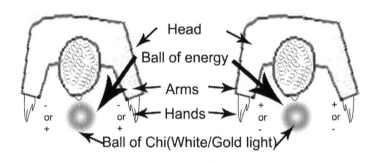

Diagram # 4 : Attraction & Repulsion of the Hands

This attraction & repulsion of the hands is done effortlessly, relaxed & w/o muscles. After getting your hands raised in the imaginary pool of water, in the previous diagram turn the palms of the hands toward each other & separated, see a plus(+) change in one hand & a negative (-) charge in the other hand & the hands will begin to come together. Before the hands come together, see the polarity in the hands becoming plus(+), plus(+) or negative(-),negative(-) & they will push apart. Then repeat the process. As you repeat the attraction – repulsion process, see a ball of parna / white or golden light building in your hands. The hands should become warm &/or with a "tingling" sensation & /or feel currents of electricity. This would be a great "pre-protocol" process for "energy heaters" and message therapists & chiropractors.

If you perform the Tai Chi "Standing Meditation" for about twenty or thirty minutes, in a relaxed state, at worst you will enter Alpha consciousness and as you become more proficient, you can attain Theta consciousness as you become "one with theChi"! The author will not describe the Tai Chi Form, a choreograph of many flowing movements done in a relaxed manner. There are books and videos on this subject. It would be immeasurably more beneficial for you to study TAI CHI CHUAN as opposed to the diluted Tai Chi Chuh. Tai Chi Chuh is not of Chinese origin and was formulated for "lazy Americans" without the necessary patience or discipline to learn Tai Chi Chuan. If you can perform the "short form" of Tai Chi Chuan in a relaxed state, you will achieve alpha consciousness and possibly attain Theta/God consciousness!

Japanese Tai Chi, known as **DOW-IN,** is another quick way to energize the body and attune to the Alpha and Theta frequencies of consciousness. This is done standing up, in the same position as the Tai Chi "Standing Meditation", and with the shoulders, arms and hands in a relaxed state. You quickly, with short strokes push both hands backward about twenty five or thirty degrees. Then you allow the hands to come forward even with your legs. This is done repetitively, many times, without stopping, You usually can quickly feel tingling and/or electricity and/or warmth building in your hands and/or body. For the Alpha and Theta benefit from this, Dow-In should be performed for twenty to thirty minutes. You can also add pulling down the white or golden light through the top of you head and down yo below the the Solar Plexus

Do (Dow)-In Standing Meditation

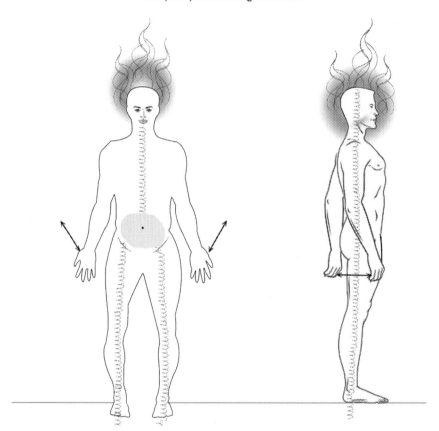

Everything here is the same as the Tai chi "standing meditation". Refer to diagram 3a & 3b.Shoulders are sloped forward & relaxed. Elbows & hands are slightly bent & relaxed, a column of white or gold light is visualized coming down through the head and spinal column into the Dantien and then down the legs & feet & into the ground. As the hands are at the side of the body, slightly separated. There from, push the hands backward, quickly but relaxed,& allow them to come forward but not past parallel to the legs. Repeat this process many repetitions & you will feel the body becoming more energized & the hands also, exhibiting characteristics of warmth, "tingling", electricity. Keep breathing down the column of light & allow to expand the ball of light .

How does Dr. Newton compare Kriya Kundalini Pranayam and the Tai Chi "Standing Meditation" and "The Backflow Meditation"? The Tai Chi "Standing Meditation is immensely easier and quicker to master and can be very powerful and can allow you to access Theta consciousness. "The Backflow Meditation" is also quicker and easier to master and likewise is powerful. However, Kriya Kundalini Pranayam, although taking much more time and effort to master, will easily take you to the deeper levels of Theta/ Divine/Superconsciousness because of the extended breathing cadence, the "Keysharee Mudra, the Eka Nylai, Sita Ushna and the Ida Pingala. PRANAYAM GIVES YOU THE KEY TO COMPLETE MASTERY OVER ALL FORCES ON EARTH!!!! The gravity of this statement is impossible to underestimate, as it were!!!! Also, Dr. Newton knows of no comparative state to Samadhii which exists in Tai Chi. There may be one of which he is unaware, however, he is deeply experienced in both disciplines!

SANSKRIT MANTRAS are similar to a Catholic Rosary but immensely more powerful since Sanskrit is considered a "SACRED LANGUAGE" due to the SONIC and VIBRATIONAL characteristics contained therein. It is special and unique in that the sounds of Sanskrit cause demonstrable effects. This is revealed when you place a speaker playing a recording of the ""Gayatri Mantra" under a table top covered with sand, it produces the geometric yantra (form), called the "Shri Yantra", considered "The Mother" of all yantras/forms for Hindus. This information has been revealed to us by Dr. Patrick Flannagan. In India, virtually every person learns the "GAYATRI MANTRA" because it is considered to have "elevated spiritual vibrations" and a gift from God to humanity! This mantra is considered to bring protection, health and prosperity to those people who daily repeat it. It will greatly aid you in overcoming all of your fears (Mem Nun Daled) from the "72 Names of God".

It is interesting to note and significant that Patanjali says in "The Yoga Sutras" that the sound "Om" will break through obstacles in your life. Basically, all Sanskrit Mantras begin with "Om" or "Aum"! DYT that this is a random coincidence? NVL (NOT VERY LIKELY)! The "elevated" beings that composed these mantras did not believe in coincidence but they were very aware of synchronistic patterns, that are constantly recurring events!

The Gayatri (short form) is pronounced as follows (phonetically):

Om Bhur Bhuval Suvaha,
Tat Savithur Varenyam (but really more like Varenyamuhm),
Bhargo Devasaya Dheemahee,
Dhiyo Yonah Prachodayat.

This should be repeated 108 times (one round) at one time, daily, in a circular repetition the same as a Rosary. Savithur is associated with the Sun. The Sun is associated with the Creator. Hermes Trimigestis, of extra-terrestial origin, in "The Emerald Tablets", also speaks about these Sun-Creator connections. Dr. Newton has seen "colicy" babies which were very agitated, calmed within a few minutes of repeating the "Gayatri Mantra". The same thing applies to agitated adults and children. After one round of "Gayatri", AT WORST YOU WILL BE IN ALPHA CONSCIOUSNESS. As you become more proficient in performing this mantra and for two or three rounds, you should ahieve THETA LEVEL CONSCIOUSNESS! You can buy a recording of this and the Mitronjaya Mantra.

The MRITYONJAYA MANTRA, has many of the same aspects and benefits as the "Gayatri Mantra" and has the same repetition requirements.

"The Mrityonjaya Mantra is pronounced, phonetically, as follows:

"Om Triumbicum Yajamahe,
Sugundam Pushte Vardhanam,
Uvaricam Eva Bandanat,
Mrityor Mukshiya Mamritat."

Alpha and Theta consciousness will ensue within the parameters discussed in regard to "The Gayatri Mantra" and "Mrityonjaya Mantra"! They will calm agitated people, create an aura of protection and will make you calm, serene and happy! What more could you want and yet you still receive the alpha/theta consciousness and the blesssings therefrom.

The matrix chart, "**ICONS: the quickening of insight**" by Fetzer and Tolman available at "www.a3dmind.com" will enscounse the viewer thereof in Theta Consciousness once natual, continual eye flutter occurs. The author has experienced using this chart and can personally recommend the effectiveness in ahcieving Theta level. There are three other charts which complement the "ICONS" chart!

With INTENSE MUSICAL PERFORMANCES, either listened to or performed by yourself or a group of musicians, your consciousness can be transformed immediately, especially if you close your eyes during the music. Many people are under the impression that calm music would transport you to the alpha/theta consciousness range. Dr. Newton has found that intenseand/or very unique music can achieve this more powerfully, at least for some people. "Brain Salad Surgery" by Emerson, Lake and Palmer, "Soul Sacrifice" and "Caravan Sera" by Carlos Santana, "Ivory Expedition" by Tom Coster, "Brain Dance" by Brandon Fields, "In A Gadda Da Vida" (long version) by The Iron Butterfly, "Break on Through" and "Light My Fire" by the Doors, "Return to Dreamland" by Sonja Jason, "Live at the Fillmore West" by the Allman Brothers Band, "Free Bird" (the long version) by Lynard Skynard, "Collection" by Yngwie Malmsteen, "Aura" by Miles Davis, "How Bizarre" by OMC, "T Louie" by ZZAH, "Uberjam" by The John Scofield Band, "Heavy Weather" by Weather Report, "Collection" by Yellowjackets, "Face First" by Tribal Tech, "Seal" by Seal, "Blood, Sweat, and Tears" (the second album, not the one with Al Kooper) by Blood, Sweat, and Tears.

Other recommendations would include "On Hearing Solar Winds" by David Hykes and the Harmonic Choir, "Opera Sauvauge" by Vangelis, anything sung by Andreas Bochelli, "Let It Bleed" and "Beggars Banquet" by The Rolling Stones, anything from the Mahavishnu Orchestra (with John Mc Laughlin), "The Koln Concert" and "The Vienna Concert" by Keith Jarrett, "Internal Combustion" by Glen Velez, "Out of the Loop" by the Brecker Brothers, "Owner of a Lonely Heart" by Yes, anything recorded or live by Steely Dan, "A Love Supreme" by John Coltrane and covered in "The Divine Flame" by Carlos Santana and John Mc Laughlin.

Still more recordings would be "Four Sides Live" by Genesis, anything live by Peter Gabriel, "Jazzpana" by Vince Mendoza and Aarif Mardin, "Downward Spiral" by Nine Inch Nails, "Rage" by Rage against the Machine, "Danzon" by Arturo Sandoval, "Return to Forever" by The Chick Corea Band, "Starship Pyramids" by Christopher Palanai, "Through the Winds" by Juan Carlos Quintero, "Karma" by Pharoh Sanders, "Below the Fold" by Otis Taylor, any music every played by Phil Upchruch, any music by Uncle Festive, any of the music by Linkin Park, all of the music by Nirvana, all of the music by Leon Russell, "Sgt.Pepper's Lonely Heart Club Band" and "The White Album" by the Beatles, "Black and White Knights" by Roy Orbison, et. al., Led Zepplin CD's (especially live recordings), any music by "Brother". There are other selections, of a smoother/mellower nature listed in Dr. Newton's, "Pathways to God" book.

Dr. Newton remembers the first time he learned to meditate listening to "Brain Salad Surgery", "Caravan Sera" and "Ivory Expedition". Listening to the music at a loud volume and with headphones, will more fully catalyze the alpha/theta consciousness effect! The author could not over recommend any of the selections listed BUT IN THE END, YOU MUST FIND MUSIC WHICH RESONATES WITH YOUR THE DNA OF YOUR SOUL! WHEN YOU ACCOMPLISH THIS, YOU WILL MOST LIKELY ENTER THE ALPHA/THETA EXPERIENCE! You need music that will take you into a "trancelike" state.

DRUMMING and PERCUSSION, by rhythmic and syncopated (offbeat) modes, can very quickly take the listener or player thereof into Alpha/

Theta consciousness. This is especially true when a rhythm is repeatedly drummed and when a counter-rhythm is performed behind the initial repeated beats. Playing with a drum circle group is an intense and enjoyable way to experience this. A true trance state can be achieved by performing and listening to drums and percussion and this trance state is Theta Consciousness. When you close your eyes, either listening to or performing music or drumming, the Theta effect can easily be magnified. Chanting and drumming, such as at a Yagna, a Hindu "fire ceremony", can powerfully uplift you into altered consciousness (Theta)! The chanting of the "Gayatri" or "Mrityonjaya" mantra or the mantra of your Satguru coupled with drum accompanyment can really pull you into Theta Divinity!

REPETITIVE CHANTING is known to create a trance-like state if it is performed over a long period of time. The same is true for TONING, which is akin to singing but without words and relying on musical sounds. Usually toning is done in a free form manner. When performed by a group in free form, the sounds of the various group members will sound disharmonic at first but over time they will meld together into a melodious performance. So, these two things will aid in achieving Theta level of consciousness.

There are also some powerful Hebrew chants/mantras from the "Key of Enoch" by Dr. Hurtak. Since Hebrew is considered the other "sacred language" besides Sanskrit, the result from repeating these is powerful and induces Alpha and Theta states of consciousness. One of these Hebrew mantras is as follows and is contained in the "Keys of Enoch", by Dr. J.J. Hurtak:

"Kadoish, Kadoish, Kadoish, Adonai, Saforoth"

The company formerly known as ZYGON, currently known as MIND TECH and SUPER LIFE created an "Ultra Meditation" Tape in the late 1980's which Dr. Newton listened to in about 1991. And within one minute or less, he was having an intense Kundalini awakening that literally enveloped his whole consciousness, both physically, mentally and spiritually. Dane Spotts created this tape and in the years it seems Super Life has been busy creating even more effective means to enable an Alpha-Theta-Delta brainwave consciousness.

In fact, Dr. Newton is sure that these tapes have little or nothing to do with brainwaves because he will show you in Chapter Eight that no function of consciousness has ever been detected in any study of the brain. Whether this disparity between Dr. Newton's perceptions and those who study "brain entrainment" such as Mr. Spotts or this is just a "semantic hurdle" created by the imprecision of our languages, undoubtedly the tape he used and the more recent offerings from Mind Tech/Super Life are profoundly and immensely effective in getting you into the Theta and even deeper, Delta consciousness. These CD's use harmonics and sound frequencies to create a "shift" in your consciousness. You want certainly want to order the "Ultra Meditation: Five Levels of Transcendence. They are available from" The Super Life Catalogue. com.

THESE TAPES, AS POWERFUL AS THEY ARE, DO NOT OBVIATE THE NEED FOR THE ASSIDUOUS PRACITICE OF KRIYA KUNDALINI PRANAYAM and THE TAI CHI "STANDING MEDITATION" because the tapes will not create the "light body" (Spirit/Prana/Chi/energy body) although they may well help catalyze the "light mind" and unleash it into your subconscious mind/computer. Also, devoted practice of the Sanskrit mantras, "Gayatri" and "Mrityonjaya" also will create frequencies which help activate the "light body". Use everything listed herein as parts of the total mixture. Make your focus "multi-directional" (a "multi trick pony") as opposed to omni-directional (a "one trick pony")!

Distance running, the author having done a lot himself, will catalyze this alpha/theta consciousness once "you break through the wall". Until this point you may be very ensconced in beta consciousness and possibly in pain!

Extreme sports such as SURFING (especially when you are "in the tube" or riding a large or very long wave), SNOWBOARDING and SKIING (especially when you are on a long run/trail or a difficult run where you handle the terrain well and do not fall), wakeboarding and water skiing (when you are in an intense run), dirt motorcycle riding when you ascend a steep, difficult hillside or traverse continuously difficult terrain, sky diving and base jumping all will pull you into theta consciousness as long as you are not afraid in these situations. Dr. Newton has had MANY EXPERIENCES SURFING, DIRT MOTORCYCLE RIDING, SNOW BOARDING and JET SKIING WHERE he ENTERED A STATE OF SAMADHII FOR EXTENDED PERIODS OF TIME! This is like theta squared or cubed! The feeling of this indescribably intense and sublime concurrently!

Even in GOLF, you can hit one or a series of shots that can put you in a state of euphoria and if you can maintain such throughout 18 holes of golf that is an achievement in and of itself. INTENSE DANCING or DANCING WITH A PARTNER ON THE BEACH AT NIGHT DURING A FULL MOON, can create a romantic feeling that ushering theta consciousness. From personal experience, Dr. Newton knows this to be ". . . certain and most true".

EXTENDED, INTENSE SEX WITH A PARTNER, where you feel like you are melding with your lover, can also elicit the theta realm in a very intense manner. And these sexual feelings can be heightened through the use of Tantric (an Asian Indian tradition), Taoist (a Chinese tradition) and Kadoshka (a Cherokee Indian tradition) techniques which are, at a minimum, from thousands of years ago!

IN SEXUAL ENCOUNTERS—IF YOU DESIRE THE FULL ("WHOLE ENCHILADA") THETA/ DIVINITY/ SUPERCONSCIOUSNESS RESULT/EFFECT—ONLY FOCUSING ON "FUN WITH FRICTION" IS NOT NECESSARILY YOUR PATHWAY and MAY ACTUALLY OBSCURE IT. All of the three traditions listed above require

you to START THE SEXUAL EXPERIENCE NICE AND EASY—
NOT HARD AND ROUGH. Taking time LAYING NAKED AND
HUGGING and CARRESSING YOUR PARTNER anywhere and
everywhere in the erogenous zones is generally the first step and should
last at least fifteen to thirty minutes or more.

Doing this in the "spooning" position where the man lays down on his
right body side slightly curled with his frontside tucked into the woman's
backside is an extremely powerful position for both partners. Then you
engage in EXTENDED, PASSIONATE KISSING. And then it should
lead to FONDLING AND STIMULATION OF ERROGENOUS
ZONES WHILE STILL KISSING/CARRESSING. This can even be
performed from the "spooning position" which is really optimal. Next,
could be for the man to PERFORM ORAL SEX ON THE WOMAN.
Men, you must not "blow your load" (ejaculate) yet or the "party is over".
The goal is the BUILD SEXUAL/SPIRITUAL ENERGY AT A SLOW
BUT GRADUALLY INCREASING RATE!

Then after AT LEAST A HALF-HOUR TO AN HOUR OR EVEN
MORE, IT IS TIME FOR THE PENIS TO ENTER THE VAGINA.
The goal for the MAN IS TO DELAY ORGASM FOR AS LONG AS
POSSIBLE (and some sources say without ejaculating. And this IS MORE
LIKELY TO BE ACHIEVED USING THE "DOG POSITION", "THE
ELEPHANT POSITION" or "TORTOISE POSITION" because the
MAN CAN CONTRACT/TIGHTEN HIS ANAL MUSCLES (Mula
Bandam/root lock). This bandam will allow EJACULATION TO
BE DELAYED FOR A LONGER PERIOD OF TIME OR EVEN
PREVENTED. The MAN SHOULD DELAY ORGASM FOR AT
LEAST TWENTY OR THIRTY MINUTES AND LONGER IF
POSSIBLE.

The man should attempt to time his ejaculation with the woman's orgasm.
If not, the woman really needs to orgasm first, because the man's job is to
"ignite" the Woman who into turn can catalyze" ignition within the man.

If you have any powers of perception or insight, you should not have to be told why this is necessary. Actaully, BOTH PARTNERS CAN HAVE EXTREMELY ENERGY INFUSED ORGASMS WITHOUT EVEN ANY PENETRATION OF THE PENIS INTO THE VAGINA BUT JUST TOUCHING AGAINST EACH OTHER at the point of entry!

Once a simulataneous orgasm has occurred or the woman first—the man second—THE COLLECTIVE PRANA/ENERGY GENERATED BETWEEN THE PARTNERS SHOULD BE "MIND SHATTERING" IN THE AMOUNT OF FORCE GENERATED AND THE NEW INSIGHTS YOU CAN HAVE INTO THINGS, which exist in the "new territory". IT CAN FEEL AS IF YOUR HEAD IS ALMOST EXPLODING! If one partner is or both partners are very PROFICIENT IN PRANAYAM BREATHING at the advanced level described within this book, ONE OR BOTH PARTNERS CAN SPONTANEOUSLY ACHIEVE THE SAMDAHIC STATE. The latter scenario is optimum because a partner not in Samadhii will not understand nor appreciate what you are experiencing and this partner will most likely distract you in your euphoric state but not if you use your Yogic powers of concentration.

The sexual positions in these paragraphs are well illustrated and described in "Sexual Secrets" by Douglas and Slinger. Even without this, accomplishing a Theta sexual state should be achieveable. Below, are depictions of "spooning" and and "The Dog" sexual position.

THE SPOONING SEXUAL POSITION

Diagram # 6a

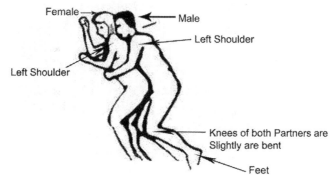

The male & female partners lay on their sides with the right shoulder down & the left shoulder up. The knees of both partners are slightly bent & it is the male's responsibility to mould his body into the female form. This done better naked than with clothes because "There is more galvanic energy/Pranic energy" with the following: "This is done better naked than with clothes because there is more galvanic energy/Pranic energy interchanged between the partners." The Penis touches the Vagina but is not inserted therein. A mind shattering orgasm is achieveable by both partners if they have been working to build the Pranic force within their bodies. This is an invaluable position for those men with erectile disfunction.

DOG SEXUAL POSITION

Diagram # 6b

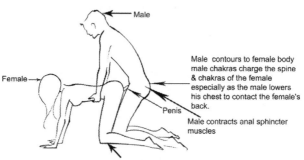

Female legs are spaced at least shoulder width apart and the male puts both of his legs between the legs of the female and the male inserts his Penis into the Vagina. Upon entry into the Vagina, the movement of the penis should be slow or random or none, for a long period of time. By this deliberate process, each partner will generate vastly more Prana and will be "blasted" into a euphoric Theta/Divine consciousness. This is the result of delaying and/or circumventing the male's orgasm. Both partners will enter a higher dimension of consciousness, provided that the female has achieved an orgasm.

This is really an optimal sexual position for the male since it is easy to contract the anal sphincter muscles so that he can delay ejaculation. When ejac. is delayed, more sexual Pranic energy is generated taking both partners to a mind shattering climax of Pranic/Theta/Divine Consciousness. THE MALE MUST NEVER REACH ORGASM BEFORE THE FEMALE. SO IT IS THE RESPONSIBILITY OF THE MALE TO USE HIS CREATIVITY/ INGENUITY TO MAKE THIS HAPPEN, HOWEVER IT DOES OCCUR!!!!

THIS IS CRITICALLY IMPORTANT AND NOT AN OPTIONAL PROTOCOL!!!!

Paul Foster Case, in "The Book of Tokens, talks about a **SEXUAL "SUPERSENSORY PERCEPTION"** that comes from the "higher centers of the brain" that create an "**interior orgasm**" as opposed to an "external orgasm" and they become an agent of "Great Magic". This is why Dr. Newton has stressed that the **HIGHER ASPECTS OF SEXUALITY ARE NOT "fun with friction" BUT RATHER A GREAT GATHERING AND UNLEASHING OF PRANA, CHI, LIFE FORCE WHICH TAKE US INTO THETA DIVINITY and SUPERCONSCIOUSNESS/COSMIC CONSCIOUSNESS.** This type of energy will allow you to make quantum leaps in understanding the spiritual dimensions and place you in the same. You will never sense these incredible things if you are only immersed in the "friction aspects" of sexuality!!!! It is the process of **SPIRITUAL ALCHEMY that occurs during intense sexual experiences.** This is certain beyond doubt!!!!

Once you become proficient in Pranayam, it is easy to enter Samadhii after an intense sexual experience. Additionally, you will be in a state in which you can access the Akashic/atomic records and receive information that may not be in books and you can easily solve difficult problems. Beyond this, you can enter parallel or alternative dimensions of existence and even invent things. You can even enter the Samadhic state after intense masturbation using bandam "root locks" (tightening of the anus) for both men and women.

Dr. Newton personally experienced these things and so for him, this is not "farout", "farfetched" or even remote theory! However, he is reasonably certain that you will not read or hear about this in other books and media about the energy dimensions and Samadhi as it relates to sexuality. Literally, much of this sexual effect information has come the the Akashic/atomic level of information. This is basically information from the Earth and the Universe that has been stored in the atomic field, similar to a computer but on a Cosmic level! This will be discussed more in an upcoming chapter on Theta abilities!

So as you become a master at living in the Theta/Divinity/Superconsciousness realm, the vibration of your person resonates at a higher frequency. THE HIGHER THE FREQUENCY WAVE, THE MORE DIVINE YOU BECOME AS DOES YOUR BODY LIKEWISE AND HENCE MORE LIGHT IS AGGREGATED IN YOUR ACTUAL PERSON—YOU CAN ACTUALLY SEE LIGHT EMANTING FROM WITHIN THE BODY, hence the "light body" which is more energy and less the illusion of matter! Other things that actuate this "light body" will be discussed in subsequent chapters such as "anointing oil" and Monatomic Gold.

Please consider the following:

Those who only find,
Will be in a bind,
And will remain as blind,
When they become mashed by the "grind"!

But those who apply,
The knowledge that is supplied,
Through a daily dedicated ply,
Will certainly learn to fly!

And fly they will,
Beyond the hill,
With the greatest of thrill,
And transcend they will!

IN OTHER WORDS, SEEKING KNOWLEDGE WITHOUT APPLYING IT TO YOUR LIFE, IS OF MINIMAL VALUE AND VIRTUALLY A WASTE OF YOUR TIME, akin to trying to herd wild Geese!!!! **THE APPLICATION OF KNOWLEDGE IS THE ONLY REAL BENEFIT FROM OBTAINING IT!!!!**

BASICALLY, WHAT HAS BEEN COVERED IN THIS CHAPTER ARE MEANS, METHODS AND PROTOCOLS THAT CAN CATALYZE THE PROCESS OF "SPIRITUAL ALCHEMY" WHICH LEADS TO THETA CONSCIOUSNESS/DIVINE CONSCIOUSNESS/ SUPERCONSCIOUSNESS/COSMIC CONSCIOUSNESS

In review:

We can use breathing techniques (Pranayam and Tai Chi),Samadhii (a natural suspension of breathing), Sanskrit mantras (extended, repetitive prayers), the "Backflow Meditation", intense musical perfromances, long distance running, extreme sports, golf, intense dancing and extended, intense Tantric sex to attain Alpha/Theta consciousness.

SO THE CREATOR HAS NOT LEFT US HELPLESS in an "excrement hole" or "up shiite creek without a paddle". THETA consciousness/Divinity REALISTICALLY ATTAINABLE NOW! You must, however, dedicate yourself to this process in a regular and disciplined manner!

START PRACTICING THE PROTOCOLS LISTED IN THIS CHAPTER NOW, ESPECIALLY PRANAYAM AND THE SANSKRIT MANTRAS. They are higly recommended by Kriya Yoga Siddha/ Satguru Patanjali, an acknowledged master of the "light body" and "light consciousness".

STOP WASTING YOUR TIME ON THE INTERNET, TALKING EXCESSIVELY ON YOUR CELL PHONE, TEXTING, "FACEBOOK". These things are just JIBBER JABBER and the MONKEY MIND GONE BERSERK AND WILL LEAVE YOU AT "SQUARE ZERO" or close thereto! Just to learn things has little value, but to practice and incorporate into your life these "learned things" is of great value AND A BLESSING TO YOU!

Learn Pranayam from Babaji's Kriya Yoga can contact online or from Dr. Newton's seminars. Even the very spiritually evolved Paul Foster Case was very emphatic that this needs to be learned under supervision!

PRACTICE PRANAYAM (if you are without medical impediment) AND THE GAYATRI AND MRITYONJAYA MANTRAS AND YOU WILL SOAR INTO THETA CONSCIOUSNESS, THE AKASHIC FIELD, SUPERCONSCIOUSNESS AND DIVINITY!!!!!!!!!!!!!!!!!!

UNTIL YOU HAVE BEEN TRAINED IN PRANAYAM, YOU CAN SUBSTITUTE THE TAI CHI "STANDING MEDITATION' or the "BACKFLOW MEDITATION WHICH YOU CAN USE AS YOUR THETA CONSCIOUSNESS PROTOCOL.

Literally, Pranayam and Samadhii will "magnetize" and infuse bodily cells with energy and light so as to stop the process of decay and bringing us to the doorstep of immortality/"light body".

There is a type of sexuality that concentrates on the building of Prana, Chi, life force instead of "fun with friction" that can elevate you into Samadhi and provide you eith great spiritual insight, knowledge, problem solving and inventiveness, especially if you are adept at Pranayam breathing!

As you elevate your vibrational frequency from practicing the Theta practices listed in this chapter, the Divinity unleashed within yourself will begin to actuate your "light body" and your aura will be increased and light will literally emante from your body which will begin the process of it being more energy and less the illusion of matter.!

IF YOU READ THIS BOOK WITHOUT REGULAR PRACTICING THE DISCIPLINES IN THE BOOK YOU ARE WASTING YOUR TIME! Make a dedicated time slot each day for this, PREFERABLY AT THE BEGINNING OF YOUR DAY and at night, if possible!

DO NOT JUST BE A SEEKER! FINDING THE INFORMATION IS ONLY THE FIRST STEP, NOT AN END IN ITSELF! FOCUS YOUR CONSCIOUSNESS AND ACHIEVE YOUR BIRTHRIGHT OF PERFECT HEALTH, UNLIMITED PROPERITY, EUPHORIA, SUPERCONSCIOUSNESS AND DIVINITY!

BASICALLY, THE CHAPTER GIVES US THE MEANS AND PRACTICES THAT CATALYZE A STATE OF "SPIRITUAL ALCHEMY" THAT TAKE US TO THETA CONSCIOUSNESS!

TTATOD (Time to awaken to our Divinity)!

CHAPTER FOUR

NOW THAT YOU HAVE ACHIEVED THETA CONSCIOUSNESS,
WHAT DO YOU DO WITH IT . . ."Let me count the ways"? HOW
ABOUT FOR HEALING AND MANIFESTING ABUNDANCE?

Few people are really happy most of the time, feel they have enough money, have optimal health and have a good self image. Some of the reasons we have discussed already! There is constant misinformation (propaganda) dispensed by governements telling you that you should work hard and pay your taxes and be obedient to the authorities. Additionally, the government wants to regulate how you think (thought crimes), how you drive (seat belts must be worn) and how you ride your bicycle and motorcycle (you must wear a helmet). Personally, Dr. Newton evolved beyond this decades ago. He knows of no person or judge in the governmental structure who is qualified to guide or judge him!

Organized religions, with the exception of the Hinduism, Buddhism, Kabbalistic Judaism, the Christian Science Church and Kriya Yoga (not a religion), never teach or emphasize just how wonderfully divine and perfect you are as Mary Baker Eddy did in "Science and Health with Key to the Scriptures" and Hermes Trismegistus did in "The Emerald Tablets") and the "72 names of God" from Exodus so completely describe for us. NOTHING COULD BE MORE DAMAGING TO A PERSON IN UNDERSTANDING THIER DIVINE BIRTHRIGHT THAN TELLING THEM THAT THEY ARE IMPERFECT AND A SINNER AND FATALLY FLAWED TO WIT! By repeating and thinking such things, inevitably they are created into our lives!

This faulty information goes directly into the subconscious mind or "mortal mind" (your personal, personal computer) and it REPLICATES MORE OF THE SAME ATROPYING AND IMPERFECT SCENARIOS IN YOUR LIFE BECAUSE IT IS PROGRAMMED TO DO SO BY US. And with such a mindset HOW COULD YOU EVER BE SUCCESSFUL IN LIFE OR EXPERIENCE HEALTH, ABUNDANCE AND PROSPERITY? The answer is self evident! "I'M NOT PERFECT, ONLY HUMAN", IS NOTHING MORE THAN THE PERPETUATION OF MEDIOCRITY AND AN INSULT TO YOUR CREATOR and DIMINISHES YOUR OWN DIVINITY!

SO, HOW DO YOU EXTRACT YOURSELF FROM THIS PERNICIOUS CYCLE/PREDICAMENT? First, you never believe anything a SOCIALIST COMMUNIST GOVERNMENT tells you BECAUSE IT HAS AN INHERENT PROPENSITY TO CONTROL YOU!!!! You may say that this does not apply to you because the USA is a democracy. And then Dr. Newton will tell you that we are supposed to live in a Republic and that, oh contrar, your "democracy" is a socialist/communistorga organization WHICH WANTS TO CONTROL YOUR EVERY MOVE AND THOUGHT.

Additionally, this applies to ALMOST ALL OF THE WORLD'S GOVERNMENTS. MORE THAN HALF OF THE COMMUNIST MANIFESTO HAS BEEN INCORPORATED INTO THESE GOVERNMENTS INCLUDING THE USA! Income tax and "thought crimes" would be just some examples! Please check back issues of the "American Free Press" or Goggle this information from the internet.

THIS IS CONSPIRACY REALITY—NOT THEORY! Remember Jesus' words, "By their works ye shall know them!" and "Seek and ye shall find". What the author detects from governmental proclamations is a malodorous stench, devoid of truth or value!!!! Warrantless wiretaps and warrantless searches of Americans and other people have existed since 9-11-2001. But you are protected by the U.S. Constitution from this, right?

Unfortunately, WRONG! Don't these drastic government actions make you safer? Well, that is their contention but YOU WOULD BE JUST AS SAFE WALKING THROUGH A MINE FIELD WITHOU A MAP. TTATYD (Time to awaken to your Divinity). The only agenda in these government actions here is that we are being bambozled into accepting the creation of the Orwellian nightmare government of which George Orwell and Aldous Huxley warned us against allowing!

There are a few governements in the world that are libertarian (NOTE THE "LIBERTY" ROOT OF THIS WORD) as the USA government was originally conceived. These might include Argentina and New Zealand. We must all demand a return to the libertarian ideal in our governments ASAP. TRULY, NO GOVERNMENT THAT HAS EVER EXISTED IS COMPETENT TO ENACT LAWS FOR ITS CITIZENS OR TO JUDGE THEM, UNLESS THEY LIVE BY THE PRECEPTS WHICH THEY ENACT (which they do not). NOT EVEN SOLOMON IS CAPABLE OF THIS! SUCH A TASK IS BETTER SUITED FOR THE CREATOR, AND ONLY THE CREATOR, NOT SOME CO-DEPENDENT LEGISLATOR or PRESIDENT who take campaign contributions (effectively legal bribes), are unduly influenced by lobbyists have extra-marital sexual liaisons and fail to fully read and comprehend the bills that they are voting on and are being signed into law! MANY OF THESE LAWS ARE LITERALLY ERODING OUR CONSTITUTIONAL FREEDOMS!!!!

SOME POEPLE FEEL WE WOULD BE BETTER SERVED BY ANARCHY than the alternative totalitarian governments under which we live! Once you ponder this seemingly insane idea is becomes alot less insane if you can take yourself to new perceptual realities! At that point, THE TRUTH OF THESE STATEMENTS BECOMES SELF EVIDENT but most poeple would be horribly terrified by anarchy!!!!

Secondly, extricate yourself from organized religions, (other than Christian Science, Kabbalistic Judaism, Buddhism, Hinduism and Kriya Yoga (not a religion), IF THEY ARE NOT "WORKING" FOR YOU. After what has been revealed in this book, the author would find it hard to believe that the "control mentality" of many religions ALLOW YOU TO ASSUME AND MANIFEST YOUR FULL POTENTIAL!! But if your religion brings you great happiness and abundance, then it is right for you!

Also, you should seriously consider DETACHING YOURSELF FROM YOUR GOVERNMENT AS MUCH AS POSSIBLE! DO NOT EXPECT ANYTHING FROM YOUR GOVERNMENT (such as favors) OTHER THAN TO BE TOLD THE TRUTH ABOUT ALL SITUATIONS, including the 9-11 government "fairytale". The over 1100 architechs and structural engineers that tell us that commercial airliners could not have caused the collapse of the "Trade Towers" are not conspiracy theorists—they are technical experts. The USA government is also a technical expert of spreading propoganda and misinformaton and disinformation but has no expertise in structural engineering! DYT?

Thirdly, demand that the GOVERNMENT STOP SPRAYING TOXIC CHEMICALS INTO THE ATMOSPHERE (chemtrails comprised of Aluminum and Barium Salts) and STOP CORPORATIONS FROM TOXIFYING OUR OCEANS, LAND AND AIR, such as the environmental disaster fiasco that British Petroleum created in the Gulf of Mexico with their "half ass" superficially cosmetic cleanup or mega debacle Japan Power created at Fukashima in the Sea of Japan releasing many thousands and probably millions of gallons of radioactive water into the ocean and plutonium into the atmosphere! Ask nothing of government or your religion, except for the excluded ones just above, because most likely it has little or nothing that will help you, unless you desired to be misled, misinformed, strictly controlled with quasi-truths and non-truths and fleeced of your hard earned money!!!! Certainly, the USA Governement has wasted obscene amounts of taxpayer funds on an endless parade of wars and bailing out corrupt banks and "investment houses" and insurance companies!!!!

Now, WE WILL USE OUR NEWLY ACQUIRED ABILITIES IN THETA CONSCIOUSNESS AND BEGIN TO REPROGRAM OURSELVES, OUR GOVERNMENT,OUR RELIGIOUS AND ILLUMINATI CULT AND EXTRICATE OURSELVES FROM THEIR RESTRICTIONS AND DISTORTIONS OF TRUTH! Please realize that the author would rather not have to even mention these disturbing truths. BUT UNDERSTAND EVEN MORE THAT IT IS DIFFICULT, IF NOT IMPOSSIBLE, TO HEAL SOMETHING UNTIL YOU KNOW THE CAUSE THEREOF! As Dr. Newton's Dean in law school, Maxwell Boas, used to say, "Forewarned is forearmed."

Let us begin with ourselves because AS WE BECOME MORE PERFECT IN OUR PERSONAL AFFAIRS, OUR GOVERNMENT WILL NATURALLY FOLLOW! Some people know, Dr. Newton included, that when you get a certain mass of people believing and acting in a certain manner, it will change society even if there is not a majority thinking and living in this manner. This is talked about in Ken Keyes book, "The Hundredth Monkey". It is claimed by different sources that as little as one percent and maybe as much as ten percent of the people in a society must think a certain way to make a change in that society. Therefore, AN ENLIGHTENED MINORITY CAN AND WILL CHANGE THEIR OWN GOVERNMENTS, RELIGIONS AND CORPORATIONS!

Mary Baker Eddy, in "Science and Health with Key to the Scriptrues", says that IF WE ARE ONE WITH GOD THEN WE ARE A MAJORITY. So the sooner we acquire this "oneness" which begins to manifest at the level of Theta consciousness, the better ourselves and world will become!

As was mentioned in Chapter One, on the atomic level, it is known, actually quite recently, that if atoms make any type of change that they will affect other atoms many kilometers away (and this is most likely true on the other side of our Earth, Galaxy, et.al.) This was measured in an experiment by physicists. If we take this to the next level, ourselves, it could be distilled in the concepts of Hermes Trismegistus when he said in "The Emerald Tablets", that things above affect things below and vice versa. So as it is with the atoms, so as it is with the humans. SO THE THOUGHTS OF A MINORITY OF HUMANS, like a minority of atoms, CAN EFFECTIVELY CHANGE THE THOUGHTS OF THE MASS OF HUMANS. This was discussed two paragraphs previously but this cannot be overly restated!

WHAT IS THE QUICKEST WAY TO CHANGE CONSCIOUSNESS, HEALTH AND PROPERITY? IT IS TO CHANGE OUR BELIEFS, PERCEPTIONS AND THOUGHTS OF THINGS! THE EASIEST AND MOST EFFECTIVE WAY TO DO SUCH IS AT THE LEVEL OF THETA CONSCIOUSNESS and THETA CONSCIOUSNESS PROGRAMMING. This is how Christian Scientists do it although they would more than likely disagree with this analysis. Nevertheless, the state that effective Christian Science healers enter is THETA WHICH DIRECTLY EQUATES WITH DIVINITY—"DIVINE MIND" which could be called "DIVINE CONSCIOUSNESS" and Mary Baker Eddy makes reference to this as THE METHOD BY WHICH SPIRITUAL HEALING OCCURS!

WE CAN DIRECTLY PROGRAM PERFECTION, JUSTICE FOR ALL AND PROSPERITY FOR ALL WITH THETA CONSCIOUSNESS and DIVINITY. You could do this with hypnosis but often times the programming "does not take" or is "incomplete" or both. Hypnosis seems to work from Alpha consciousness. TRUE SPIRITUAL HEALING AND PROGRAMMING OCCURS IN THETA AND NOTHING ELSE WILL BE DIVINELY ALIGNED TO COMPLETE AN EFFECTIVE SPIRITUAL HEALING PROCESS, regardless of the method or modality utilized UNLESS IT IS DELTA CONSCIOUSNESS and then you are in SORUBA SAMADHI (perpetual Samadhic Divine consciousness) or sleeping!

PERFECTION BEGETS PERFECTION AND THETA BEGETS THE QUALITIES OF PERFECTION WHICH ARE DIVINITY AND SUPERCONSCIOIUSNESS AND COSMIC CONSCIOUSNESS!

ORGANIZED RELIGION (other than Christian Science, Kabbalistic Judaism, Hinduism, Buddhism and Kriya Yoga [not a religion]) CREATE and JUSTIFY MEDIOCRITY, DEPENDENCE, SICKNESS/ DISEASE and PHYSICAL and MONETARY IMPOVERISHMENT and SPIRITUAL CONFUSION ABOUT THE REAL NATURE OF MAN AND THE PHYSICS OF CREATION and THE NATURE OF THE CREATOR (an atomic force-field)! Whereas, the FOUR LISTED RELIGIONS AND KRIYA YOGA ALL DO NOTHING BUT SPEED YOUR SPIRITUAL EVOLUTION, although they will not refer to "atomic forcefields", to Theta/Divine Consciousness and the immortal "light body." Some people knew this even many thousands and even millions of years ago! Their ideas are liberally dispensed throughhout this book!

People who feel stressed from lingering problems only have this stress and these problems BECAUSE THEY ARE UNAWARE OF THEIR INHERENT DIVINITY AND THEY ARE UNAWARE OF THE TRUE NATURE OF THEIR CREATOR/GOD WHO CREATED THEM PERFECTLY. REALISTICALLY, WHY WOULD PERFECTION BE CAPABLE OF CREATING ANYTHING OTHER THAN CORRESPONDING PERFECTION? Are "Fallen Angels" a misinterpretation from one language to another? All religions claim that God is good and great and so this God gave man "free will" so that he could descend to the level of a dunkoff? THIS MISGUIDED CONCEPT MUST HAVE EMANATED FROM A DISORDERED MIND AND THAT SURELY IS NOT THE MIND OF GOD!

Now, after belaboring these points, Dr. Newton will reveal the process of SPIRITUAL/THETA HEALING!

WHEN YOU ARE IN THETA CONSCIOUSNESS YOU ARE ALIGNED WITH WHAT MARY BAKER EDDY CALLS THE DIVINE MIND. WHEN YOU ARE IN CONSONANCE WITH THE DIVINE MIND, COSMIC CONSCIOUSNESS, SUPERCONSCIOUSNESS and AKASHIC CONSCIOUSNESS YOU ARE IN THE STATE OF HEALING OR IN A STATE TO PERFORM HEALING!!!!

Therefore, for "Theta Consciousness Healing™" to occur the following protocol will assist you to that end:

1. You must be grateful, and expressive of such, for everything that you already have received in your life! This is because **GRATITUDE "PRIMES THE PUMP" OF HEALTH AND PROSPERITY** SO THAT THE CREATOR KNOWS YOU ARE IN A STATE TO RECEIVE MORE "BLESSINGS" in your life!

2. Next, you **MUST KNOW THAT YOU ARE AT THETA LEVEL**/thinking/receiving consciousness. THIS CAN BE A **TRANCELIKE STATE** AND THE MORE YOU RESIDE THEREIN, THE MORE AWESOME YOUR HEALING EFFORTS WILL MANIFEST!!!!

3. This is most certainly achieved through:

   a. The **Gayatri or Mrityonjaya Mantras** for at least 108 repetitions
   and/or

   b. Three rounds (48 repetitions) of **Kriya Kundalini Pranayam** with one complete breathing cycle:

      (1). As close to thirty seconds as possible with the "**Kecharee Mudra**".
      (2). The eyes in the "**Eka Nylai**" positions for each breath.

   c. Twenty to thirty minutes of the **Tai Chi "Standing Meditation**.

d. Twenty to thirty minutes of the "**Backflow Meditation**".

e. Looking at "**ICONS**: The Quickening of Insight" matrix chart available from "www.a3dmind.com" until a state of natural eye flutter is achieved for ten to fifteen mins.

f. Optimally, Theta Consciousness is achieved in **Samadhi**i!!!!

4. **If you are a beginning spiritual healer, you would be most benefitted by performing "a." and "b". If you had time for only one of these Pranayam would be your best choice. If you have not learned Pranayam from an experienced teacher, then the Tai Chi "Standing Meditation" or "The Backflow Meditation" are alternative choices.**

5. Now you begin the **PROLOGUE TO THE SPIRITUAL HEALING PROCESS** which is surrounding yourself in a "**forcefield of positivity**" which includes:

a. Repeating "The Emerald Tablets" of Hermes Trismesgutis (this is the Sir Issac Newton translation; the author wanted to use the version by PaulFoster Case, overseen by the Builders of the Adytum but there were too many requirements to make this feasible:

"Tis true, without lying, certain and most true that which is below is like that which is above and that which is above is like that which is below to do the miracles of the one thing (authors's note: this means that above and below are a "single thing" as translated by Kriegsman in his tranlation of the Phoenecian interpretation of the "Emerald Tablets"). And as all things have been arose from one by mediation of one: so all things have their birth from this one thing by adaptation (author's note: this means things are constantly regenerated as was stated by Kriegsman). The Sun is its father, the moon its mother, the wind has carried it in its belly, the earth its nurse. The father of all perfection in the whole world is here. Its force or power is entire if it be converted into earth (author's note: Case says in his translation that our perfect father consumes the entire world).

Separate thou the earth from the the fire, the subtle from the gross sweetly with great industry. It ascends from the earth to the heaven again it descends to the earth and receives the force of things superior and inferior. By this means ye shall have the glory of the whole world, thereby, all obscurity shall fly from you. Its force is above all force for it vanquishes every suble thing and penetrates every soild thing. So the world was created. From this are and do come admiraable adaptations whereof the means (or process) is here in this. Hence I am called Hermes Trismegist having three parts of the philosophy of the world. That which I have said of the operation of the Sun is accomplished and ended".

b. Reciting "**The Patterns on the Trestleboard: The Truth About Self**" by Paul Foster Case (listed in Chapter One in paraphrase form LISTED IN CHAPTER ONE, PAGE FORTY SIX.

c. Using specific symbols from the "**The 72 Names of God**" from Exodus 14, verses 19-21 as follows:
We are starting on the next to last line of the names and going backwards to the top line which is a formula for spiritual/Theta physical healing and manifestation wherein you need to repeat the three word Hebrew symbols as follows:

(1.) Connecting to the Light (**Hey Resh Chet**)

(2.) The Certainty that God is always there for us for (**Ayin Resh Yod**)

(3.) Finding the God in the Bad (**Resh Hey Ayin**)

(4.) Allows us to see the big picture (**Aleph Nun Yod**)

(5.) Which allows us to overcome our fears (**Mem Nun Daled**) [**this is the most crucial name since fear is that thing which separates us from our Creator** and **manifests sickness and prevents healing**!]; this name occurs in the middle of the "72 Names" and certainly not by coincidence!

(6.) Which makes the impossible possible (**Vav Vav Lamed**) [this symbol is similar to a backwards 911, possibly a universal call for help!

(7.)   Which removes obstacles (**Yod Chet Vav**).

Now we move up to the first lines for the formula for spiritual/theta healing:

(8.)   Fixing your past, through "time travel" if necessary and creating happiness in your life! (**Vav Hey Vav**).

(9.)   From this state of happiness, your energy (prana) is boosted (Yod Lamed Yod)! This statement and its effectiveness can be verified through Kinesolical muscle testing.

(10.)   From this state of increased energy, miracles are created (**Samesh Yod Tet**); The healer Jesus was in this state as denoted by the halo (pranic energy field) which surrounded his head and body in pictures of him!]

(11.)   And after you have performed "miracles" your negative thoughts are eliminated (**Ayin Lamed Mem**)

(12.)   And from this state of emotional balance, healing occurs (**Mem Hey Shin**)

(13.)   And this healing process can be aided by subsconscious messages (dreaming, lucid daydreaming, accessing the Akashic/atomic energy field akin to the great healer, Asclepias!) (**Lamed Lamed Hey**)

(14.)   And thus we restore things to their perfect state (**Aleph Kaf Aleph**)

(15.)   And we defuse any and all negative stress (**Kaf Hey Tav**)

d.   Repeating the "**Scientific Statement of Being**" on page 468 "**Science and Health with Key to the Scriptures**" by Mary Baker Eddy which basically says there is no matter, which is only an illusion! This is IMPORTANT BECAUSE IT IS MUCH EASIER TO "HEAL" SPIRIT, ENERGY, PRANA AND CHI THAN IT IS TO PERFECT MATTER, WHICH IS A FLAWED CONCEPT OF MISINFORMED MEN!!!!

Now you have established a positive field of perfect thought and perception which you will use in the spiritual/theta healing process. So with your eyes gazing upward to the "third eye" or inside of your head) perform and think the following:

1. **PERFORM KINESIOLGY "muscle testing"** on yourself or your patient/subject to know what you need to remove and/or add to the subconscious mind of the subject (see muscle testing diagram that follows).

2. Then you begin the healing procedure by stating: Creator I ask that you REMOVE, on the conscious and subconscious level my own and my relatives and ancestors, DNA (your personal energy field blueprint), karma, and at the Akashic/atomic level, any and all thoughts that:

   (a.) That your creation is material, imperfect with limited abundance;

   (b.) The creation of humanity is material and imperfect

   (c.) That I personally (or your patient/subject) is material, imperfect, subject to sin/ disease/ death/ malfunction/ pain/ suffering,/breakage/ aging; list any particular malady you may be treating and list the appearance of poverty and/or lack, if it is an apparent condition.

   (d.) That I/patient am/are unworthy the have and bask in your perfect creation.

3. In place of these things, Creator I ask you instill, on the conscious and subconscious and in my own and my realtives and ancestors, DNA, karma and at the Akashic/atomic level:

   (e.) That your creation is Spiritual, energy, Prana, Chi, light vibration and unlimited abundance and without doubt, perfect as per "The Emerald Tablets" of Hermes Trimegistus, "The Patterns on the Trestleboard: the Truth About Self" by

Paul Foster Case, "The 72 Names of God" from Exodus 14, verses 19-21, "Science and Health with Key to the Scriptures" by Mary Baker Eddy and the highest concepts of Kriya Yoga as per Krishna in the "Bhagavad Gita", Patanjali in "The Yoga Sutras", Tai Chi and Taoism.

(f.) That all of these things apply to humanity in general BEING CREATED OF SPIRIT BY GOD AND FROM A PERFECT TEMPLATE.

(g.) That all of these things apply to me specifically (or your patient/subject) and that only perfection, health, unlimited abilities and boundless prosperity are my true nature and Divine birthright!
ANYTHING IN MY BODY WHICH NEEDS HEALING OR REPLACING OR NEEDS TO BE REGENERATED IS AND HAS OCCURED. Any and all emotions which have caused any and all ailments are being released and eliminated!

(h.) That I personally (or your patient/subject) are the embodiment of and created in the image and likeness of our Creator, created in perfection and from Spirit, energy, Prana, atoms

(i.) Then you must remove the programs of imperfection, matter, sickness, disease and lack of prosperity on the level of your personal beliefs, the level of DNA, the Akashic/Atomic level, and the level of Spirit, energy, Prana, Chi, light and vibration. Then you must do the same process again as you install the programs of perfection, Spirit, prana, chi, perfect health, perfect appearance and functioning body and exhaustless prosperity on the personal belief level, the DNA level, the Akashic/Atomic level, and the Spirit, energy, Prana, Chi, light and vibration level.

When you go through this process see yourself removing a computer disc with the removed information from your personal computer and see a new disc with the perfect programming entering your personal computer!

Then say, let this be done, let it be! EXPECT RESULTS; THINK AND TALK WITH POSITIVITY. IF YOU DO OTHERWISE, SAY "CANCEL, CANCEL" TO UNDO NEGATIVE THOUGHTS OR UTTERANCES!

      (j.) Powerfully assert your worthiness to have all of this (after all it is your Divine right)!

THIS PROTOCOL IS POWERFUL ENOUGH TO HEAL OR CHANGE ANY CONDITION KNOWN TO MAN OR WOMAN! This is the PROCESS OF ALCHEMICAL HEALING! If your first treatment does not get the desired results, check that you have adhered to the listed protocol above and then re-enact the treatment procedure. Also, be sure that you are in a verifiable state of Theta. "THETA CONSCOUSNESS HEALING" WILL WORK AS WELL IN CREATING ABUNDANCE IN OUR LIVES AS IT DOES FOR HEALING!!!! You simply must change from the healing perspective to the abundance/property perspective. And, in fact, Dr. Newton does both of these things concurrently!

THE TWO TYPES OF KINESIOLOGY MUSCLE TESTING
The Arm Method (Tested by another person)

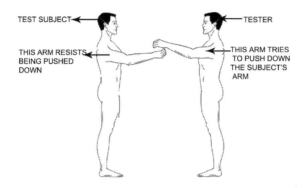

Diagram # 7a

The purpose of this is to access the subconscious/personal computer-brain by asking "yes" & "no" questions. First questions are asked of the test subject that the answer to the questions are already known. So questions are asked that are true & false. The tester asks these questions while pushing down on the subjects are out stretched straight in front of this body, with the subject resisting the 'push down" usually a correct answer will prevent the arm from being pushed down while an incorrect answer allows the arm to be descended. By this method, you can decode bodily ailments among other things by asking "yes" & "no" questions. Always be in trance like state to obviate personal bids.

FINGER METHOD OF MUSCLE TESTING

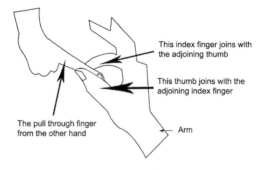

Diagram #7b

The same protocols occur as per above expect that the looped finger & thumb resist being separated by the finger on the opposing hand. This method allows self testing .Always try to be in a trance like state to obviate personal opinion bias.

It is true that the subconscious mind can become emeshed in "toxic mind" recordings that keep "looping" in our lives. Linda Joy Rose talks about this in detail in her book, "Your Mind: The Users Manual. She recommends hypnosis as a way of eliminating these "recordings"; the results that the author has seen from hypnosis are hit or miss because its works at the level of Alpha Consciousness whereas Theta/ Divine consciousness always works/heals/manifests within the framework and parameters described in the protocol above. REALIZE, as was covered in Chapter Two, THAT IN THE THETA HEALING PROTOCOLS THAT YOU VERY WELL MIGHT NEED TO REMOVE EMOTIONAL PATTERNS FROM THE HEALING SUBJECT WHICH HAVE ATTACHED TO THE PATIENT FROM RELATIVES AND ANCESTORS, traced back as far as they go in the past!!!! THIS COULD BE APPLIED TO CHRISTIAN SCIENCE HEALING TREATMENTS LIKEWISE!!!!

CHRISTIAN SCIENCE SPIRITUAL HEALING works equally effective and can be part of the protocol just above BUT CAN STAND ON ITS OWN IN AND OF ITSELF. Theta Healing is more formulized whereas Christian Science healing is somewhat more open to interpretation— there is not a "hard and fast" formula but it is effective when done with CONVICTION AND FEARLESSLY. Mary Baker Eddy was the first modern person to assert that ALL IS GOD which she equates to DIVINE MIND. And that ANYTHING WHICH CONTROVERTS THIS, which she called error or mortal mind, is FALSE TESTIMONY or AN ILLUSION which tries to block out or obfusticate Spirit, God. If you work with this, with a REAL CONVICTION, not a" half baked" effort, you will heal with this perspective provided by Mrs. Eddy. She says, and correctly so, that SPIRIT FILLS ALL SPACE (omnipresent [all presence]) and is omnipotent (all powerful) and omniscient (all knowing) and this leads to healing.

Dr. Newton knows this works since he employed this viewpoint numerous times not only to heal but to solve problems and to create prosperity! And this would have been even easier and more certain if he had had a means to verify that his consciousness was in Theta/Divinity/Superconsciousness as has been provided in this book!

Also, the Neurolinguistic Programming protocol of "SWISHING" can be used in a crucial healing situation where you just do not have the time for "Theta Healing" or Theta Consciousness Healing" protocols. This is described in "Pathways to God: Experiencing the Living God in Your Everyday Life", in the chapter on Neurolinguistic Programming.

DO YOU HAVE TO DO THE LISTED THETA TECHNIQUES TO BE IN THETA CONSCIOUSNESS? No, you do not and many Christian Science practitioners work from this level, often without knowledge thereof. HAVING THE TECHNIQUES AND PROTOCOLS LISTED, HOWEVER, SURE MAKES YOUR HEALING MISSION MORE CERTAIN AND PROBABLY EVEN MORE EFFECTIVE! Who would not like to have a verifiable standard from which to work from? It creates more confidence and a greater certitude that you will get results. AND HEREIN LIES THE BENEFIT THEREOF! Using verifiable criteria to validate Theta consciousness always is superior to guessing if are in this state of Divinity!!!! CONFIDENCE BEGETS RESULTS! ALSO, as was mentioned in Chapter Three, ANY HEALING PROCESS WILL BE MAGNIFIED AND MORE QUICKLY EXPEDITED IF YOU ARE IN A STATE OF SAMADHI!!!! THUS, IT BEHOVES US TO BECOME INITIATED INTO AND DAILY PRACTICE KRIYA YOGA SO THAT WE CAN BENEFIT FROM THE ADVANTAGES OF THE SAMADHIC CONSCIOUSNESS!!!! Those who do not see this as self evident are not paying attention to the preponderance of evidence that has been presented in this book!

Dr. Newton intended to give an example that seemed to be contrary or contradictory to the Theta techniques to raise consciousness and provide healing, regarding a musical performance by Reverend Kim Clement. On the evening of 9-23-11, Rev. Clement was on a TBN television program where he was singing and chanting and actually repeating a simple mantra, although the author is sure that Clement would not agree with the "mantra" designation. Anyway, by looking into Clement's eyes, Dr. Newton could see and feel that Rev. Clement was in Theta level Consciousness. And it was apparent that much, if not all, of the audience was also in Theta. YET, SINGING, CHANTING and MANTRA ARE THETA CONSCIOUSNESS TECHNIQUES. An ancillary point can be made here, however, that you do not need to be a Yogi or a Hindu priest or a Buddhist priest to reach Theta Consciousness! History is rife with examples where Christians and Moslems and Jews and Buddhists and Hindus have done so likewise! Unfortunately, this is perceived by an insignificant amount of people!

Now we are prepared to COD (Create our Divinity—not fish), as it were, in the next chapter!

So in review:

Only the Creator is qualified to judge you—not your religion and not your government! You are perfect and not a sinner but if you believe otherwise, it will be recorded in your subsconsious and you will manifest sickness, disease and lack of abundance and properity!

We must extricate ourselves from the control our governments and religions other than Christian Science, Kabbalistic Judaism, Hinduism, Buddhism and Kriya Yoga (not a religion) because only these things will usher our spiritual evolution into Theta Consciousness and the "light body"!

IT ONLY TAKES AN ENLGITHENED MINORITY TO CHANGE THE POPULATION AT LARGE. This is in conformance with Ken Keyes "The Hundredth Monkey".

SO AS WE PERFECT OURSELVES THE RESULT IS THAT OUR GOVERNMENTS AND OUR RELIGIONS WILL INEVITABLY FOLLOW OUR LEAD!

To heal, quickly and powerfully, we need to be in Theta/Divinity/ Superconsciousness.

This is aided by repeating the GAYATRI and/or MRITYONJAYA Sanskrit Mantrasat least 108 times for each mantra.

Theta is accelerated and established even more powerfully doing 48 REPETITIONS OF PRANAYAM as per standard operating procedure with thebreaths being at least 30 seconds each using the Kechare Mudra and the Eka Nylai Mudra.

The TAI CHI "STANDING MEDITATION" could be substituted for Pranayam as could the "BACKFLOW MEDITATION" but you most likely will not achieve as deep a Theta trance.These need to be done for twenty to thirty minutes.

Using "ICONS: The Quickening of Insight" until the condition of continual eye flutter can also be used to estabalish Theta Consciousness.

OPTIMALLY, THETA CONSCIOUSNESS WILL BE ACHIEVED IN SAMADHI!!!!

For beginning, even advanced healers, you should perform one of the Sanskrit Mantras and Pranayam as proscribed.

Then, once Theta has been firmly anchored in your consciousness, to envelop yourself in a "FORCEFIELD OF POSITIVITY", repeat "THE EMERALD TABLETS" of Hermes Trimegistus. Memorize this two paragraph "gemstone" because you will use it many, many times.

Next repeat "THE PATTERNS ON THE TRESTLEBOARD: THE TRUTH ABOUT SELF" by Paul Foster Case or Sir Issac Newton. Likewise, memorize this too.

Subsequently, repeat the preamble symbols from "THE 72 NAMES OF GOD" from Exodus 14, verses 19-21.

Then go up to the top line of "THE 72 NAMES" and repeat the eight names on this line of the formula for PHYSICAL HEALING.

Then proceed through the Theta conscioiusness protocol to heal or use a Christian Science protocol. Then fearlessly know the results desired will occur! Let it be so! The more you focus on the positive ideas and concepts listed in this book, the more it will be so! THE MORE YOU ARE AT THETA LEVEL THE MORE YOU ACHIEVE AND CREATE!!!!

IN THE STATE OF SAMDAHI, ANY HEALING PROTOCOL WILL OCCUR QUICKER AND WITH MORE EFFECTIVENESS AND COMPLETENESS!!!!

YOU WILL PROBABLY NEED TO REMOVE EMOTIONAL PATTERNS FROM RELATIVES AND ANCESTORS WITHIN THETA HEALINGS PROTOCOLS FROM RELATIVES AND ANCESTORS, as far back as they can be traced, which could be more than the seven generation rule generally accepted in "Theta Healing"!!!!

CHAPTER FIVE

A NEW PARADIGM, ARCHETYPE, TEMPLATE OF THE BODY OF LIGHT AND THE SPIRITUAL MAN IN THE "IMAGE AND LIKENESS OF GOD": THE PROCESS OF "SPIRITUAL ALCHEMY"!

In the "Key of Enoch", Dr. J.J. Hurtak talks about the vibrations and electro—magnetic energy on our Earth being intensified so as humanity can take the form of the "Adam Kadmon Archetype" (perfect humans) and as has been described in "Science and Health With Key to the Scripture" by Mary Baker Eddy and from "The 72 Names of God" from Exodus 14, verses 19-21. We have also found this in "The Emerald Tablet" by Hermes Trismegistus and "The Patterns on the Trestleboard: The Truth About Self". Also, it has been revealed how KRIYA KUNDALINI PRANAYAM, as explicated in "The Bhagavad Gita" and "The Yoga Sutras", ELECTRIFIES AND INFUSES THE BODY WITH FIRE/LIGHT AND MAGNETISM. THIS WOULD CERTAINLY DESCRIBE A "SPIRITUAL ALCHEMICAL" PROCESS! Additionally remember, it has been revealed in "Chapter One" how atoms seem to function with perfection and with precision and that everything in the Universe is comprised of them.

If our world and we are comprised of atoms, as they are, then our worlds and we must also mirror this atomic perfection—DIVINE PRECISION AND ORDER which is revealed many times over ON THE ATOMIC AND SUBATOMIC LEVEL. When you look into a Helium ion microscope you see beautiful geometric forms in many different permutations of triangles and the full spectrum of colors included in these. And these reoccuring triangles are the basis of our humanly engineered bridges and buildings. This is hardly a coincidence but rather a DIVINE RECURRENCE THROUGHOUT ALL CREATION SINCE THE TRIANGLE IS THE STRONGEST TEMPLATE OR PATTERN KNOWN IN ENGINEERING AND CONSTRUCTION. You also see recurring triangles in many of the "crop circles". So we can see, through the replication of the triangle at many levels of creation, that it is divinely inspired and "authorized", as it were.

Platinum Crystal Matrix

This picture truly depicts what Dr. Hurtak is saying about the pyramid being a recurring shape on the atomic level and it shows the nine geometry forms of creation as per the treatises of Valery P. Kondratov

About four decades ago, in "**The Keys of Enoch**", Dr. Hurtak talked about how pyramidal crystals and molecules occur over and over again on the atomic level of creation. We have confirming evidence from the work of Valery P. Kondratov, in her online treatises, "**Geometry of a Uniform Field**" and "**Fabric of the Universe**" **and the picture of the Platinum crystal, just preceeding**. And Dr. Hurtak also talked about how as the vibration intensity became stronger on Earth, it would cause a physical TRANFORMATION in the COMPOSITION OF OUR BODIES to a state of LESS DENSENESS and MORE LIKE SPIRIT. As was mentioned just previously, he discussed man being reformed into the "ADAM KADMON ARCHETYPE" representing a DIVINE TEMPLATE. Well, guess what has been revealed to us? Some physicists and scientists (of Russian and French origin) have been studying an event in the center of the "Milky Way" Galaxy since the 1970's and describe how there is an "ENERGY BOOST" that has been directed at and OCCURING IN OUR PLANET and the planets in our solar system.

There are likelwise Gnostic texts, possibly Pleadean in source, that describe a "**garment of light**", which most likely correlates with the concept of the "light body" and a "divine human template". This is discussed in detail in "The Secret of Sion**", b**y William Henry. This is just adding to a preponderance of evidence which cross correlates and cross validates what has been discussed previously in the chapter and this book!

In consonance with what has been occurring on our planet at this very time, there is a gradually increasing intensity is an electromagnetic energy and a forcefield and gravity that is bombarding our planet and this can and has been measured!!!! AGAIN, WHAT IS BEING DESCRIBED, AND WHAT IS OCCURRING IS AN ALCHEMICAL PROCESS, as the folowing paragraph provides verifying evidence!

David Wilcock talks about these things in his book, "Source Field Investigations", and also reveals that it can be scientifically proven that OUR DNA HAS CHANGED by a factor of over 6% in the last one hundred years. This would not just happen unless there was something CATALYZING this CHANGE IN THE ELECTROMAGNETIC "FORCEFIELD" in which we live, because at our essence, we are comprised of electromagnetic atoms. And the energy bombardment from the "Milky Way Galaxy", just discussed, certainly should be enough of a catalyst to accomplish this DNA "mutation"/enhancement.

Richard Hoagland, of "The Enterprise Mission" has chronicled this "event" more completely than anyone else the author has encountered! This increased energy is called TORSIONAL or HYPERDIMENSIONAL ENERGY and on Earth, we are in a transition which will align us with the galactic center of our "Milky Way" Galaxy on or around 12-21-2012 (there is some doubt now as to the exact date and some scientists and astronomers feel the date could be closer to 11-11-2011 because of differences between our Gregorian Calendar and the Mayan Calendar [codex]). And as each day passes, OUR BODIES HAVE THE POTENTIAL OF BECOMING LESS MATERIALIZED AND MORE SPIRITUALIZED/ ENERGIZED/ CHARGED WITH PRANA! Actually, OUR BODIES WERE ALWAYS INFUSED ONLY WITH PRANA/SPIRIT! Remember the game we came to Earth to play described by Rabbi Berg in the Prologue (to tranform ourselves back to our perfect form)?

While we are experiencing this vastly increased influx of torsional or hyper—dimensional energy (increased Prana), we will most likely be subject to intense extremely severe weather events and geomantic and geologic disturbances manifesting as earthquakes, volcano eruptions, tsunamis and intense spikes of electromagnetic energy coming to Earth from our Sun and our "Milky Way" Galaxy. Earthquakes and volcanos are known to be activated by intense electormagnetic spikes coming from the Sun and now from our Galaxy. This is why animals react chaoticly just before volcanos and earthquakes are activated because they navigate by magnetic leylines that circumnavigate our planet, which are scrambled and/ or re-oriented during the "spikes". ACTUALLY, INTENSE WEATHER EVENTS AND GEOMANTIC AND GEOLOGIC DISTURBANCES

DR. ROBERT J. NEWTON, J.D., N.D.

ARE TAKING PLACE RIGHT NOW ON A VERY LARGE SCALE. To date, solar "spikes" probably have caused the earthquakes in Haiti, Chili, New Zealand and Japan!

Also, there will be political uprisings/civil wars in many countries as is occuring at this very time. There COULD likely be famine due to weather extremes, crop failures and Illuminati medling and there could people dying en mass. This is the BAD NEWS.

The GOOD NEWS, which more than negates the "bad news", IS THAT THESE INCOMING INTENSE ENERGIES WILL MAKE SPIRITUAL EVOLUTION AND HUMAN ENLIGHTENMENT VASTLY EASIER TO ATTAIN BECAUSE THE ENERGY OF THE CREATOR WILL HAVE AN EVEN STRONGER "PULL"/FORCE ON US. Think of God as a magnet with a positive charge and ourselves as a magnet with a negative charge that are being irresistibly pulled together. Now electrify these magnets and they become exponentially stronger as they become electromagnets. Originally, Dr. Newton received this idea metaphorically but it could actually be very real from a physics perspective. The realization of the "LIGHT BODY" and IMMORTALITY in this lifetime, IS WITHIN OUR GRASP RIGHT NOW DESPITE WHAT WE HAVE BEEN TOLD OR BELIEVE TO THE CONTRARY! In a sense, the CREATOR is "POWERING UP" ITS MAGNET so that we can be RECONNECTED IN A "DIRECT LINK" TO GOD as the Creator intended us to be!

SO, NOW IS THE TIME TO TAKE ADVANTAGE OF THIS OPPORTUNITY FOR US PROVIDED BY THE CREATOR! TTATOD (time to awaken to our Divinity)! In business there is a maxim that when a good opportunity comes along you should "jump on it". Now it is the right time for us to do the same, likewise for our spiritual evolvement! THE CONDITIONS FOR SPIRITUAL AND PHYSICAL ENLIGHTMENT AND IMMORTALITY ARE REACHING AN OPTIMAL POSITION not seen on Earth for 13,000 years due to increased electormagnetic energies (Prana) focused on our planet from the center of the "Milky Way Galaxy", as we know from the investigations of Richard Hoagland, among others. SOME INVESTIGATORS FEEL WE MAY HAVE BEEN GIVEN A PASSAGE FROM THE KALI YUG, a cosmic cycle of unenlightenment, to the SATYUG WHICH IS THE HIGHEST LEVEL OF CONSCIOUSNESS! Please refer to "The True History and Religion of India" for a fuller explanation of the "yugs" or "yugas".

Commensurate with this, humans will have vastly stronger powers of telepathy and other psychic abilities. As a result, lying or being deceitful or being disingenious will no longer be an effective way of dealing with other humans because you will be immediately "outed"/exposed in your attempted subterfuge! Unbelievable healing powers and inherent health will be possessed by humans. Moreover, if you would like these abilities NOW, and you most certainly might, YOU CAN HAVE THIS RIGHT NOW—YOU DO NOT HAVE TO WAIT UNTIL 12-12-2012 (OR 11-11-2011).

How does this occur? It happens by taking our CONSCIOUSNESS into the THETA/DIVINE/SUPERCONSCIOUSNESS via the information and protocols covered in previous chapters of this book!

But what is the MECHANISM THAT TRANSFORMS OUR BODY INTO BEING MORE LIKE SPIRIT, energy, Prana, Chi, light, vibration WHICH FORM THE "LIGHT BODY" and lessens our interplay with our perception of dense, imperfect, deteriorating matter within our bodies? Once, again, it is the process of TAKING OUR CONSCIOUSNESS INTO THE THETA/DIVINE/SUPERCONSCIOUSNESS state of being! And this occurs with the PRACTICES AND PROTOCOLS set forth in the previous chapters. Certainly, and it would be impossible to overstate this, that KRIYA KUNDALINI PRANAYAM WILL UPLIFT YOUR CONSCIOUSNESS AND LITERALLY BEGIN THE PROCESS OF THE CATALYZATION OF THE "LIGHT/ENERGY

BODY! This may not sound very easy and may seem "farfetched" yet we know undoubtedly that this occurs on the level of atoms and "atomic force"—that they are already at a level of Divinity! ATOMS ARE MICRO "LIGHT BODIES" LITERALLY, which Sir Issac Newton knew centuries ago (mentioned earlier in thie text), and AGGREGATED THEY FORM MACRO "LIGHT BODIES" which are us Earthlings, among others. It would be wrong to underestimate just how powerfully this "light body" can occur when your CONSCIOUSNESS APPROACHES THE LEVEL OF DIVINITY OR THE THETA OR THE ATOMIC STATE/ LEVEL! Once again, an ALCHEMICAL PROCESS OF SPIRITUAL EVOLUTION is being described here! **And it follows the laws of physics and chemistry!!!!**

So to GET TO THIS STATE, WE NEED CONTINUAL PRACTICE OF KRIYA KUNDALINI PRANAYAM, KRIYA DHYANA (meditation) and VOLUMES OF REPETITIONS of "The GAYATRI mantra", "The MRITYONJAYA mantra", "The Babaji Mantra" and the "Ram" mantra, AS WELL AS OTHER SANSKRIT MANTRAS INTO WHICH YOU SHOULD BE INITIATED BY A KRIYA YOGA MASTER, such as Yogi Govindan Satchidanada. One of these other Sanksrit mantras, the RAM MANTRA, has been demonstrated by practitioners, thereof, to be a "MAGNET" FOR ACCUMULATING PRANA AND LIGHT IN OUR BODIES as is the "Gayatri" and "Mrityonjaya" mantras!!!!These practices are considered as essential in "The Yoga Sutras" by Kriya Yoga Siddha (Satguru/ MahaAvatar), Patanjali. These then lead us to Samadhi and the "light body" in an eternal state of functioning, AT LEAST IN SORUBA (continual) SAMADHI! THESE THINGS 'RESTORE US TO OUR PERFECT STATE' (Aleph Kaf Aleph)!

And if we can get ourselves into a DAILY ROUTINE of performing the above practices, we will feel "incomplete" when we do not perform them, because as we establish the Kriya Yoga routine we begin to feel an enhanced energy presence within ourselves!!!! There is not only a sense of feeling more energy in our bodies, there is a SENSE THAT WE ARE CONNECTED

TO AN IMMENSE PRESENCE BEYOND OURSELVES. We are then ESTABLISHING AN ENCHANCED LINK WITH DIVINITY and this is when we begin to really comprehend that a wonderful tranfromation is occurring, some of which are listed below!

Although this was stated in previous chapters as related by MahaAvatar/ Siddha Patanjali in the "Yoga Sutras" and Krishna in the "Bhagavad Gita" and the "Mahabarata" and Goswami Kriyanada in "The Spiritual Science of Kriya Yoga", there are many beneficial results from Pranayam breathing. Basically you have Oxygen and blood infusing the body with more Prana/God charged life force via your extended Pranayam breath. Even more important is that Prana is infused into the spinal cord and its corresponding nerves and there is a magnetic oxidation/force and fire (Yagna) and beams of light which are cumulatively dematerializing the body (as it were) and you are activating the body's Spirit, energy, Prana, Chi, God charged life force. In India this has been KNOWN AS FACT FOR AT LEAST 5100 YEARS AND QUITE LIKELY HUNDREDS OF THOUSANDS OF YEARS AND MILLIONS OF YEARS, among Yogis.

Please realize that civilization in India has existed in an unbroken time line for 1.9 billion years—YES ALMOST TWO BILLION YEARS as is listed in the "Vedas" and "Upanishads" and "The True History and Religion of India" by Swami Saraswati. Unfortunately, most all archaeologists are completely uninformed about this and if they know it they derisively dismiss it. Still ignorance and summary dismissal of something do not disprove it but rather expose the gross incompetence of purported "expert" archaeologists who need to WTFU (wake the fork up)! When a mind becomes "closed", it cannot "feed" itself and like a mollusk, such as a muscle that cannot open, it will atrophy and die! So that is what is occurring to many archaeologists today.

In your spare time, you can listen to the music that Dr. Newton has listed in Chapter Three as Alpha/Theta inducing. Dr. Newton will repeat that BY PRACTICING THESE DISCIPLINES YOU "RESTORE YOURSELF TO YOUR PERFECT STATE" (Aleph Kaf Aleph) from "The 72 Names of God".. THE ONE THING THAT WE DO NOT NEED IS ALCOHOLIC BEVERAGES, CANNABIS AND OTHER DRUGS, PSYCHEDELIC OR OTHERWISE BECAUSE THEY WILL IMPEDE THE UNFOLDING OF DIVINITY WITHIN YOURSELF! UNDOUBTEDLY! This statement is "CERTAIN AND MOST TRUE"! If people feel otherwise it is only because of their drug induced lack of clarity! They are unaware that they have dug a pit into which they have unwittingly fallen!

As we dedicate ourselves to the Theta/Divine/Superconsciousness practices and protocols just discussed, and with the torsional/hyperdimensional electromagnetic energies "flooding" the Earth now, the vibrational frequency of our bodies becomes increased. And this higher level of energy INDUCES and INCREASES the auric/etheric/ Pranic energy around the body and MORE LIGHT WILL ACTUALLY EMANATE THEREFROM and it will be detectable with human sight with your eyes out of focus. Now the process "enlightenment", as it were, to recreate the "light body" has begun as has the process to discard the illusory material body! This was dicussed previously in Chapter Three. So remember:

From atoms you came,
And from atoms you remain,
And from atoms only energy is released,
So atoms relegate matter to a state of deceased.

It is especially important to note that as you are PERFORMING KRIYA KUNDALINI PRANAYAM, you are COLLECTING MORE PRANA (electro-magnetic life force) in your body as discussed by Goswami Kriyananda is his book, "The Spiritual Science of Kriya Yoga". Additionally, our blood is charged with plus and minus electrical charges which DOES TRANSPORT PRANA THROUGHOUT THE BODY. So while almost everyone else is looking at this from a perspective of physicality/

dense matter, Dr. Newton sees the OVERRIDING IMPORTANCE OF THE ENERGY ASPECTS of these two processess (BREATHING and BLOOD CIRCULATION) and from the PRANIC/Chi/life force aspects. Also the nervous system and its related nerves distribute Prana/Chi throughout the body!

We know, from the pictures from Kirilian photography (pictures of the energy field surrounding the body) that ONCE PRANA ESCAPES FROM/LEAVES YOUR BODY PERMANENTLY, THE BODY CEASES TO EXIST. There are NO KNOWN EXCEPTIONS to this and it includes animals and plants/trees! Even when in the state of "Samadhi, where breath, heartbeat and blood circulation are suspended, Prana is still infused in and surrounding the body, although you may still harbor suspicions as to the validity of this statement!

However, once you have experienced Samadhi, and probably only after you have been in this state, will you know the truth of this proclamation as does the author and other practitioners of Kriya Yoga! Know that there is NO INTENTION TO DECEIVE you or lead you astray. Rather there is an AGENDA TO RECAST YOU IN YOUR DIVINE FORM—a form that we seem to have drifted away from, as it were!!!! Actually, as has been noted previously, you could say that HUMANITY HAS "LOST IT'S WAY" and forgotten about its inherent perfection!!!!

As was similarly stated in the previous paragraphs, Dr. Newton has detected, contrary to the perceptions of medical science, that BREATHING AND BLOOD CIRCULATION SUPERCEDE PHYSICAL FUNCTION and importance and ESTABLISH THE HIGHER FUNCTION OF PRANA, Chi, energy and the Spirit realm through which this Divine Energy circulates throuhout our bodies! OXYGEN MAY WELL AID OR EVEN BE CRUCIAL IN THE DISPERSAL OF PRANA IN THE BODY. Also the author has REVEALED A PREPONDERANCE OF EVIDENCE that our TRUE NATURE/reality of our being is as DIVINE HUMANS—not degraded, decaying, material, malfunctioning body units. We actually know as A CERTITUDE THAT ATOMS ARE ONLY ENERGY AND THAT WE ARE ONLY COMPRISED OF THEM! So once again we are faced with the inescapable STARK REALITY THAT WE ARE ONLY ENERGY/PRANA/CHI/SPIRIT!!!

Jay Lakhani, a physicist, in "Challenging Materialism" printed in "Hinduism Today" in the July/August/September 2011 issue says: "The reason material reality appears so solid and objective is that not only is the world of appearance incredibly self-consistent, it is shared universally by all observers." From this we could conclude that THE WIDELY ACCEPTED BELIEF IN MATTER OR PHYSCIAL FUNCTION IS THE RESULT OF THE GENERAL MASS BELIEF OF THIS AND NOTHING ELSE. SO THESE ASPECTS OF MATERIALITY COULD LITERALLY BE AN ILLUSION as Dr. Newton described the effect of a MIRAGE, APPEARING REAL, BUT UPON CLOSER INSPECTION THE APPEARANCE OF REALITY IS DISPELLED as discussed earlier in this book! OR IT COULD BE THAT BY CHANGING OUR PERCEPTION AND THUS our CONSCIOUSNESS, WE TRANSCEND TO ANOTHER CONCEPT OF REALITY SUCH AS ENERGY, PRANA, CHI and SPIRIT AND WE NEGATE THE EXISTENCE OF DENSE MATTER AS A FACTOR IN OUR LIVES! Our consciousness may well shift into an alternative dimensional reality or actually a higher dimension such as the fourth dimension, WHICH IS ACTUALLY EASIER THAN YOU MIGHT THINK, once you have the foundation for this which is provided by Kriya Kundalini Pranayam, the Tai Chi "Standing Meditation" and the "Backflow Meditation"!

Also, no part of brain has ever been located which established the function of consciousness as Jay Lakhani, a physicist, points out in the same article (it appears to be true, however, the brain can indicate our state of consciousness, as routine research has established)! He says later in the article from above: "Trying to explain the quantum in terms of matter fails because it is trying to capture reality through appearance. Such stuff could be written off as poetry if it were not so incredibly close to what quantum and consciousness are pointing at. If we were to ask a physicist to give a physical interpretation to the quantum function, he will immediately say it is the probability of its existence. Trying to explain the quantum in terms of matter fails because it is trying to capture reality through its appearance. The reason why neuroscience struggles to capture the essence of consciousness is that it ends up focusing on what we are conscious about, rather than on what consciousness actually is. This again is an attempt to capture reality through its appearance."

AND THESE STATEMENTS ARE WHY THE AUTHOR IS DENOTING "THETA" A STATE OF CONSCIOUSNESS AS OPPOSED TO A BRAINWAVE. Although there are brainwave chaaracteristics in "Theta Consciousness", Akashic insights are revealing to the author that the brain is an indicator of "THETA LEVEL" as a MEASURING DEVICE as to "THETA REALITY" as opposed to Theta actually emanting from the brain (our personal, personal computer)!!!! THIS, THEREFORE, LEAVES US TO LOOK ELSEWHERE FOR "THETA CONSCIOUSNESS". And SINCE ATOMS are the "BUILDING BLOCKS" of all creation and the CREATOR IS ENSCOUNSED and ENCOMPASSED in the "ATOMIC FIELD" of these atoms, THIS IS WHERE WE COULD NATURALLY BE LED TO KNOW FROM WHENCE "THETA CONSCIOUSNESS" EMANATES!!!!

Lakhani also says in his article, "**Most physicists are so fixated on matter that it is almost impossible for them to think outside of a materialistic box.**" And elsewhere in his article he quotes physicst John Searle who says that **materialism exists because science does not want to challenge its materialistic assumptions** (this is paraphrased and not directly quoted).

So for Dr. Newton and physicist, Jay Lakhani and John Searle, conventional physics and neuro-science have failed to perceive the nature of the body, human consciousness and reality because **THEY HAVE ASSUMED MATTER TO BE AN INHERENT REALITY WHEN IN FACT PHYSICISTS HAVE IGNORED THAT NO MATTER HAS BEEN**

DETECTED EVEN IN THE BEST OF ATOMIC COLLIDERS, in Hadron Switzerland.

The ASSUMPTION OF MATTER BY CONVENTIONAL PHYSICS IS INHERENTLY UNSCIENTIFIC because of its INHERENT MATTER/ MATERIALISTIC ASSUMPTIONS and THIS APPLIES TO CONSCIOUSNESS LIKEWISE!!!! This has been revealed through a preponderance of "quality evidence revealed in this book! As has been stated several times previously in this book, MATTER IS A MIRAGE— AN ILLUSION, JUST AS MARY BAKER EDDY REVEALED IN "SCIENCE AND HEALTH WITH KEY TO THE SCRIPTURES" over one hundred and thirty five years ago! At the time of this revelation, virtually everyone thought Mrs. Eddy was "looneysville". MATTER IS NOTHING MORE THAN A CREATION OF THE CUMULATIVE "THOUGHT FIELD" BY THE MAJORITY OF HUMANITY!!!! To the author, it is sad and yet comical watching physicists being frustrated by not finding "dense matter". REPEATING THE SAME FAILED PRESUMPTIONS IN A SEQUENTIAL MANNER WILL STILL REVEAL THE SAME FAILED CONCLUSIONS, TIME AFTER TIME!!!!

SPIRIT, ENERGY, PRANA, CHI ARE THE REAL REALITY—NOT CONSTANTLY DETERIORATING MATTER which cannot be formed from the atoms God created, which are the "building blocks" of the Universe and this idea is closely described by Sir Isaac Newton when he describes the composition of "light" as streams of minute particles! It is also discussed in "The Bhagavad Gita" and even "The Yoga Sutras" when it discusses "Gunas" which are considered cosmic energies of "light, motion and mass". DYT (Do you think) THAT THIS COULD DESCRIBE ATOMS AND PHOTONS AND PHONONS?

There are many other dimensions and alternate/parallel dimensions where this is likewise applicable. IN FACT, IT IS THESE VERY ATOMS THAT ALLOW OTHER DIMENSIONS AND ALTERNATIVE/PARALLEL

DIMENSIONS TO EXIST, BECAUSE THE ELECTROMAGNETIC ENERGY OF THE ATOMS IS OMNIPRESENT/ PERVASIVE WHEREAS MATTER BASICALLY IS NOT and DETERIORATES FROM THE FORMS THAT IT IS SUPPOSE TO REPRESENT!!!! It is basically certain that it is more difficult for matter to "travel" through "space" than it is for pure atomic energy, considering the factors of resistance and composition!

THE FACT THAT WHEN IN THE ADVANCED THETA STATE OF SAMADHI, WITHOUT BREATHING OR BLOOD CIRCULATION, NEITHER THE BODY OR BRAIN ARE HARMED, STRONGLY SUPPORTS THE CASE FOR THE NON-MATERIAL, SPIRITUAL (ENERGY) HUMAN BEING! This will not be accepted by the medical establishment and they will tell you that your brain will be damaged without oxygen after about four minutes. NEVERTHELESS, DR. NEWTON, AS WELL AS MANY KRIYA YOGIS HAVE PERFORMED THIS FOR UP TO SEVERAL HOURS AND EVEN LONGER WITHOUT BRAIN DAMAGE—IN FACT THE BRAIN OR YOUR CONSCIOUSNESS IS UNHARNESSED FROM ITS PERCEIVED LIMITATIONS BECAUSE YOUR CONSCIOUSNESS IS IN A COMPLETELY DIFFERENT DIMENSION—THETA/DIVINITY—WHICH IS VASTLY DIFFERENT FROM THAT WHAT WE ARE NORMALLY ACCUSTOMED! And this is when our "fun" and enlightenment (as it were) really begins!

Within this framework, as was stated previously in this chapter, it is still possible and in fact likely that Prana/Chi/life force is carried throughout the body by Oxygen and that this Oxygen may well cause Prana/Chi/life force to be magnified in the body. With Samadhii, however, we probably have a "Maha Prana" or "Meta Prana" (both of these meaning a BEYOND PRANA—A MORE INTENSE or HYPER PRANA/Chi) process of SUSTAINING THE BODY. And/or we could have an "Intra Pranic" effect where different nurturing properties of Prana/Chi/life force are unleashed in an anerobic (lack of oxygen) condition. The many books on Kriya Yoga and Taoism that Dr. Newton has encountered do not mention this subject so he is literally going into the Akashic/atomic field of information for these insights but he still feels they are essentially correct as presented but uncorroborated at this point in time in this dimension. In the case of Samadhi, you do not have to know all of the physics involved to experience this condition.

Related to this, IT IS COMPLETELY WITHIN THE REALM OF POSSIBILITY AND ACTUALITY TO REGENERATE limbs, teeth, joints, organs, etc. in the HUMAN BODY! Dr. Robert Becker, in "The Body Electric", discussed how he and his team of scientists regenerated the amputated legs of Salamanders on numerous occasions through electrical stimulation. This most likely was the result of the electrical nature of atoms being activated or more highly energized by electrical stimulation to reform a leg. There would not be a compatible resonance for this to occur unless the essence of animal and human bodies were not fundamentally electrical!

LITERALLY, LIMB REGENERATAION COULD BE ACCOMPLISHED BY USING TECHNIQUES FROM KRIYA KUNDALINI PRANAYAM, QUI GONG, TAI CHI AND REIKI or any other energy based healing protocol. This could also possibly occur with "frequency specific micro-current" treatment! Certainly it has healed numerous other maladies of the human body! The only thing that would prevent this is the MASS BELIEF THAT IT CANNOT BE DONE! Did you ever hear THAT THE FOOL DID NOT KNOW IT COULD NOT BE DONE SO HE/SHE WENT AHEAD AND DID IT ANYWAY? Did you know that THE "FOOL" IN THE TAROT CARDS IS NOT PEJORATIVE BUT ACTUALLY AN EXALTED SEEKER AND ABSORBER AND UTILIZER OF KNOWLEDGE, GOING FEARLESSLY WHERE OTHERS DARE TO TREAD?

As has been discussed elsewhere in this book, we know from Kirilian photography that once a human limb has been amputated or part of a leaf has been cut, there remains an energy template of the amputated limb or cut part of the leaf which can be discerned with human sight with your eyes out of focus. So as well as electrical stimulation, other protocols such as Reiki, Qui Gong, Kriya Kundalini Pranyam "healing" lasers such as "Q Laser", accupuncture and magnetic accupuncture should be able to regenerate limbs, joints, teeth, organs, etc. in the human body. Also, this should be possible with the "AIM program" (radionics) and "Sound Signature" (sonic vibrations), from the John Keely research using musical notes (covered in the "Journal of Vibratory Physics") and the Dinsbaugh protocols of light and color therapy. Additionally, it is possible through the spiritual healing protocols of Christian Science, Theta Healing and Theta Consciousness Healing. This is because the essence of these healing modalities is PRANIC-ELECTRICAL STIMULATION!

The Swiss physician, Paracelsus, said that "discordant" states of the human mind lead to disease and lack of health and this is very similar to what Louise L. Hays has explicated in her book, "You Can Heal Your Life", in which EMOTIONAL MODIFICATION is used as a healing modality. What Paracelsus used to ameliorate these maladies was herbal remedies, color therapy and sonic protocols. This would include many of the healing modalities discussed in the previous paragraph! BUT REGARDLESS OF THE MODALITY USED, THE MEANS (modality) IS JUST A CATALYST WHICH BRINGS US TO A HIGHER STATE OF CONSCIOUSNESS!

THIS IS POSSIBLE BECAUSE ALL OF THE HEALING PROTOCOLS LISTED IN THIS CHAPTER, STIMULATE ELECTRICITY AND MAGNETISM JUST AS DR. BECKER WAS DOING. KRIYA KUNDALINI PRANAYAM ALSO EXPONENTIALLY RAISES THE ELECTROMAGNETIC POTENTIAL IN THE HUMAN BODY SIMPLY THROUGH ADVANCED BREATHING TECHNIQUES, AS WAS JUST DISCUSSED IN THIS CHAPTER. Likewise, certain Sanksrit mantras produce this same elevated electromagnietic potential in the body, especially the "Gayatri Mantra", the Mrityonjaya Mantra and the "Ram Mantra".

We are basically talking about a CATALYTIC PROCESS. WHAT WAS PREVIOUSLY THOUGHT TO BE IMPOSSIBLE IS WITHIN THE REALM OF THE POSSIBLE NOW through the advancements in science, quantum physics and mechanics and metaphysics and the "spiritual sciences". It has just been revealed in this chapter the real possibility of immortality and the regeneration of body parts.WHAT WAS ONCE A "FAIRYTALE" IS NOW FAIRLY ACHIEVEABLE, as it were!!!!

Additionally, cytopathologist, Dr. Nadaraja, states in "Kauai's Hindu Monastery" newsletter of June 2011, that recent research indicates that Telomerase activity is known to repair damaged DNA. And this telomerarse phenomenon is catalayzed by meditating, chanting SANSKRIT MANTRAS, Rosary, Aramaic Hebrew chants, the singing of holy songs and intense religious ceremonies (such as pujas) THIS IS SCIENCE REALITY—NOT SCIENCE FICTION! SANSKRIT MANTRAS HAVE BEEN REAL AND PRACTICED FOR THOUSANDS AND LIKELY MILLIONS OF YEARS! This concept is similar to what Dr. Hurtak was talking about in "The Keys of Enoch" when he discussed the power of Aramaic Hebrew Chants to raise the body to a higher spiritual/ energy level! Telomerase is an energy that attaches itself to the end of the strands of DNA. DNA is part of our personal computer code and encoded "memory chips" of some sort!

Dr. Newton will even take the idea of telomerase activity in repairing DNA to the next level. Bascially it has been revealed to him, in an Akashic manner, that DNA IS CREATED AND/OR MODIFIED BY OUR THOUGHTS AND OUR EMOTIONS AT THE SUBCONSICOUS LEVEL (your personal, personal computer). And somehow, our thoughts and emotions elicit a binary code, of which the DNA is comprised and thusly this code creates and/or modifies DNA!!!! One thing that we do know for sure is that when telomerase activities such as mantras, stimulate this process, LDL Colesterol is lowered. This was proven in a study by Drs. Dean Ornish and Jue Lin, et.al, which was published online and was published in Dr. Ornish's book, "Dr. Dean Ornish's Program for Reversing Heart Disease". This would indicate that some type of **DNA modification is occurring** and thus adds credence to Dr. Newton's contention above, because a **mantra will definitely change your emotions to a state of positivity!** This has been proven repeatedly by those people who recite mantras, including the author!

PLEASE TAKE TIME TO STUDY, LEARN, PRACTICE, PRACTICE, PRACTIVE, PRACTICE and MEMORIZE WHAT HAS BEEN PRESENTED IN THIS CHAPTER AND BOOK! Wean yurself from the internet, Facebook, texting and cell phones (think of all the extra band space we will avail to other people!). Use these devices sparingly! Otherwise we could continue to be imprisoned in the illusion of imperfect and decaying matter, physical maladies and the lack of prosperity for all people because we are not practicing the protocols that will allow our trancendence of our perceived limitations! View the new ideas presented here in the context of "The Hundredth Monkey" written by Ken Keyes where the more people that perceive and believe and act upon an idea the more likely it is to become established in the "mass consciousness". We need to direct our consciousness to REACTIVIATING THINGS TO THEIR ALREADY PERFECT STATE OF BEING (Aleph Kaf Aleph from the "72 Names of God" from Exodus)!

TTATOD (Time to awaken to our divinity)!!!!

In summary:

We now know that the electro-magnetic and vibrational energies are increasing as talked about by Dr. Hurtak in "The Keys of Enoch" and Richard Hoagland through "The Enterprise Mission".

And we know that these energies will create a favorable condition for creation of the "Adam-Kadmon" archetypal body, described by Dr. Hurtak, in much the same sense as the perfect man described by Mary Baker Eddy in "Science and Health with Key to the Scriptures", "The 72 Names of God" from Exodus 14, verses 19-21, "The Emerald Tablets" of Hermes Trismegistus, "The Patterns on the Trestlboard: The Truth About Self" by Paul Foster Case and the energizing ourselves through electricity and light through the practice of the Kriya Kundalini breathing regiment! THESE THINGS CREATE AN ALCHEMICAL STATE OF TRANSFORMATION TO THE "BODY OF SPIRIT".

This will result in human abilities being expanded including unbelievable healing abilities, vastly enhanced pyschic abilities including being able to "read" a person and access to atomic/Askashic knowledge obtained from the "atomic field"/"Akashic records".

These abilities occur at the level of Theta/Divine/Superconsciousness and are aided by the Theta protocols and practices discussed in this book. These practices in conjunction with the torsional/ hyperdimensional energy "flooding" our Earth raises our vibrational frequencies leading to an increased auric/etheric/Pranic field around the body and our bodies literally emanate more light and we become less emeshed in illusory matter! Again, we have a process of "spiritual alchemy" occuring here!

You do not need to wait for 12-21-2012 OR 11-11-2011 to access these abilities and an increased energy/light body—literally, as it were!

Kriya Kundalini Pranayam uses the breath to augment the level of Prana/ Chi (the life force of God) in our bodies and the blood to transport this Prana more powerfully throughout the body and brain/personal, personal computer. The nervous system and its related nerves also serve this function.

Matter only seems to exist, says physicist Jay Lakhani because of the widely held belief by humans that it is a real phenomena. Matter is a mirage—an illusion JUST AS REVEALED IN "SCIENCE AND HEALTH WITH KEY TO THE SCRIPTURES" BY MARY BAKER EDDY.

There is no part of the brain which has been located as a point where consciousness occurs. Therefore intelligence, invention, creativity might well emanate from the Creator through its "atomic field" rather than your brain!

"THETA CONSCIOUSNESS" IS ONLY INDICATED BY THE BRAIN—NOT CREATED THEREFROM!!!!

REALITY CANNOT BE DEDUCED FROM APPEARANCE AND ONLY FROM ACTUAL VERIFIABLE MEASUREMENTS. THUS, REALITY MUST BE AN ATOMIC FIELD—ENERGY, PRANA, CHI, SPIRIT which we can measure and actually detect!

The fact that after suspending breathing and blood circulation in the body in the advanced Theta state of Samadhi, neither the body or the brain deteriorates, STRONGLY INDICATES THAT THE BODY IS NOT MATTER BUT RATHER SPIRIT, ENERGY, PRANA, CHI—THE REAL REALITY!

Also, we know from Dr. Becker's work and from Kirilian photography that it is within the realm of ACTUALITY for humans to regenerate limbs, joints, teeth, organs etc. within their bodies by Prana/Chi protocols and through electrical stimulation and electrical frequencies, sonic vibrations, "healing" lasers such as "Q Laser", the "AIM program, accupuncture and magnetic accupuncture, Kriya Kundalini Pranayam, Qui Gong, Reiki, John Keely protocols of musical notes, the Dinsbaugh protocols of colored light, "Frequency Specific Micro-currrent" therapy and through spiritual healing such as Christian Science and Theta Consciousness Healing BECAUSE OF THE ELECTRICAL, MAGNETIC and LIGHT

INDUCING NATURE OF THE ABOVE LISTED PROTOCOLS! This could regeneration could be facilitated by the Richway Bio-mat even though Richway makes no such claims

WE ALSO KNOW THAT DNA CAN BE REPAIRED BY MEDITATION, CHANTING (SANSKRIT MANTRAS such as "Gayatri", "Mrityonjaya" AND "Ram), THE SINGING OF HOLY SONGS AND PUJAS (religious ceremonies) because of a Telomearse phenomenon!

Also, DNA can be created and/or modified through our thoughts and emotions!!!!

Louise L. Hay's book, "You Can Heal Your Life", uses emotional modification to effectuate healing, as does Christian Science "treatment!!!!

Additionally, we know that Swiss physician, Paracelsus, used herbal remedies, color therapy and sonic protocols to lift his patients from "discordant" states of mind so that he could heal them!

We have evidence from Gnostic texsts that have references to "a garment of light" depicting the human body as per the research of William Henry in "The Secret of Sion".

Chapter Six

CREATING THE SPIRITUAL WORLD ORDER AND TEMPLATE
(ALEPH KAF ALEPH [Restoring things to their perfect state])
AS OPPOSSED TO WHAT WE SEEM TO HAVE RIGHT NOW!

How we create this SPIRITUAL WORLD ORDER, as it were, that sets us free figuratively and literally, IS BY OUR OWN EVOLUTION TO A HIGHER PLANE OR STATE OF CONSCIOUSNESS OR DIMENSIONAL REALITY—TO LIVE AT THE LEVEL OF THETA/DIVINITY/SUPERCNSCIOIUSNESS/COSMIC CONSCIOUSNESS AS MUCH OF THE TIME AS IS POSSIBLE. The course and protocols by which this can be done was exhaustively discussed in Chapters Three and Four. So how does this happen? Well, IT HAPPENS AS WE RESIDE, more and more, IN THETA/DIVINE/ SUPERCONSCIOUSNESS. This will happen more frequently as our consciousness is uplifted by the Theta Consciousness protocols listed in Chapter Three.

THE PROTOCOLS NEED TO BE PRACTICED ASSIDUOUSLY, in the same manner that people devote themselves to "texting". THE MORE DILIGENTLY DEVOTED YOU ARE TO THIS, THE MORE TIME YOU WILL RESIDE IN THETA CONSCIOUSNESS UNTIL IT MORE OR LESS BECOMES YOUR NATURAL LEVEL OR STATE OF BEINGNESS! This is NOT AN EXAGGERATED CLAIM but an actual and basic PROVEABLE TRUTH! And you can prove this to yourself by following the previous protocols in this book BUT YOU MUST PRACTICE THE PROTOCOLS DAILY AND EVEN BI-DAILY!! Otherwise, we do not have the means of potential proof which verfies this in our own consciousness! So basically you must perform this yourself to prove its worth to you!!!!

Now, could we be helped by extra-terrestial intervention, as some people have suggested? As bizarre as this may seem to many people, the answer is quite possibly YES! It has happened before as listed in Zecharia Sitchin's and Eric Von Donnagen's, David Wilcock's and Robert Temple's books, among others. It most likely occurred in India 5100 years ago in the epic known as "The Mahabharata" which involved Krishna and Arjuna and over 300,000 years ago in The Ramayana" involving Ram and Hanaman. There is also evidence of this occuring in Eygpt, Greece, Sumer (Iraq), Mexico and Peru but not limited thereto.

The Cherokees, the Blackfoot and the Hopi Indians state that their learnings and teachings were from the stars and some of the tribes have glyphs that would lend credence to these claims. The Dogon tribe in Africa claimed they were taught by extraterestials from Sirius as detailed in Robert Temple's book, "The Sirius Mystery". In the Mormon religion, Joseph Smith was given sacred stone tablets from Moroni, who was described as an angel but who could have been of extraterrestial origin, as it might be difficult for a being of pure energy, such as an angel, to transfer a stone document to someone, here on Earth. Some the ancient descriptions of extraterrestials are depictions of beings who emanted light from their bodies. Therefore, it is certainly conceivable that an ET could be mistaken for as an "angel"!

If and when these "higher beings" come to interact with us, to uplift us, THERE WILL BE AN INTENSE CAMPAIGN OF DISINFORMATION TO SCARE YOU FROM INTERACTING WITH THEM BECAUSE THEY THREATEN THE EXISTING CORRUPT POWER STRUCTURES (Illuminati cult, organized religion and governments) WHICH THE AUTHOR HAS ALREADY DISCUSSED. The only thing you can know with certainty from these disingenious sources is that their interets always take precedence over our best interests and we must critically dissect every utterance they proclaim and every action they take and know that it is more than likely based on excrement and deceit!!!! THE ILLUMINATI CULT CONSIDERS US IGNORANT AND "HERDABLE" as cattle and the reason they get away with this is because we allow it to happen!

IRRESPECTIVE OF THIS, THE CHANGING OF OUR PERCEPTION OF OURSELVES CHANGES OUR WORLD—FIGURATIVELY AND LITERALLY!!! EXTRATERRESTIAL HELP MIGHT ALREADY BE HERE NOW BUT CURRENTLY IN A BENIGN FORM, as observers as opposed to actors! Some people at a high intelligence level which is respected by the author, such as David Icke, claim that the Illuminati cult is actually of extraterrestial origin, having been here for centuries and maybe millenia. This is detailed in, "HUMAN RACE Get off Your Knees: The Lion Sleeps No More". It is imperative that we humans do the "heavy lifting" in our transformational process! Nevertheless, extraterrestial knowledge and insights would certainly be invaluable for us to evolve ourselves to our highest potential! David Wilcock, in his book "The Source Field Investigation", assiduously documents the history of extraterrestial involvment with our planet. And so IT APPEARS THAT THIS INTERACTION WITH "SPACE BEINGS" HAS OCCURRED FOR THOUSANDS AND POSSIBLY MILLIONS OR EVEN BILLIONS OF YEARS, at least in India!

But if we do this ourselves, without extraterrestial intervention, how is our perception enhanced and uplifted to a HIGHER, THETA CONSCIOUSNESS? This is ACCOMPLISHED by UTILIZING the INFORMATION, TECHNIQUES and PRACTICES listed in the previous chapters. We inculcate the concepts of Christian Science in "Science and Health with Key to the Scriptures" by Mary Baker Eddy. We study and memorize and apply the concepts of "The Emerald Tablet" by Hermes Trismegustis. We learn and apply the concepts of "The Patterns on the Trestleboard: The Truth About Self" by Paul Foster Case. We learn to read and memorize Hebrew so that we can speak and visualize

"The 72 Names of God" from Exodus 14, verses 19-21, to perform this at will and any time. This happens when we study "The Yoga Sutras" by Satguru, MahaAvatar and Siddha Patanjali. When we pursue "The Bhagavad Gita",when we immerse ourselves in "Thirumandiram" by Satguru, MahaAvatar and Siddha Thirumoolar. THESE THINGS ARE "CATALYSTS" THAT FACILITATE AN ALCHEMICAL REACTION. AND IN A CHEMICAL REACTION, "CATALYST" IS USED TO SPEED UP THE RESULTS OF THE REACTION of the chemicals involved. The reaction desired here is Theta transformation and uplifting of our consciousness and bodies!

The "CHEMICALS" are the THINGS WHICH WE PRACTICE such as the disciplines of Kriya Kundalini PRANAYAM, Kriya DHYANA meditation and Kriya ASANAS (stretching postures). OTHER "CHEMICALS" are the "GAYATRI", "MRITYONJAYA", "RAM" and "BABAJI" Sanskrit Mantras that we repeat at least 108 times continuously and do this every day. MORE "CHEMICALS" are the study and practice the Tai Chi "STANDING MEDITATION", the "BACKFLOW MEDITATION" and when we LISTEN to and/or PERFORM MUSIC and DRUMMING. Still other "chemicals" are added to the mix such as extreme sports, dancing, singing, playing musical instruments, running, intense sexual energy couplings (not group sex or things related thereto such as "one night stands"). THESE "CHEMICALS" ARE BENEFICIAL INGREDIENTS IN THE TRANSFORMATION OF OUR CONSCIOUSNESS, in a manner of speaking, and the "CATALYSTS" THAT SPEED THIS TRANSFORMATION ARE IN THE PARAGRAPH ABOVE. So there is an alchemical process occurring in this process of "spiritual chemical elevation"!

SO WE DECREASE THE TIME OF THE "CHEMICAL REACTION" OR "THE LEARNING CURVE" BY ADDING, as one example "THE EMERALD TABLETS" OF HERMES TRISMEGUSTIS TO THE PRACTICE OF KRIYA KUNDALINI PRANAYAM. THEN WE CAN ADD "SCIENCE AND HEALTH WITH KEY TO THE

SCRIPTURES" TO THE PRACTICE OF THE TAI CHI "STANDING MEDITATION". The combinations do not necessarily have to be as the descriptions above but THESE ARE USED TO ILLUSTRATE POSSIBILITES! CERTAINLY AN ACCELERATED CHEMICAL REACTION WOULD RESULT FROM COMBINING "THE YOGA SUTRAS" AND "THE BHAGAVAD GITA" AND KRIYA KUNDALINI PRANAYAM since they are all CLOSELY INTER-RELATED and actually interconnected! Yet any of the sources of study and guidance and any of the disciplines and protocols can be combined beneficially to facilitate an accelerated spiritual and physical transformation!

These studies and disciplines/protocols will make us better people. THIS WILL HAPPEN NATURALLY AND YOU WILL NOT HAVE TO "STRAIN" TO HAVE THIS MATERIALIZE!!!! These things REMAKE US IN THE IMAGE AND LIKENESS OF OUR CREATOR/GOD. And as we REPERCEIVE OUR INHERENT DIVINITY/Spirituality WE RESTORE OUR WORLD to its PERFECT STATE (Aleph Kaf Aleph). This may seem difficult or ridiculously unrealistic but it is not if WE BECOME FANATICALLY POSSESSED ABOUT RECLAIMING OUR TRUE AND SPIRITUAL NATURE. THIS WOULD BE A GOOD OBSESSION BECAUSE IT CREATES THE DISCIPLINE TO ACHIEVE THIS "SPIRITUAL MISSION"! With the discipline to perform the practices in the paragraph above, ALL OF OUR DIVINE BIRTHRIGHTS AND ABILITIES AND OUR INHERENT PROSPERITY COME TO FRUITION! Or, we could continue on our path of disfuntionality? We can begin to create our "LIGHT BODIES" and enter the realm of THETA/DIVINE CONSCIOUSNESS because of the COMBINATIONS of the "CATALYSTS" and the "CHEMICALS" and AT AN ACCELERATED PACE. The catalysts are the key to this process of acceleration!!!!

TTAFOS (time to awaken from our slumber)!

Also, Richard De Wolf, on the "Coast to Coast" radio show related how from American Indian sources via interdimensional contact (extraterretial) that there will be a large interdimensional vortex focused in the "Four Corners" are of the USA on 11-11-11 that will go through to the other side of the Earth in the Indian Ocean. It is claimed that this will help cleanse and rebalance our polluted and abused planet and help to alleviate the intense weather and geophysical disturbances we are experiencing right now. Dr. Newton intends to be at this location on this date and most likely several months before to make a before and after comparison of the vortexial energies! This vortex (similar to a tornado but comprised of Prana without wind [actually Prana can also is wind]) is an intensely spinning electromagnetic energy in a "cross form" of energy and light which is detectable using "etheric sight" techniques. This vortex is said to emanate from the planet Sirius, with a "feminine" (nurturing) energy field. Sirius "B" is considered by some people to be our "sister" planet and this would make this idea more realistic, if there is an interconnectedness with Earth and Sirius.

Dr. Newton hopes this does in fact occur for our general welfare because the Illuminati has already taken "care" of themselves from a survivalist perspective! One thing we know as a certainty is that the "Four Corners" area has a higher gravity (which is electromagnetic in its constitution) and higher magnetic forces than surrounding areas. This was discovered in a University of Texas at El Paso study entitled, "Integrated study of basins in the Four Corners area" conducted by Olunide, Olarvirmi, Foybota. Dr. Newton is feeling that there is at least a seven and more likely a twelve leyline magnetic intersection (in "cross form") in a vortex that already exists in this area. This information of a "cross form" in a vortex came to the author from Dr. John Brandenbury, a plasma physicist, that was conveyed on the "Coast to Coast" radio show on 9-1-2011. When dowsing rods are used to measure a vortex, at the vortexial center the dowsing rods will move in a circular, clockwise motion in the Northern Hemisphere of our Earth.

There would most certainly be a goemantic propensity for a vortex under the circumstances just described for this area. So the existing Earth vortex could definitely be an attracting force for the interdimensional vortex, since the existing magnetism in this area would be an attractant for an intersellar magnetic force and presence.

Dr. Newton feels strongly that this interdimensional electromagnetic force could be a "trigger" for earthquakes and volcanos, despite its purported "feminine" nature and this event being touted as a way to mitigate the severe weather and geological disturbances (earthquakes, tsunamis, erupting volcanos). As has been mentioned previously, this is because strong electromagnetic forces are known as a geological trigger for these events and this is why animals act strangely just before the occurence of these events since they are very aware of this presence, which becomes "skewed" during an electrical "spike". This is especially true for birds who navigate by electromagnetic leylines as was previously discussed in another chapter. WHATEVER OCCURS, AND NOTHING IS CERTAIN UNTIL IT ACTUALLY DOES HAPPEN, WE ARE ASSURED THAT OUR CREATOR IS ALWAYS PRESENT AND HELPING US THROUGH ANY SITUATION as per Ayin Resh Yod (the certainty that God is always there for us [from "The 72 Names of God" from Exodus])!

There are many Biblical, Mahabarata, and Ramayana accounts of "servants of God" experiencing this exact thing just stated where people were helped in surviving "impossible" situations! "The 72 Names of God from Exodus can literally be your "lifesaver" if the "shiite hits the fan" if you have memorized these names before facing a crisis. So the author perceives from this situation that it is NECESSARY AND SELF EVIDENT THAT YOU NEED TO MEMORIZE THESE "NAMES OF GOD" SO THAT YOU ARE ALREADY PREPARED FOR ANYTHING THAT MIGHT OCCUR!!!! At Theta level learning this is an easy task!

Actually, after writing this, the author is feeling ashamed of all of the times he felt that God had left him up "Shiite Creek" without a paddle or that "life is unfair and God does not care" when in fact it was his lack of perception and Theta conscousness that led to such an incorrect and distorted view of the Creator! And so it has been for many, actually most of us! This might be why Jesus proclaimed, "Go and sin no more." Or, let us expunge our ignorance and know we are ALWAYS ONE WITH GOD!!!! "The 72 Names of God" from Exodus 14, verses 19-21, are a template of frequencies by which we achieve this ONENESS WITH OUR CREATOR!

Dr. Newton will construe this concept of "sin" differently than to what you have been accustomed. Dr. Michael Jensen says that the NOETIC EFFECTS OF SIN HAVE PREVENTED US FROM KNOWING THINGS ABOUT OUR SELF AND THE WORLD AND GOD. So what he is describing, but more like implying, is that SIN HAS LEFT US IGNORANT OF OUR OWN DIVINITY! So for Dr. Newton, this translates to SIN IS IGNORANCE AS OPPOSED TO TRANSGRESSIONAL ACTS. However, what the author has concluded probably would not receive concurrence from Dr. Jensen because of his more limited perspective than that of the author! Nevertheless, the author thanks him for his insights about the noetic effects of sin!

Jesus must have been telling us to SHED OUR IGNORNACE ABOUT THE PERFECTION OF GOD'S CREATION AND OUR OWN PERFECTION. The author keeps returning to Mary Baker Eddy's steadfast position in "Science and Health with Key to the Scriptures" that WE WERE CREATED in the "PERFECT IMAGE AND LIKENESS OF GOD" and as was related in the first chapter of Genesis. Unless this perfect God is a buffon, a bubala, or bombastically erratic, man never could have descended into a state of trangression against his own Creator. Perfection inherently defies any state of imperfection or degeneration or denigration. AND WHEN WE VIEW THE OPERATIONAL CHARACTERISTICS OF PERFECTION DISPLAYED BY ATOMS, WE CAN KNOW THE INHERENT VALIDITY OF THIS STATEMENT, especially when you view atoms through an electron (Helium Ion) microscope, from which there is a photograph in Chapter Five!

Astronomer and author, Robert Temple states in "The Sirius Mystery", there is a METHODICAL OCCURRENCE AND PRESENCE THAT PERVADES THE UNIVERSE. Gee, the author really does not have to wonder who might be the controlling force of this! Would you believe God, through atomic force? All of this has been verified by the work of astrophysicist, Dr. Hugh Ross, as was previously discussed. Also, we know from the work of physicist David Boehm that the Universe is a detailed hologram and not solid as we have been deluded into believing. As Boehm states, you can cut a Rose flower in half and still create a whole new Rose from a remaining half. This possibility is obviated if the Rose was bound by a "physical /material" form!

So, thank God, fortuitously for us, the Creator is not a buffon, a bubala, or bombastically erratic because the workings of the atomic field prove otherwise, as per the treatises of Valery P. Kondratov in "The Geometry of a Uniform Field", "The Fabric of the Universe" and "The Confirmation of Nine Energies of Egyptian Tradition", published online. So what Kondratov has revealed is the nine recurring geometric forms of atom creation and the nine energies of atomic creation, which were previously discussed in Chapter One.

Additionally, as Hermes Trismegustis says in "The Emerald Tablet", that which is below is that which is above so that this perfection elevates from "below" where atoms reside to "above" where we reside! THE ATOMIC FIELD PROVES THE PERFECTION OF THE CREATOR AND POSSIBLY EVEN THE EXISTENCE OF GOD. But for sure, it proves that there is a force that controls the atoms, which can be discerned anecdotally, so for the lack of a better name, let us call it God and/or Controller and/or Creator!!!! OTHERWISE, **WITHOUT THIS "CONTROLLER"**, ATOMS WOULD NOT COALESCE INTO MOLECULES and FORMS/TEMPLATES (aggregates of molecules). RATHER,THEY

WOULD DISPLAY CHAOTIC CHARACTERISTICS WHICH COULD NOT CREATE ANYTHING LARGER THAN ONE LONELY, SINGLE ATOM AND WE HUMANS WOULD NOT EXIST, or for that matter, as it were, any and all other objects!!! Certainly, this is an idea to cogitatively comtemplate!

In summary:

The SPIRITUAL WORLD ORDER will be CREATED BY OUR OWN EVOLUTION INTO THETA/ DIVIITY/SUPERCONSCIOUSNESS. THE MORE WE CREATE PERFECTION IN OURSELVES, THE MORE OUR WORLD BECOMES PERFECT IN ITS OWN RIGHT!

World evolution could be aided by ET intevention and it has happened in the past in India, Eygpt, Greece, Sumer (Iraq), India, Mexico and Peru; also there were ET interactions between the Cherokee, Hopi and Blackfoot Indians and the Dogon Tribe in Africa. Also, this could apply to Mormon theology

If ET intervention materializes, there will be a disinformation campaign by the Illuminati cult to discourage us from interacting with these visitors!

WE LIFT OUR OWN CONSCIOUSNESS THROUGH STUDYING "SCIENCE AND HEALTH WITH KEY TO THE SCRIPTURES", "THE EMERALD TABLETS" OF HERMES TRISMEGUSTIS, "THE PATTERNS ON THE TRESTLEBOARD: THE TRUTH ABOUT SELF", "THE 72 NAMES OF GOD" FROM EXODUS 14, VERSES 19-21, "The Yoga Sutras", "The Bhagavad Gita" and "Thirumandiram". These "STUDY SOURCES" are LIKE "CATALYSTS"!

WE FURTHER LIFT OUR CONSCIOUSNESS, to the realm of the Creator, THROUGH PRACTICING KRIYA DHYANA MEDITATIONS, KRIYA KUNDALINI PRANAYAM, KRIYA

ASANAS (stretching exercises), RECITING THE "GAYATRI" AND MRITYONJAYA" MANTRAS and studying the HIGHEST ASPECTS OF NON-THEISTIC HINDUISM. Additionally, consciousness is elevated by practicing the TAI CHI "STANDING MEDITATION", the "BACKFLOW MEDITATION", MUSIC, DRUMMING, RUNNING, DANCING and INTENSE SEXUAL COUPLING. These disciplines/protocols are LIKE "CHEMICALS"!

WHEN WE ADD THE CATALYST (studies) TO THE CHEMICALS (practices such as Pranayam, Sanskrit Mantras, etc.) WE SHORTEN OUR "LEARNING CURVE" AND WE EVOLVE IN THETA CONSCIOUSNESS AND "LIGHT BODY" ACTIVATION AT AN ACCELERATED RATE!

These things will remake us in the "image and likeness of God" and restore us to our perfect state (Aleph Kaf Aleph from "The 72 Names of God" from "Exodus").

IT TAKES OBSESSION TO GIVE US THE DISCIPLINE TO SUCCEED IN OUR SPIRITUAL MISSION AND RECLAIM OUR DIVINE ABILITIES AND PROSPERITY AND HEALTH!

There is the strong possibility of an interdimensional/interstellar electormagnetic energy vortex being established in the "Four Corners" area of the USA that will help cleanse the earth and mitigate our severe weather patterns but it could also trigger earthquakes and volcanos.

There is existing scientific validation that is a measurable level of "higher gravity" (which is electromagnetic in its constitution) and higher magnetism already existing in this "Four Corners" area; this would mean that there is already a geomantic propensity for there to be a powerful leyline intersectional vortex to currently exist in this area!

ALTHOUGH WE MAY EXPERIENCE A TIME OF TRAVAIL, WE CAN KNOW WITH CERTAINTY THAT GOD IS ALWAYS WITH AND GUIDING US (Ayin Resh Yod) from "The 72 Names of God from Exodus. This has been shown in stories throughout the "Bible", "The Mahabarata" and "The Ramayan", among others!

SIN IS NOTHING MORE THAN OUR IGNORANCE ABOUT THE PERFECTION OF GOD'S CREATION AND OUR OWN REFLECTED PERFECTION AND HAS NOTHING TO DO WITH TRANGRESSIONS!

THE ATOMIC FIELD PROVES THE PERFECTION OF THE CREATOR AND POSSIBLY EVEN THE EXISTENCE OF GOD and certainly that there is some force that controls the atoms, which can be proven anecdotally! If there was not a CONTROLLING FORCE OF THE ATOMS, THEY WOULD ONLY EXIST SINGLY AND WE HUMANS WOULD NOT EXIST!!!!

From the work of physicist David Boehm, we know that the Universe is a detailed hologram and not solid in any way, shape or form!

CHAPTER SEVEN

IS IMMORTALITY IN THIS BODY BEYOND THE ABILITY/ ATTAINABILITY OF MAN?CAN THIS ULTIMATE ALCHEMICAL PROCESS OF BODILY IMMORTALITY BE ACHEIVED?

Since we have at many examples of immortality in the last many millenia, being Ram, Krishna, Mithras, Osirus, Attis of Phrygia, Dionysis, Jesus the Christ, and NogaBaba, the answer to the chapter title would be NO! Also, in the Kriya Yoga lineage, we have this immortality attained by Satgurus and MahaAvatars-Siddhas Babaji Nagaraj, Boganathur, Agastyr, Thirumoolar, Rama Devar, Kokanavar, Valmiki as well as hundreds of other Siddhas in this lineage. Many people will counter with the ASSERTION that they are "ONLY HUMAN AND THEREFORE NOT PERFECT AND THAT THEY WILL EVENTUALLY DIE" and so this concept of perfection is irrelevant to this lifetime!

Dr. Newton will counter with JESUS' STATEMENT which says: "GREATER WORKS THAN THESE SHALL YE DO ALSO!" Every Christian Scientist knows this statement and the readers of this book should "take this statement to heart"! WE SHOULD ACTUALLY AIM TO SURPASS THE WORKS OF JESUS, AS HE EXHORTED US TO DO and by doing so WE ACTUALLY HONOR THE CHRIST!

Otherwise his "mission" and example were without purpose because neither he nor anyone else "can wipe away your "sins" (which could be nothing more than ignorance as was discussed in Chapter Six) and provide you with "salvation" BECAUSE DOING SO WOULD VIOLATE GOD'S LAWS OF PHYSICS WHICH ALSO INCLUDES KARMA, including Jesus' "Golden Rule" ("Do unto others as you have them do unto you!")! This could be rephrased to say, treat others well so that you can be treated likewise! YOU, AND ONLY YOU, CAN PROVIDE YOUR SALVATION AND EVERYONE EVENTUALLY GETS THIS ANYWAY—IT IS INEVITABLE—as it well should be! OMG, now we can actually be saved and liberated by our own actions? Yes, truly you do not need your pastor or your priest for this or any other religious or philosophical personage, although a Yogic master or a Christian Science teacher may be able to help you with such!

Certainly this goes against the prevalent thought patterns presently coveted by many people. The author gets no satisfaction from "raining on your parade". He remembers when likewise he experienced having his parade "rained on". Then again, he is not the person who foisted these phantasmogoric, disjointed thought patterns and scientific inaccuracies upon you or himself!

DR. NEWTON WILL TELL YOU THAT THOUGHTS ABOUT AND JUSTIFICATION OF MEDIOCRITY AND FALLABILITY AND IMPERFECTION WILL INEVITABLY BEGET THESE SAME PATHETIC QUALITIES. PLEASE READ THIS STATEMENT AGAIN AND AGAIN UNTIL YOU REALLY COMPREHEND IT! When WE lower ourselves into ACCEPTING AND FOLLOWING IMPERFECT MODELS, WE PERPETUATE MORE OF THE SAME as Mary Baker Eddy so lucidly pointed out in "Science and Health with Key to the Scriptures" where she talks about "the imperfect models of Man"! Follow the perfect examples and models of Mrs. Eddy and Krishna and Ram and Patanjali and Thirmoolar and Kriya Yoga, "The Emerald Tablets" of Hermes Trismegistus, "The Patterns on the Trestleboard: The Truth About Self" by Paul Foster Case and "The 72 Names of God" from Kabbalistic Judaism! Do we really want to devote ourselves to mediocrity?

Will this take us to an awareness of our perfectly created beingness? NVL (not very likely!)

CONVERSELY, FOCUSING ON THE PERFECT NATURE OF MAN, AS HAS BEEN ALREADY REVEALED IN THE PREVIOUS PARAGRAPH OF THIS BOOK, BEGETS GREATNESS, GRANDEUR, SUCCESS, HEALTH, BLISS AND EUPHORIA, SAMADHI AND SORUBA SAMADHI! Dr. Newton craves the latter of these scenarios and would be astonished if virtually everyone did not likewise desire the same! The only problem would be that we DO NOT FEEL WORTHY TO HAVE THIS OR AFRAID TO HAVE IT. And considering the blatant, excrementally laced misinformation that most of our churches and governments have dispensed, this is completely understandable! BUT THIS IS NOT AN INSURMOUNTABLE OBSTACLE "in any way shape or form"!!!!

We know that after Mary Baker Eddy passed from her body it lasted for many months without deterioration or decomposition. This also occurred with Paramahansa Yogananda, a Kriya Yoga Avatar asscociated with The Self Realization Fellowship, whose deceased body also replicated the effects of the body of Mrs Eddy. THIS IS DIRECT EVIDENCE OF THE OPERATION OF ALCHEMY. It would appear at, least in large part, that Mary Baker Eddy in "Science and Health With Key to the Scriptures" was correct in her statements in the "Scientific Statement of Being" on page 468 that man is not "material" but rather "spiritual", which is energy as transliterated by Dr. Newton.

AS A NOTE TO READERS OF THIS BOOK, YOU REALLY WOULD BE DOING YOURSELF A FAVOR TO GIVE THIS "Science and Health . . ." AN UNPREJUDICED AND DEDICATED READING! Christian Science is not a "cult" as the Christian orthodoxy would have you believe AND THEY BENEFIT FROM YOUR IGNORANCE THEREOF BUT WE DON'T!! But certainly the Illuinati is an "elistist"/ oligarchial cult and more than many of our present religions perpetuate the mediocrity discussed throughout this book! Why keep ourselves "imprisoned" by blantantly unenlightened people and organizations, UNLESS A STATE OF IGNORANCE IS PREFERRABLE?

According to William Haney, who was a guest on George Noory's "Coast to Coast" radio show on 5-30-2011, there is an "ANOINTING OIL" which CAN AID in this PROCESS of IMMORTALITY OF OUR BODIES. What is being referred to is a way to regenerate the body in a manner more powerful than Human Growth Hormone, Testosterone, Colostrum, Shark and Bovine Cartilage AND WOULD HAVE STRONG ALCHEMICAL PROPERTIES. Haney claims that he has found in his research that this "anointing oil" is CREATED AT THE CENTER OF OUR SUN and other STARS. Also he has found indications that the Eyptian priests used this oil on Osirus, who attainted immortality of the body. Haney stated that we can CREATE "anointing oil" in our OWN BODIES. Further, Haney states there are indications that MARY MAGDALENE put this ANOINTING OIL all over JESUS' BODY AFTER HIS CRUCIFIXION. Also, Haney stated that he found in his reasearch that ARCH ANGEL MICHAEL ANOINTED ENOCH WITH THIS OIL and that ENOCH'S BODY SHONE AS LIGHT and that he could time travel between the stars! This sounds like teleportation, done in a "light body". So, we could surmise that "anointing oil" is akin to an agent of immortality!!!!

Since the "Gayatri Mantra" is an exultation/praise of Savithur, the Hindu representation of the Sun, would it be too far fetched to speculate that saying this mantra repeatedly for extended periods of time may well activate this "anointing oil" in us? Could this mantra have caused Siddha Rama Devar to have activated this oil to catalyze himself into a state of Soruba Samadhi/immortality? We know that the recitation of Sanskrit Mantras was Rama Devar's path to enlightenement and immortality! Dr. Newton's Akashic feeling is that this is more than a distinct possibilty.

In ancient Greece, Helios, representing the Sun likewise, was revered. For the Mayas, Misol Ha was a Diety and a representative of the Sun. In ancient Eygpt, the Sun was revered and represented by Ra, Helios and Auten and you can see depictions thereof in the many Eyptian temples and tombs in Luxor but not limited thereto. The Sun was worshiped by all Native American Indians. At the very least it can be said that the Sun was extremely important to many ancient cultures—actually all of them. Is this just a random coincidence? You mean there is no synchronicty (reoccurence)? NVL (not very likely)!!!!

THE IMPORTANCE OF THE SUN AS A RECURRING SYNCHRONICITY IS NOT SOMETHING TO BE IGNORED! There is an OVERWHELMING OCCURENCE of this devotion to the Sun and for good reason! THIS IS NOT SUPERSTITIONAL FANTASY or DRUG INDUCED HALLUCINATION! It is a common thread through diverse civilizations that were cognizant of its inherent validity! Many, if not all of these civilizations, were highly advanced beyond our own because in extraterretial interaction with beings far evolved and spiritually enlightened beyond ourselves!

Also, it is a known fact that "Vitamin D" emanates from the Sun and is absorbed into the human body through the skin and seems to be necessary not only for physical health but more crucial for emotional health. It is also known that most sunscreens block the abosorbtion of "Vitamin D" into the body and this was being discussed by Nora Gidowskus on the "Coast to Coast" radio show on 06-21-2011.

"Vitamin D" may be an "anointing oil" talked about that is produced by the Sun or it could be a component thereof. Essentially, ANYTHING COMING FROM THE SUN IS GOING TO CONTAIN INTENSE PRANA/CHI/"LIFE FORCE" and COULD IN FACT CATALYZE IMMORTALITY and AT A LESSER LEVEL, AT LEAST NURTURE THE BODY. This was the reason for the creation of the "Gayatri Mantra", a prayer and praise of the Sun, the most powerful sources of energy in our solar system. Dr. Newton has seen research from articles in the "American Free Press" that INCIDICATE THE SUN'S RAYS DO NOT CAUSE SKIN CANCER and it is A NUTRITIONAL PROBLEM RELATED TO A DEFICIENCY OF ANTIOXIDANTS AND VITAMINS AND MINERALS IN THE BODY. Louise L. Hay might well call it an emotional problem and rightly so. But what better way to make a lot of money than by scaring people into believing that Sun does cause Cancer? A lot of Dermatologists will say that these statements are irresponsible and yet they make a lot of money saying this! Is it not EQUALLY IRRESPONSIBLE TO IGNORE THE SUBSTANCIAL BENEFITS OF SUN EXPOSURE WITHOUT SUNSCREEN? DYT (Do you think)?

You must make your own decision about this. Dr. Newton has noticed a synchronistic pattern that indicates people, especially older people, are terrified of the Sun and supposedly the Sun is creating Melanomas and Sarcomas in their skin. And yet the Sun was revered by virtually all ancient civilizations! How did they ever survive without sunscreen? They must have consumed enough anti-oxidant foods! Wow, what a novel concept? EVEN BETTER, THEY MIGHT NOT HAVE FEARED THE SUN BUT RATHER WORSHIPED THIS FIERY ORB! How unfortunate they were to not have a government, such as that in Austrailia, to pass laws that you must "protect" yourself from the Sun! How did the "ancients" ever survive without governmental directives? AS A CERTAIN TRUTH, THAT WHICH YOU ARE AFRAID OF WILL HAVE A HIGH PROBABILITY OF MANIFESTING IN YOUR LIFE!!!! This likewise applies to Melanomas. This fear may well be mutating and reprogramming the DNA computer code, actually creating skin Cancer!!!! This statement is made within the context of what was covered near the end of Chapter Five,

Despite all of the digressions on this topic, the point being emphasized is THAT YOU NEED TO ABSORB SUNLIGHT THROUGH YOUR SKIN WITHOUT SUNSCREEN FOR AT LEAST PART OF THE DAY TO BE EMOTIONALLY AND PHYSICALLY HEALTHY

UNTIL YOU ATTAIN SORUBA SAMADHI. If dermatologists are outraged by this, it can be explained by their lack of holistic understanding! Were this not true you would not have a disproportionate level of suicide in Scandanavian countries where there is little sunlight during the winter months! Es todo (that's all) should be the summation of this because it is self evident when viewed in an unbiased manner, without a fear based mentality!!!!

This was mentioned several paragraphs previously but needs to be re-emphasized that we know from the Kriya Yoga traditions that Siddha Rama Devar attained Soruba Samadhi (immortality) focusing on the continual recitation of Sanskirt Mantras. Dr. Newton has not accessed any information via Earth which sources which would empirically prove which mantras Rama Devar repeated. BUT HE IS QUITE CERTAIN THAT ONE OF THEM WOULD HAVE HAD TO HAVE BEEN THE "GAYATRI MANTRA" since it is considered "THE MOTHER OF ALL MANTRAS" by Yoga and Hinduism. And it is possible that this was the only Sanskrit Mantra recited by MahaAvatar, Satguru Siddha Rama Devar! Virtually every Hindu and most Yogi's which Dr. Newton has known, either knows or knew the "Gayatri" simply because everyone in India knows the auspicious power connected thereto, which is protection, inducive of health and Pranic energization of the human body! So this could be another indication of the Sun—"anointing oil" and immortality connection! IF "ANOINTING OIL" DOES EXIST, and after the previous discussions in this chapter it seems it is more than possible, IT SHOULD SURELY BE PRODUCED BY THE MANTRA THAT EXALTS THE SUN, "THE GAYATRI MANTRA", in light of the fact that "anointing oil" is believed to be originated in the Sun!!!!

There is also the regenerative process of the body from Hinduism and Yoga called KAYAKALPHA. The process of Kayakalpha takes approximately nine months and invovles using a secret combination of herbs which are taken while the subject human rests during this entire process. Dr. Newton's feeling is that there is credibility in these statements. But for the population at large, the problem is that we do not know the specifics of the herbal combinations, nor does anyone know that the author has queried about this. This is not even discussed in Babaji Nagaraj's, "The Death of Death" THIS KAYAKALPA PROTOCOL MIGHT WELL INCLUDE "ANOINTING OIL" SUCH AS "BINDHU" AND/OR THE "GAYATRI MANTRA". This statement is definitely within the realm of possibility and even probability! It might also include the ingestion of "Occinum Sanctum" AKA "HOLY BASIL"! Every Hindu person the author has encountered wants "Holy Basil" growing on their property, as it is considered as very auspicious presence!!!! It certainly has strong medicinal qualities This information probably supercedes superstition and is based on historical and anecdotal experiences regarding this plant, of which the author has experience growing and using as an emotional palliative (creating calmness).

Additionally, WE KNOW THAT SATGURU, MAHAAVATAR, AND SIDDHA, BABAJI NAGARAJ, ATTAINED SORUBA SAMADHI through the practicing of KRIYA DHYANA Yoga (specific meditations), PRANAYAM (a protocol of special breathing and techniques already listed in this book) and SAMADHI (a living state of breathlessness for extended periods of time). There are reports from people at the Kumba Mela (a very special religious celebration in India) that Babaji makes an "appearance" there and can time travel and move himself through different dimensions. BUT THEN AGAIN, SO CAN WE when we WUTOD (wake up to our Divinity)!

Also, one of the Kriya Kundalini Pranayam Breathing techniques involves circulating "Bindhu" with the Pranayam breath. Yogi Govindan Satchiananda taught us in Kriya Yoga classes that "Bindhu" helps in alleviating our accumulated Karma (transgressions against others). Dr. Newton has had trouble with this concept of the elimination of Karma but could understand this if "Bindhu" is likewise an "anointing oil" and that these two things could operate in tandem. His strong Akashic intuition is that "BINDHU" IS AN "ANOINTING OIL, REGENERATING

THE BODY TO A STATE OF ENERGY/LIGHT AND EXPANDING CONSCIOUSNESS TO ITS NATURAL STATE OF DIVINITY!!!! This would be a further indicator of the power of advanced Pranayam techniques AND THE ALCHEMICAL TRANSFORMATION THAT IS THE RESULT THEREOF! THEREFORE, IMMEDIATELY—IF NOT SOONER—LEARN PRANAYAM FROM "BABAJI'S KRIYA YOGA" (internet accessable) or in Dr. Newton's seminars. The "early bird" gets the Pranayam!

Additionally, Zecharia Sitchin in his various books about an extraterrestial culture, detailed in historical records in Sumer, came to Earth and were fanatical about extracting as much Gold as possible from our planet and were very successful in doing so in Africa. Recently in Africa, monumentally huge goldmines have been found which do not "fit in" with our existing record keeping. Are these just anomalies? NVL (not very likely)!

IT IS NOW KNOWN THAT MONATOMIC GOLD CAN RAISE A PERSON'S CONSCIOUSNESS WHEN INGESTED (possibly to Theta level over a period of time), and will RAISE THEIR ENERGY LEVEL (Prana, Chi, life force) of their body (the life force is easy to measure with dowsing rods). It appears that these extra-terrestials, from the planet Nibiru, knew of these properties possessed by Gold and they ingested it in the Monatomic form and were possibly even able to ingest and absorb enough so that their skin actually turned into the color gold from their bodies being infused with Gold. As a comparison it is known that when people ingest large amounts of colloidal Silver that their skin can turn "blue-greenish", which becomes the oxidized color of Silver!

It is also known that this culture from Nibiru, known as Ananaki, interacted with the old Egyptian dynasties. And the Egyptians always made their statues, depicting gods who the Ananaki were considered (actually they were demi-gods) out of Gold because the color of their skin was probably in fact gold from their voluminous consumption of this metal. These

Ananaki are reported in the records from Sumer (ancient Iraq) to live 800 to a 1000 years, the same length as early Biblical figures such as Methusala and Moses. Is this a mere coincidence? Probably not, as they might well have been Ananaki also! It definitely would have been easier for Moses to have "manna" falling from an Ananaki spaceship than from the heavens of space, in the quest to feed his poeple. This is not Biblically conventional yet within the realm of the possible as per the books of Zecharia Sitchin, Robert Temple, Von Donagen, and David Wilcox, among others!!!!

After digressing again, the point trying to be made here is that MONATOMIC GOLD COULD VERY WELL BE AN "ANOINTING OIL"/longevity extender/immortality agent! Additionally, eating CAYENNE and other hot peppers or TINCTURES made from the same, could also be a type of "ANOINTING OIL" because they augment the ciruculation of blood throughout the body. It is known by some herbalists, including the author, the Cayenne tincture will immediately stop a heart attack or stroke, although such is not even listed in "The Herbal Physicians Desk Reference". As was previously discussed, blood helps transfer Prana through the body. And Prana helps "lighten" and "enlighten" the body! Also, "Occinum Sanctum" AKA "Holy Basil" could also have the "anointing" properties but the author is not aware of the mechanism that would make it so!

Additionally, Aloe Vera, stabalized Oxygen, Hydrogen Peroxide (H_2O_2 and water from "The John Ellis Water Machine" (also H_2O_2) could be considered "anointing oils", in a sense, since they are highly oxygenated substances. As has been discussed elsewhere in this book, OXYGEN SEEMS TO BE SUBSTANCE BY WHICH PRANA/CHI/LIFE FORCE CAN BE MORE FULLY INTEGRATED INTO OUR BODIES. And this is the necessary ingredient to creating a "light body" or a body of energy as oppossed to a body of degenerating matter!

Also, in the "Keys of Enoch", Dr. Hurtak talks about AdenoTrioPhosphate (ATP) as an expander of consciousness and a regenerator of the human body. This might also fall into the category of "anointing oil". This is available as a stand alone supplement and also in "Alpha PXP forte", extremely concentrated rice bran containing Polysaccharides and Peptides, which appears to be a precursor to ATP. The author's experience with these two substances indicates that they are an effective consciousness and Prana (life force) enhancers but the process is gradual and hardly noticeable at first. So if you use these things, you must have patience to see results!

But, if we DAILY FOCUS our efforts upon the practice of Kriya Yoga ASANAS, Kriya Kundalini PRANAYAM and the Kriya DHYANA Meditations, FIRST THING IN THE MORNING, we would be on the ROAD TO IMMORTALITY sans the ingestion or exposure to "outside substances" such as "anointing oil" and Monatomic Gold. If we daily repeat the "Gayatri Mantra" and/or the "Mrityonjaya Mantra" for at least 108 rounds in one session, we will be on the ROAD TO IMMORTALITY. If we repeat these mantras while doing menial tasks or walking or hiking or biking or golfing, or surfing or motocycle riding or driving, among others, we will be in THETA consciousness and on the ROAD TO IMMORTALITY. THESE THINGS ARE NOT BEYOND YOUR CAPABILITIES IF YOU ARE MOTIVATED! AND MOTIVATIONS YOU HAVE ALREADY BEEN GIVEN IN ABUNDANCE!

Personally, the author is tired of reaching a state of quasi-enlightenment, dying shortly thereafter and then reincarnating as a hapless baby and then being educated by spiritually braindead educators and parents and controlled by codependent, spiritually inferior people in business and government! **NITTTTSI** (NOW IS THE TIME TO TRANSCEND SUCH IDIOCY)!!!!

The above recommended practices are more productive and beneficial use of your time as compared to partying, internet searches, Facebook, Twitter, texting, blabbing and gossiping on your cell phone or watching television! WHY WASTE YOUR TIME ON BETA "JIBBER JABBER"? Why let the "monkey mind" distract you from reaching your Divine nature? OMG, TTATYD (Time to awaken to your Divinity)! DO NOT LET TECHNOLOGY ENSARE YOU IN ITS CLUTCHES as it is already doing to many of us!

Dr. Hurtak says in "The Keys of Enoch", that the Egyptian Calendar Stone ends to 2012, signifying a new Earth cycle. This is in conjunction with our solar system and our Earth aligning with the center of Milky Way Galaxy, on or about 12-21-2012, which is the end of the Mayan Calendar Stone. Thus what is occurring is that there is more hyperdimensional/torsional energy /electro-magnetic energy/Prana entering our Earth which gives a "boost" to our efforts of transformation (talked about in a previous chapter about changing from pathetic, error prone humans to the Divine beings that we are as the Creator made us)! THIS IS THE OPPORTUNITY/ DEAL OF MANY LIFETIMES because new cycles and increased energies/ consciousness bombarding Earth. Use this OPPORTUNITY well! IMMORTALITY, of your existing body, IS WITHIN YOUR GRASP, NOW! Use your road maps/pathways which include "Science and Health With Keys to the Scriptures", "The 72 Names of God from Exodus", "The Emerald Tablets" and the "Patterns on the Trestleboard: The Truth About Self", "The Yoga Sutras", "The Bhagavad Gita" and "Thirumandiram" so that we do not need to keep reincarnating on Earth in a new body time after time, attending the same party with the same underachieving actors and actresses)!

KNOW THE TRUTH AND LET IT MAKE US FREE FROM THE IMPERFECT MODELS OF UNENLIGHTENED MEN AND WOMEN! Or we could stay ignorant and indifferent and that would suit the Illuminati cultists and organized religions and national governments just fine.

TO ANSWER THE SECOND QUESTION OF THIS CHAPTER TITLE, YES, WE CAN ACHIEVE THE ULTIMATE ALCHEMICAL TRANSFORMATION TO THE IMMORTAL ENERGY/"LIGHT BODY"!

TTATOD (TIME TO AWAKEN TO OUR DIVINITY)!

In summary:

We know immortality of the body is a real possibility because of Jesus, Ram, Krishna Mitrha, Osirus, Attis of Phrygia, Dionysis, NogaBaba, Babaji Nagaraj, Agastyr, Boganathur, Thirmoolar, Rama Devar, Valmiki, Kokanavar and many other Kriya Yoga Siddhas.

Jesus exhorted us to surpass his works so obviously you can do so (he wasn't just taunting us)!

There may be several "anointing oils" which aid in the process of immortaility!

One of them could be "Bindhu", which is a protocol of Kriya Kundalini Pranayam AND WOULD HAVE ALCHEMICAL TRANSFORMATIONAL PROPERTIES, eliciting bodily immortality!

Another "anointing oil" is Monatomic Gold, which was used by a visiting extra-terretial culture, the Ananaki, which could definitely be considered similar an "immortalith agent", since the these people lived 800 to 1000 years or more as related in Zecharia Sitchin's books and also most likely in the "Old Testament"!

Rama Devar, a Kriya Yoga Siddha (Avatar), attained Soruba Samadhii (immortality) through the recitation mantras and one of them may have been the "Gayatri Mantra", which is a prayer to the Sun, could aid in producing "anointing oil".

Bindhu, part of the Kriya Kundalini Pranayam protocol of breathing, may also be an "anointing oil"!!!!

Cayenne and other hot peppers, eaten or taken as herbal tinctures, and "Occinum Sanctum" ("Holy Basil") could also have "anointing oil" characteristics!

Aloe Vera and Hydrogen Peroxide and "John Ellis Water" could also be types of "anointing oil" since they are laden with Oxygen which can carry more Prana into the body and infuse it therewith!

Dr. Hurtak, in "the Keys of Enoch", discusses how AdenoTrioPhosphate can uplift our consciousness and infuses our bodies with more light, helping to create the perfect "Adam Kadmon archetypal" body!

Babaji Nagaraj, a Kriya Yoga Siddha (Avatar), attained Soruba Samadhii(immortality), through practicing Kriya Dhyana meditations and Kriya Kundalini Pranayam and Kriya Asanas (physical exercises).

So practicing the regimens of Rama Devar, Babaji Nagaraj, Kokanavar, Boganathur, Agastyur, Thirumoolar, Valmiki and other Kriya Yoga Siddhas will aid us in the quest for immortality! Thus it behooves us to become proficient in the protocols of Kriya Kundalini Yoga!

Also, the fact that increased concentrations of Prana via torsional and hyperdimensional energies from the "Milky Way" Galaxy are entering our Earth make the evolution to perfection/immortality easier to achieve.

So now is the time to take advantage of this rarely occuring state of intense Prana as per 12-21-2012 (or 11-11-2011), which are time frames for the end of the Mayan and Egyptian Stone Calendars. This signifies the start of a new Earth cycle of a higher conscsiousness when overlayed with the increased hyper-dimensional energies bombarding Earth at this time. THUS, OPPORTUNITY IS KNOCKING AT OUR DOOR!!!!

Use the maps and pathways of "Science and Health . . .", "The 72 Names of God", "The Emerald Tablets", "The Patterns on the Trestleboard . . .", "The

Yoga Sutras", "The Bhagavad Gita and Kriya Yoga to guide and tranform you to Theta/light consciousness and bodies!

WE CAN ACHIEVE THE ULTIMATE ALCHEMICAL TRANSFORMATION TO AN IMMORTAL ENERGY/"LIGHT BODY"!

TTBRIOD (time to be reformed into our Divinity)!

Chapter Eight

IS IT POSSIBLE FOR US TO HAVE PSYCHIC POWERS AND SUPERNATURAL ABILITIES?

Having psychic and supernatural abilities ARE THE RIGHTS OF MEN, ENDOWED BY THEIR CREATOR. YOU LITERALLY WERE BORN WITH VARIED PSYCHIC ABILITIES BECAUSE YOU INCARNATED IN A STATE OF ALPHA AND THETA CONSCIOUSNESS! Many of these abilities focus in the Alpha consciousness realm. They would include the "reading of auras", communication with relatives, friends and others who are discarnate, rudimentary telepathy and receiving psychic impressions from another person's objects (psychometry) and dissolving clouds.

More advanced psychic abilities, rooted in Theta consciousness, are "remote viewing", pure spiritual healing (Christian Science and Theta based healing which are actually essentially the same thing), advanced telepathy (where you can "read" someone like a book, "Light Speed Learning" (absorbing entire books in several minutes), going into paralell and higher dimensions, reading the Akashic or atomic records, Samadhi, Kundalini "awakening", invisibility, teleportation and weather modification (beyond dissolving clouds), manifestation of objects from the ethers (spiritual realm).

How do you know when you are in Alpha consciousness, considered by many scientists to be a brainwave between seven to ten or eleven megahertz? You will be relaxed and breathing slowly and possibly in a state of benign happiness. Beyond doubt, the Tai Chi "standing Meditation", Kriya Kundalini Pranayam, Kriya Dhyana meditations, the "Backflow

Meditation", the recitation of Sanskrit mantras and the listening to and performing of complex or repetitive musical and compositions allow you to access the Alpha state. Also, wearing a pyramid made from metal rod, on your head, will for almost all people intensify/magnify your psychic abilities. These are available from "Paradyne" and from "Metaforms". Pyramids will focus your consciousness in Alpha, if not Theta, so they are useful for our purposes here! Dr. Newton used a Copper rod pyramid coated in Gold, Silver and Titanium often in developing his own psychic abilities back in the 1980's. The result for him and his students was always beneficial!

The use of pyramids and crystals such as Quartz and Tourmaline, which are pietzoelectric (statically electrified) and the use of Lapis and Sugulite are covered in depth in Dr. Newton's "Pathways to God" book. This book should be in its second printing at the same time or shortly after this book is available.

READING AURAS, the energy field around a person's head, is achieveable by making your eyes go out of focus and of course if you are myopic (near sighted) so much the easier this practice becomes. When first attempting "aura reading" it is easier done in a very dimly lighted place. Every person has an aura or they are not incarnate on Earth. A person with a body teeming with Prana will have a larger aura than someone who is low energy or depressed. Usually you will see a white light appearing as the aura and sometimes you will see colors. If your subject-person has a purple or blue cast to their aura, you know they are spiritually uplifted/evolved. If you see a red cast then you know your subject is angry and/or agitated. This is as valid as way to read someone as is "body language". When you become proficient and confident in your aura reading ability, you might be able to read auras with your eyes in focus.

Also related to reading auras, you may be able to see discarnate entities and/or "ghosts". These you will usually see as amorphic forms—not actually bodies—but nevertheless detectable on a ceiling or wall. You may even see energy forms in nature—sometimes even at night.

With COMMUNICATION WITH DISCARNATE ENTITIES you need to be in a relaxed state. Such communcation is not difficult since there are such entities constantly around and about everyone. Also, all of the FOURTEEN DIMENSIONS which scientists have discovered and postulated about in "The Membrance Theory" and "The String Theory", ARE ALL STACKED AND/OR OCCUPY THE SAME SPACE as our so-called third dimension. So, essentially THERE IS VERY LITTLE, IF ANY, DISTANCE BETWEEN OURSELVES AND THE DEAD.

Such communication with discarnate entities happens routinely in the dream state which accesses Alpha and Theta frequencies. Some people believe the veil/ membrane between the dimensions lessens during Halloween and there must be some validity in this with all of the attention directed to ghosts during this period of time. In Mexico, Halloween is known as "Dia De Los Muertos" ("Day of the Dead"), which is more appropriately named than Halloween. This interdimensional communication often just comes "out of the Blue" so be constantly vigilant to "incoming messages". If you concentrate on the face of a departed person, you can often summon communication with them. Don't expect talking from them out loud. THE COMMUNICATION WILL COME USUALLY AS THOUGHTS AND PICTURES RATHER THAN WORDS. You can get a different perspective on things with interdimensional communication. So, once someone has "died", you do not really lose the possibility of communication with them!

TELEPATHY, which is UNSPOKEN-MENTAL COMMUNICATION BETWEEN INDIVIDUALS, is a very useful and precise way to communicate considering how abstract and ambiguous most languages are especially including English which truly is a mishmash hodgepodge melangue of a "tongue". It is well known that twins have this ability inherently and they know what each other is thinking and how they are feeling. In the Alpha state, you can at least have a general feeling of what someone is thinking. At Theta level, it is more like you can get inside of someone's head. You will most likely be quite unsuccessful in telepathy if you try too hard to do it. Relax, use the Alpha-Theta protocols and telepathic communication can occur.

WE MIGHT AS WELL BECOME PROFICIENT AT TELEPATHY BECAUSE IN THE COMING YEARS IT WILL BE A VERY PREVALENT MODE OF RELATING TO PEOPLE. Also, YOU HAVE THE MEANS TO KNOW IF SOMEONE IS LYING TO YOU OR BEING DECEITFUL! And as Yogi Govindan Satchidanada often says, "people who TALK TOO MUCH WASTE A LOT OF PRANA" (which is Divine energy and Divine intelliegence and Divine consciousness)! Additionally, these incessant "talkers" seem trapped in Beta Consciousness—the level of "mindless babble".

PSYCHOMETRY is a way to uncover information about another person by holding an object that they have on their person all the time and you put it in your left hand generally (because it is usually the "receiving" mode of most humans) and you receive "impressions"/information from the object. Although this sounds difficult, and Dr. Newton remembers his trepidation on his first attempt at Pyschometry, it is not difficult to receive information about another person in this manner. Dr. Newton has been in classes in Psychometry where every person in the room was successful in "reading" things about their subject. YOU MUST ONLY RELAX AND LET THE INFORMATION FLOW TO YOU IN AN EFFORTLESS MANNER AND TRUST THAT IT IS and WILL!

DISSOLVING CLOUDS is something that Yogi Govindan Satchidanada always has his students do collectively in "Level Two" Kriya Yoga training. Dr. Newton remembers his first time taking "Level Two" and wondering, "how the hell are you supposed to dissolve a cloud?" Well, we were successful and the second time he participated in "Level Two" all he could think about was dissolving clouds again. Basically, you focus Prana through your eyes, as you breathe it down through your head, and in a gaze or a trance a group of people can easily make a cloud go away by keeping their focus constantly on that form.

Actually, A GROUP OF PEOPLE COULD MAKE A VIOLENT STORM GO AWAY and with what we have been experiencing weatherwise recently, this is a more than TIMELY AND USEFUL ABILITY! Could one person perform a comparable feat? Yes, most of them are or were in India, Prana masters of Kriya Yoga and Hindu Avatars such as the recently deceased Satchi Sai Baba! In the "Nature of Personal Reality", Jane Roberts channelled information from the Akashia records which indicated that people as a group actually create the weather! So THAT WHICH CAN BE CREATED CAN BE UNCREATED/NEGATED! This scientifically and psychicly true!

Now, let us examine the THETA PSYCHIC ABILITIES. You were born in Theta consciousness and functioned at this level until you were five or six years old and your schooling "pounded it out of you". At your core, your soul, THIS IS YOUR NATURAL STATE OF BEING AND CONSCIOUSNESS! How do you know you are in Theta consciousness, which is in the range of 4 to 7 megahertz! If your are a master of Kriya Kundalini Pranayam in that you can do 3 rounds (48 repetions) at a more than thirty second per breath breathing cadence with Eka Nylai, you are most likely in Theta consciousness. The way to know for sure is to have yourself tested with an EEG (electro encephlagram) or you can validate this through the occurence of NON-FORCED EYE FLUTTER AS YOU PULL YOUR EYE FOCUS UP TO YOUR MID-FOREHEAD ("third eye" area).

If you can do the "Gayatri" or "Mrityonjaya" mantra for at least 108 continuous repetitions where it becomes "automatically" repeated and you are entering a trance-like state of consciousness, you are most likely in the Theta state. This state will be aided by the light and sonic perfection you activate as you are chanting these Sanskrit mantras. If you are performing the Tai Chi "Standing Meditation" or the "Backflow Meditation for twenty to thirty continuous minutes, you are likely entering Theta Consciousness!!

If you are listening to or performing intense music, you could access Theta. If you are in a drum circle and/or chanting circle for a long period of time (at least one half to one hour in length), you could likewise enter the Theta state. IF YOU HAVE DOUBTS HOW THIS IS ACHIEVED, PLEASE REREAD CHAPTER THREE. Also, when your eyes are in the Eka Nylai positions, you can be reasonably certain you are in Theta level. If your eyes flutter naturally, when you turn them up—just your eyes and not your head, you can be certain of Theta Consciousness!

REMOTE VIEWING is a Theta ability in which you focus your consciousness on a specific geographical area and you try to view what is occurring now in "real time" and even in the future. This requires a STRONG CONCENTRATION and DEVELOPED POWERS OF VISUALIZATION. The United States government and other world governments have had and/or have remote viewing operations.The application of this power is awesome, especially when you engage in "future viewing" or looking into the future. IT IS NOW KNOWN THAT BIRDS USE REMOTE VIEWING TO NAVIGATE (as well as magnetic leylines). And it is further known that ALL PEOPLE CAN REMOTE VIEW FOR THREE OR FOUR SECONDS! To do it for longer you must put yourself in a very relaxed, trance-like state of consciousness and then you visualize the area or place of which you want to view. The more you are in Theta, the more successful, vivid, detailed, and accurate your viewing will be. Anything which takes you into future events is at best only a possible scenario because things can change before they actually occur!

SPIRITUAL HEALING, either Christian Science healing or Theta Consciousness healing, we have covered thoroughly in Chapter Four. Dr. Newton would just like to add that if Spiritual type healing comes slowly the healer is not in a deep Theta level and/or he has not dealt with his own and/or his patient's FEARS or factors of "WORTHINESS" to be healed. So you will need to focus on eliminating these things. The best way Dr. Newton has found to do this is "Mem Nun Daled" (overcoming your fears) and "Hey Hey Hey" (self-esteem) from "The 72 Names of God" from Exodus 14, verses 19-21.

Again, Dr. Newton will mention how Mary Baker Eddy in "Science and Health with Key to the Scriptures", repeatedly states that you MUST OVERCOME YOUR FEARS FOR HEALING TO OCCUR. She stated that this is accomplished by SEEING YOURSELF BEING CREATED PERFECTLY in the "IMAGE AND LIKENESS OF GOD" and that we are Divine Spirit, not matter, and nothing else! IT IS JUST THIS SIMPLE AND ANYONE WHO TELLS US OTHERWISE IS MISINFORMED. The misinformed would include just about all the other sources and people we know!

Also, Spiritual Healing/Theta Healing occur more powerfully if the healer is in the deep Theta level of Samadhi! The same is true if your consciousness is in an alternative and/or parallel dimension. These dimensions can encompass the state of Samadhi but are not limited thereto! Also, you can use kinesiological muscle testing to zero in on information related to a healing treatment where you are uncertain of the diagnosis to use and where you need to test the effectiveness of a healing treatment! The process is described below in the section regarding the AKASHIC/ ATOMIC RECORDS.

ADVANCED TELEPATHIC ABILITIES are akin to being able to "GET INSIDE OF SOMEBODY'S HEAD" as was mentioned earlier in this chapter. It is similar to "READING SOMEONE LIKE A BOOK". You will know what they are thinking and even before they say it or not. You will know whether you are being lied to or someone is be disingenious. The sooner more people acquire/open up this ability within themselves, the better. Dr. Newton remembers a time when he used a small pyramid on his head to intensify his telepahtic abilities. He knows this would aid others

AS IT FOCUSES PRANA WHICH AIDS IN ELICITING THETA CONSCIOUSNESS! These pyramids are available from Paradyne and from Metaforms.

"LIGHT SPEED LEARNING" is a method of ABSORBING INFORMATION in an entire book in several minutes and this is definitely achievable from the state of THETA CONSCIOUSNESS. In a two and one third day seminar, they bombard you with Theta stimulus "brainwaves" (which Dr. Newton feels is more akin to consciousness). They also teach you Theta enhancing techniques and practices. Dr. Newton knows that this is possible, despite what say the rampant skeptics, and you are liberated from the laborious process of "reading" books which can be better spent reading auras! Thomas and Jane Morton, presenters of this seminar, can be contacted via the internet at "Light Speed Learning".

Also related to this, is ABSORBING INFORMATION FROM STUDYING. If you have become proficient in "LIGHT SPEED LEARNING", your study time will be vastly shortened. But even sans this ability, if the theta practices in this book are performed, it will vastly aid in INFORMATION RETENTION and RETRIEVAL. Also, doing your studying just before your sleep cycle will aid in the retention and retrieval of information because we start the transition to Alpha and Theta even before we attempt to sleep!

Going into PARALLEL or ALTERNATIVE DIMENSIONS is something which we often do during the sleep state. Dr. Newton is hypothesizing that this is the MAIN FUNCTION OF SLEEP AND THAT THIS IS AN IMPORTANT FUNCTION BY WHICH HUMANS KEEP THEIR LIFE "IN BALANCE". By "balance" the author means that you need to keep in touch with yourself in other parallel or alternative dimensions where you also reside. Dr. Newton used to feel guilty sometimes when he took a nap or went to sleep earlier than he desired. Now, however, Dr. Newton sees these things as a NECESSARY INTERDIMENSION LINK WHEREBY WE STAY IN TOUCH WITH OURSELVES IN

OTHER DIMENSIONS AND HAVE VITAL AND NECESSARY INFORMATION REVEALED TO US THAT WE CAN USE IN THIS DIMENSION. Actually, the author has learned these concepts from the Akashic records—they are not in any book he has read nor does he believe that this full concept is explicated in any other publications exactly like this. BASICALLY, WHAT HAPPENS IN OUR DREAMS IS LIKELY SOMETHING THAT IS ACTUALLY HAPPENING TO US IN A PARALLEL DIMENSION AND NOT A FANTASY OR JUST A SYMBOLIC EVENT!!!!

These other dimensions are EASILY ACCESSED IN THE THETA CONSCIOUSNESS OF KRIYA DHYANA MEDITATIONS, KRIYA KUNDALINI PRANAYAM, SAMADHI AND A KUNDALINI AWAKENING and even during intense sessions of the TAI CHI "STANDING MEDITATION", "THE BACKFLOW MEDITATION" and RECITATION OF THE "GAYATRI" AND "MRITYONJAYA" SANSKRIT MANTRAS. This can also occur in the state of "lucid daydreaming". Some "experts" on this subject feel that you need to remember to leave a figurative rope or SOME TYPE OF TRACER if you desire to find your way back here—if you so desire to return! The author has not had any problems without using a "tracer".

Specifically, how this is accomplished consciously should not be revealed here but rather in a seminar type controlled environnement. Just remember, this naturally happens during your sleep state consciousness and can equally occur in waking Theta consciousness! This is sometimes referred to as QUANTUM LEAPING and by taking yourself into a parallel universe, you can bring back developed abilities from an alterante dimensions and apply these to this dimension, thus making you more informed and talented.

Also, you should know that the USA government, through the DARPA and Project Pegasus, and the Russian government was/are intensely involved in dimension "shifting"/traveling. The USA government has used a "Chronolizer", an octagonal holographic structure powered by an intense electo-magnetic field (external power source) moving the consciousness of human subjects and even their bodies in alternative/ parallel dimensions ("quantum shifting" or "quantum leaping"). This information can be accessed at "Project Pegasus.net and is compiled by Andrew Basiago.

Also, an entire naval ship was teleported from one port to another in the "Philadelphia Experiment". There were some rather bizzare events related to this and you can Goggle information about this event. Basically, this feat was accomplished through a parallel or alternate dimensional shift. This is discussed more completely, several paragraphs below under the heading of "TELEPORTATION".

Additionally, it should be discussed, that when people get older and display the so-called dysfunctional mental state of Alzhiemer's Disease, Parkinson's Disease, and Dementia, **they are not in a state of mental degeneration, as has been widely promulgated by so-called medical researchers/ experts.** The author is aware that brain scans show the brains of people of the the listed maladies above, as being "abnormal". While there is an "abnormal condition occurring, it is the fact that the people displaying the symptoms of the three listed "diseases" above, are in fact **consciously co-existing in two or more dimensions, concurrently.** So while the proclamations of such people may seem incoherent babble, in the other existing dimension, it is most likely coherent and devoid of babble. **The real dilemma here is that these so-called mentally malfunctioning people have already partially transitioned into "a state of death! Before you summarily dismiss this radical but possibly cogent explanation, take some time to ruminate on this.** Dr. Newton will tell you that he has never seen this information in any book or earthly source**!!!!**

Accessing the AKASHIC/ATOM RECORDS is a process whereby your consciousness is in the realm of Theta and it allows you to receive information beyond what is normally possible. You can receive information that can give you insight and solutions to problems and make you more creative via mental communication which does not exist from human sources. This is very useful for tracking historical events which are not covered by our human records. Akasha is mentioned in ancient Indian texts called the "Vedas" and is a Sanskrit word which means "cosmic sky". Satguru and MahaAvatar Siddha Patanjali in "The Yoga Sutras" refers to this concept as "celestial hearing", which is the same thing. As you can keep your consciousness anchored in Theta for extended periods of time, which is induced by the techniques and disciplines of Pranayam and Sanskrit mantras, Akashic information will come to you in your daily life. Often this occurs while you are doing another job or task or thinking about something else unrelated to the new incoming information!

MahaAvatar and Sasguru Siddha Patanjali says in "The Yoga Sutras", that "celestial hearing" (AKA 'Akasha') comes from being proficient in Sanyama. Proficiency in Sanyama comes from the mastery of Dharana and Dhyana which are Kriya Yoga meditation tehcniques/practicies and also from Samadhi, which is the result of the mastery of Kriya Kundalini Pranayam. So this would be the Kriya Yoga approach to accessing the Akashic records, and from the original source of this concept. WHAT HAS JUST BEEN DISCUSSED SHOULD MOTIVATE US TO BECOME FANATICAL ABOUT PRACTICING THESE THETA ACCESSING DISCIPLINES, especially Kriya Kundalini Yoga!! If Dr. Newton had this insight himself, sooner in his this life, he would have been more devoted to this at an earlier age because of the incredible benefits related to accessing Akashic information!!!! Parts of this book have been received and guided by such information!

Through the technique of KINESIOLOGY, WE HAVE A MEANS TO VALIDATE OR INVALIDATE INFORMATION THAT MAY COME TO US VIA AKASHIC SOURCES and in the SPIRITUAL HEALING PROCESS. This is an invaluable and accurate means to cross verify information received. Kinesiological muscle testing is easily performed by putting the thumb and index finger together with a strong "grip" and asking "yes" and "no" questions. First, a test question is asked to which you know the answer such as your age. You ask a question about your actual age and notice the response as you try to pull your other index finger through the loop you have created on one hand with the thumb and index finger listed previously. Either the opposing index finger will pull through the loop or it will not. For most people it will not pull through although this is irrelevant because if your "system is wired differently". as you are only establishing a reliable measuring system. Then ask if you are of an age which you are not. For most people, they will pull the opposing index finger through the loop but again this is irrelevant because you are establishing a measuring system.

So you establish the standard for "yes", whether you were strong or you could pull through the loop and are weak and then "no" will be vice versa/ the opposite. Actually, this is such a usefull technique that you can use it in many different situations in your life such as trying to locate objects or to discern the state of mind of another person. For this to be effective, it is preferrable to be in a "trancelike" state so as to be detached and disinterested in the actual results because it can be "mind influenced"! Refer to "Diagram #7, in Chapter Four for pictorial depection of Kinesiology muscle testing.

Also, you can use dowsing rods to perform the same yes and no questions as you can do with a pendulum from a Quartz, Tourmaline or Topaz crystal. You test questions you know the answer to so that you can determine what movement of dowsing rods or a pendulum indicate "yes" and "no" answers, as per the Kinesology muscle testing. Then ask actual questions about things to get verifiable answer. THE CAVEAT HERE, IS THAT YOU SHOULD BE IN A NEUTRAL, TRANCE-LIKE CONSCIOUSNESS BECAUSE IF YOU HAVE STRONLY PREJUDICED IDEAS ABOUT AN OUTCOME, YOUR THOUGH PATTERNS COULD GIVE YOU INACCURATE RESPONSES!!!!

So how does this Akashic process work? From Dr. Newton's Akashic insights and from insights from the "Keys of Enoch" by Dr. J.J. Hurtak and from information in "The Akashic Experience" by Ervin Laszlo, the atomic field (or the aggregate of atoms of which everything is comprised) store all the information and events which have ever occurred on this planet and the entire Universe and the parallel counterparts therefrom. The atoms perform the same "role" as the Silicon (Quartz) chips that store information in our human computers. Dr. Hurtak maintains, as Dr. Newton believes he mentioned earlier in this book, that there is a computer at the center of the Universe where all information in the Universe is stored. Many years ago, Dr. Newton considered Dr. Hurtaks idea about this was considerably closer to "looneyville" than actual reality. Now he views it quite oppositely!

Virtually all significant and probably insignificant inventions, art, music, engineering marvels, problem solving comes via the Akashic information "freeway"! Frank De Marco, on the "Coast to Coast" radio show discussed this same idea about receiving information of the Universe via the "Cosmic Internet". The author believes De Marco's ideas are accessable via the human Internet. Mary Baker Eddy, discoverer of the Science of Christianity via Christian Science, would most likely refer to this as "Divine Mind". Other sources have referred to this as "Universal Mind" or "Cosmic Consciousness". But whatever you call it, there is this VAST FIELD OF INFORMATION THAT CAN BE ACCESSED AND HAS BEEN ACCESSED BY OUR GREATESTS THINKERS AND MINDS—SCIENTISTS, INVENTORS, ARTISTS, MUSICIANS, PHILOSOPHERS AND WRITERS AMONG OTHERS!

Dr. Newton has found this Akashic information invaluable and very useful in the composition of this book! This also seems to be a way by which atoms, chemicals, animals, viruses and bacterias communicate with each other through an interrelated field of energy. Having your hair long and having facial hair will provide "antennas" which will give you an extra advantage in culling Akashic information. This is an important tenet of Kriya Yoga and Rastifarian disciplines, which is not coincidental since many great prophets have had long hair and or beards.

SAMADHI has already been discussed in Chapter Three. Again, this is the next level of Theta Consciousness/Divinity/Superconsciousness/Cosmic Conscioiusness after you become proficient in Kriya kundalini Pranayam. This means that you can perform at least 3 rounds (48 repetitions) of Pranayam and each breath repetition takes at least 30 seconds and 40 seconds or more is even better and YOU PERFORM YOUR PRANAYAM EVERYDAY, WITHOUT EXCEPTION. The completion of this Pranayam protocol will naturally lead you to Samadhii without having to go through the process that Kriya Yogi's teach. Your breath will naturally stop or be extremely shallow and light and your heart will stop beating. Your body and your brain are being sustained by Prana (life force energy) and possibly a Maha Prana (beyond the Pranic realm) or an Intra Prana (an unknown force within the Prana).

Exactly how this occurs is not completely clear and may legitimately defy description because of linguistic and semantic limitations. But IT IS CERTAIN THAT THIS STATE OF BEING, SAMADHI, GIVES A STRONG INDICATION THAT THE TRUE NATURE OF THE BODY AND BRAIN IS LIGHT/PRANA/CHI, QUALITIES THAT DEFINE AND/OR DESCRIBE THE CREATOR! If this was not true, the body would expire in Samadhi and YET IT DOES NOT!!!! In Samadhii, YOU ACHIEVE AN INNER PEACE WHICH IS HAUNTINGLY SUBLIME! So again, you are rewarded for your devotion to PRANAYAM BREATHING WHICH YOU NEED TO PRACTICE ASSIDUOUSLY EVERY SINGLE DAY and in the amounts prescribed!

KUNDALINI AWAKENING has also already been discussed in Chapter Three. And INTENSE PRANAYAM PRACTICE is a PORTAL to this extremely useful and integral to this process. In Dr. Newton's first experience with Kundalini Awakening, he had some guidance in entering this process. GUIDANCE FOR YOUR FIRST KUNDALINI "TRIP" IS INVALUABLE SINCE YOUR ARE ENTERING A STATE OF HYPERPRANA where it feels LIKE YOU ARE BURNING UP, although you are not, and you will be DISORIENTED BECAUSE YOU

ARE ENTERING ANOTHER DIMENSION such as occurs in an LSD "trip".! "Normal tasks" are tedious or impossible to perform whereas "cosmic consciousness"/Divinity can be accessed with virtually no effort!

If your are proficient in Pranayam, you can also enter Kundalini Awakening through using a BRAIN ENTRAINMENT CD BUT THIS SHOULD BE STRONGLY DISCOURAGED UNTIL YOUR BODY IS FIRST INFUSED WITH PRANA VIA KRIYA KUNDALINI PRANAYAM AND SAMADHI. Dr. Newton used a cassette tape produced called "Ultra Meditation" by Zygon (now known as Mind Tech and Super Life) and it immediately transported him to his second "trip" to Kundalini. Dr. Nick Begich and the Monroe Institute have also produced CD's for brain entrainment.

Also, Dr. Newton entered a Kundalini awakening lying on several different types of magnetic pads/beds. If the magnetic pad is powered by an external electrical source it will work more powerfully and the results will come sooner! Dr. Newton entered the Kundalini state on his first day of Level One of Kriya Kundalini Pranayam training. Extremely few people can remain anchored permanently in Kundalini because of various commitments and rudimentary duties they must perform which are difficult to accomplish in this highly altered consciousness and hyper state of energy! Once you have entered Kundalini with stimulating help (directed "brain entrainment"/magnetic beds or pads), it will be easier to re-acheive it without these aids at a later time.

INVISIBILITY can be achieved by IMMERSING AND MERGING YOUR BODY IN THE ATOMIC FIELD. This can be achieved by RAISING/INCREASING THE PRANA IN YOUR BODY. This can happen partially or completely IN A STATE OF KUNDALINI OR SAMDAHII. This is a natural ability of the Kriya Yoga Siddhas because in part or in whole they have merged their consciousness with the Creator! A type of invisibility can also occur by pulling your consciousness and body into an parallel or alternative dimension. In "The Yoga Sutras", MahaAvatar and Satguru Siddha Patanjali says that invisibility is achievable when we enter the state of Sanyama which allows us to break contact with the eye of the observer with the refracted light from our body. Sanyama is the result of mastering Dharana and Dhyana which are Kriya Yoga meditation techniques and from the breathless state of Samadhi which is the result of mastering the Kriya Kundalini Pranayam breath.

TELEPORTATION (moving your body and/or consciousness just below the speed of light) can be achieved as per everything discussed in the above paragraph on invisibility. There are "transit portals" that run in conjunction with the magnetic leylines on our Earth, our Solar System, our Galaxy and our Universe that facilitate this process. Extra-terretial visitors use these portals, which are electromagnetic vortexes, to move their spacecraft just below the speed of light to cover long distances in a very short span of time. Sometimes, they dispense with the spacecraft and arrive "au natural", as it were. These "transit portals or electro-magnetic vortexes are also called "worm holes".*To be successful in teleporting from one place to another, you must keep your consciousness just in front of the photonic field of light or you will not be able to project yourself. Again, the exact protocol for this is better suited for a seminar/workshop dealing with this.

WEATHER MODIFICATION can be accomplished by individuals or groups of like-minded people through their mental intent. It was previously discussed how clouds can be dissolved. Additionally, they can also be created as can rain. This is not accomplished at Alpha consciousness but rather at Theta consciousness so these abilities come from being a master of Kriya Dhyana, Kriya Kundalini Pranayam and Samadhii. They also come from extended sessions of the recitation of the Sanskrit mantras such as the "Gayatri" and "Mrityonjaya". At this Theta/Divine Consciousness/Superconsciousness level you begin to manifest on what you focus your thoughts and how you direct your attention.

Humanity has the ability to mitigate or negate intense weather events as was discussed earlier in a preceding paragraph about dissolving clouds. So, a small storm would take less Prana/energy to downgrade or eliminate. A hurricane or tornado could be mitigated or dissolved through a group of people focusing Prana/energy with their gaze from a trance-like state to achieve storm annihilation. LEST YOU THINK THIS IS WAY TOO FARFETCHED and LOONEY, THE USA GOVERNMENT HAS ALREADY ACHIEVED SUCH WITH THEIR ELF (EXTRA LOW FIELD GENERATOR COMPLEX) IN ALASKA.

This is an array of 144 antennas, interconnected with an intensely powerful electrical power source. Dr. Nick Begich, among others, has much knowledge about this and you can Google this information. Also, as well as the USA (in Alaska), Russia and China have such ELF generators and Dr. Newton would not be surprised if India and Israel have them likewise. Unfortunately these ELF generators can also create violent weather and earthquakes and cause volcanos to erupt, among other things like blasting holes in the Ionisphere! A note to readers wary of this information: just because you have not heard or do not have previous knowledge of this disturbing information, does not mean that these things do not exist! Please it is TTATYD (Time to awaken to your Divinity)!

As for MANIFESTATION OF OBJECTS FROM THE ETHERS, this is not overly difficult if it is done in a deep state of Theta Consciousness. Basically, you must first visualize what you wish to materialize. You can do this through the construction of a template of your desired object from beams or rods of light. Then as you visualize this, reciting the "Gayatri" or "Mrityonjaya Mantra" or even the continusal repeating of "AUM" or "OM" will create the sonic activation that catalyzes something into a useful manifested object. Basically, manifestation is a Yogic power and therefore you need to be an adept in Kriya Yoga and specifically Kriya Kundalini Pranayam and Samadhi! MANIFESTATION IS BEST ATTEMPTED AND MORE POWERFULLY ACHIEVED WITH A GROUP OF LIKE-MINDED PARTICIPANTS!!!!

In summary:

The foregoing psychic abilities described are developed in the realm of Alpha and Theta consciouisnes/ Divinity/Superconsciosness.

Alpha abilities are the reading of auras, communication with discarnate entities, rudimentary (simple) telepathy are facilitated and developed by meditation, the recitation of "Gayatri" and "Mrityonjaya" mantras, Kriya Kundalini Pranayam, the Tai Chi "standing Meditation" and listening to or performing intense/complex/repetitive music or wearing a pyramid on your head doing any or all of these disciplines concurrently!

Theta abilities are remote viewing, spiritual healing (either Christian Science or Theta Consciousness), advanced telepathy where you can "read someone like a book", "Light Speed Learning", taking yourself into parallel or alternative dimesnions, "reading" the Akashic/atomic records, Samadhii, Kundalini awakening, invisibility, teleportation, modifying weather and manifestation of objects from the ethers.

These Theta abilities are fostered by the Theta disciplines of Kriya Kundalini Pranayam where you can do three rounds (48 consecutive repetitions) with your breathing cycle for each repetition at least thirty to forty seconds or more, Samadhii, Kundalini awakening, the "Gayatri" or "Mrityonjaya" Sanskrit mantras for at least 108 continuous repetitions and possibly double or triple that amount, the Tai Chi "Standing Meditation" for at least one-half or more, listening to or performing intense, complex and/or repetitive music for at least one-half to one hour or more or wearing a pyramid on your head or doing all of these disciplines concurrently.

Remember, you incarnated in Alpha and Theta consciousness so you already know how to do use these psychic abilities in your subconscious (your personal, personal computer). You now have the power to re-access this!

The disciplines and protocols in this book are realigning you with your existing Divinity (Aleph Kaf Aleph [restoring things to their perfect state!]). They are "maps" and "pathways" back to our Divine birthright!

Chapter Nine

WHAT HAPPENS WHEN YOU DIE?

First and foremost, YOU CAN NEVER DIE BUT YOUR FORM CAN CHANGE AS CAN THE DIMENSION WHEREIN YOU EXIST! A famous physicist/scientist, Tom Bearden, once told Dr. Newton he could prove through mathematics that it is impossible to die". Everything else he told the author has been verified as valid so the author is inclined to believe Bearden's mathematical claims. Actually, this could be proved by Einstein's E=mc2 (Energy= mass and the speed of light, squared) which explains why "Matter can neither be created nor destroyed". This E=mc2 is also the First Law of Thermodynamics. This could also be explicated as E (Energy) =P(Prana [which also moves at the speed of light]) A (Aum [Divine sonic vibration])2 or E=PA2! Also equivalent to these is Gottfried Liebnitz's E=mv2 which equates to Energy equals mass velocity squared!!!!

Although most Christians believe that Jesus' mission was to die for their sins and provide for their redemption, Mary Baker Eddy in "Science and Health with Key to the Scriptures" states that this was not Jesus' mission. She states that Jesus was more akin to a guide for us. Dr. Newton would agree that Jesus did die for our sins if the word "SIN" is defined as IGNORANCE OF OUR INHERENT DIVINE BIRTHRIGHT!!!!

No one in the past or present probably ever spent as much time in devoted study of the Bible than Mrs. Eddy, except Sir Issac Newton. She states emphatically that JESUS WAS THE "WAYSHOWER" OF THE EXISTENCE OF THE PERFECT, IMMORTAL MAN OF WHICH WE IN FACT ARE. Dr. Newton asks, in a rhetorical sense, why would the

165

Creator waste its time making sinful, imperfect man, unless the Creator is flawed itself? If this was true, then excrement could well be more Divine than Man! IT IS STUNNING AND INCOMPREHENSIBLE THAT SO FEW PEOPLE HAVE PERCIEVED OR COMPREHENDED THIS and so many people have resisted Mrs. Eddy's powerful insights! This incomprehension is detrimental in relation to the resistance we offer to comprehending it!

In "The Patterns on the Trestleboard: The Truth About Self", Paul Foster Case tells us in statment number nine THAT WE BASE OUR LIFE IN A FIELD OF ETERNITY. Statement number ten says SPIRIT PERMEATES OUR FLESH." So Paul Foster Case is telling us, similar to Mary Baker Eddy, that our flesh is in fact Spirit, which we have deemed to be energy, Prana, Chi, et. al. and that the form of Spirit is eternal.

Hermes Trismegustis tells us in "The Emerald Tablets", talking about the Creator, that God is AN OVERWHELMING PRESENCE THAT OVERPOWERS ALL SOLID THINGS AND THAT THIS IS HOW OUR WORLD WAS CONCEIVED. AND THIS APPLIES TO EVERY TYPE AND ALL ASPECTS OF CREATION. It should be self-evident that WE HUMANS ARE ONE OF THOSE TYPES OF CREATION, as well as plant kingdom, animals, angels etc. And as one of those adaptations, ourselves, God penetrates us to our core Spirit/energy, monadic (spark of God) level. So since God is Spirit (energy) this penetration into purported solid things (like a body) might not be so "solid" as we have considered it to be. This is fortuitous and beneficial for us ALTHOUGH THIS IS BASICALLY UNPERCEIVED BY HUMANITY AT THIS POINT IN TIME!!!! But this will become blantantly self-evident in the near future!

In "The 72 Names of God", from Exodus 14, verses 19-21, the fifty ninth name of God is "Hey Resh Chet" (connecting to the light). The forty sixth name of God is "Ayin Resh Yod" (the certainty that God is always there for us). And the seventh name of God is Aleph Kaf Aleph (restoring things to their perfect state). So when these names arranged together into an amalgamation this is what is formed: WE HAVE A GOD WHO HAS CREATED A FIELD OF LIGHT AS A COMPONENT OF THE "ATOMIC FIELD" and we have a certainty that it has, is and WILL EXIST INTO THE FUTURE and that these things will REAWAKEN US TO THE PERFECTION OF OUR CREATOR/God and that WE OURSELVES LIKEWISE REFLECT. Further we can deduce that SINCE THIS GOD IS IMMORTAL (as aspected by it's light), WE MUST LIKEWISE RELFECT THIS IMMORTALITY. And if you still doubt the reality of this, you might wish to "Dial God" (Vav Vav Lamed) for verification which makes the impossible possible.

These names of God are powerful and were set in what is considered one of the two "sacred languages that we have which is Hebrew—Sanskrit being the other "sacred language". Both of these languages almost certainly were brought to us by "elevated/illuminated" beings from other star systems who were not "under the veil of ignorance" by which we incarnated here on Earth. THIS EXTRA-TERRESTIAL PERSPECTIVE HAS PROVIDED US WITH OUR SALVATION AND INHERENT DIVINE BEINGNESS!!!!

Now, many astrophysicists might counter that all is not light as Paul Foster Case claimed. But it might well be true that "BLACK HOLES" ARE NOT ACTUALLY "BLACK" but ARE LIKELY A SPECTRUM OF LIGHT WHICH HUMANS CANNOT SEE AT THIS POINT IN TIME. A comparable analogy would be dogs being able to hear high frequency sounds which humans are unable to perceive auditorily, at least on the conscious level of being. If we make our eyes go out of focus as in the reading of auras, we might be able to see light in the "black holes" that comprise Galactic centers. We might also be able to perceive that sonic vibrations from these "black holes" or a state of intense or hyper-Divinity that might emanate therefrom.

Regardless of this, we know that these "black holes" are an intense electromagnetic field of energy and we know that fire and light are an inherent part of this type of energy, WHICH IS A FORM OF YAGNA! THUS, "BLACK HOLES" DO NOT NEED TO BE FEARED AS NEFARIOUS OR DANGEROUS TO US!!!! Certainly, they could be used as portals or "worm holes" to "time travel" great distances in a very short period of time!!!! That we would be destroyed travelling through them only would apply to a "material man" and not the spiritual, energy "Prana-man"

We need to continually focus our consciousness on the fact that our essence is light, as per Number Eight in "The Patterns of the Trestleboard: The Truth About Self" and as explained in Photonic or Particle Physics. This light can at times be hidden but not destroyed since as Albert Einstein stated, "Energy can neither be created or destroyed" and as stated in the First Law of Thermodynamics or E=mc2 or E=PA2 or E=mv2!!!! So the people who scoff at the idea that people have auras (light fields) around their bodies, may have to re-examine their skepticism SINCE LIGHT IS AN INHERENT PART OF CREATION!!!! And it is an INHERENT PART OF OUR CREATION WHICH MAKES OUR "SOUL-ESSENCE", US, INDESTRUCTABLE, just as the three mathematical formulas in this paragraph indicate!!!!

So, in summary we know:

That it is impossible for us to "die"/be terminated since we are Spirit/Prana/Chi/life force/energy which cannot die but can change its form in another dimension where we may exist.

Tom Bearden, physicist, claims to be able to prove mathematically you cannot die and is inherent in Einsteins' E=mc2 and the First Law of Thermodynamics or Dr. Newton's E=PA2 (Energy equals Prana Aum squared) or Liebnitz's E=mv2!

Mary Baker Eddy, in "Science and Health With Key to the Scriptures" that Jesus came here to show us that WE ARE PERFECT AND IMMORTAL as he, himself, is also considered.

Paul Foster Case, in "The Patterns on the Trestleboard: The Truth About Self", tells us that Spirit (which is energy) . . . . "is embodied in our flesh."

Hermes Trismegustis, in "The Emerald Tablets" tells us that the "strong force" (God) . . . . "pentrates every solid thing" which can include our bodies which are not nearly as solid as we consider.

"The 72 Names of God" indicate to us that God has created a field of light within the atomic field which is certain to continue and this can allow us to restore things to their perfect state!

Although scientists might contend that all is not light because of the existence of "black holes" but this could appear true only because we cannot see into this spectrum of light. Also the electromagnetism that comprises these black holes contains fire and light (Yagna or Agna). THESE "HOLES" SHOULD NOT BE FEARED! They could be used for "time travel"!

YOUR REAL ESSENCE AND YOUR BODY IS LIGHT WHICH CANNOT BE KILLED OR DIE, as per Paul Foster Case and Photonic Physics!

LIGHT IS A PERMANENT ASPECT OF CREATION, OCCURING OVER AND OVER AGAIN and we are a part of this and what makes us immortal and is expressed in our auric/etheric "light field".!THIS MAKES OUR "SOUL ESSENCE", US, INDESTRUCTIBLE as the mathematical formulas in this chapter indicate!!

Chapter Ten

WHERE DO YOU GO WHEN YOU "DIE"?

First you cannot die. But even if your body is "dying" and you are changing more to a Spirit or energy form whereby you are transiting to another dimension of creation, you really cannot go very far because all of the dimensions exist in the same space we are occupying in this third dimension. This is explained in "The String Theory" and "The Membrance Theory" as they both reveal how FOURTEEN DIMENSIONS EXIST CONCURRENTLY IN THE SAME SPACE and this might not even account for parallel dimensions and Galaxies and Universes!

This concept will take most people into a very uncomfortable "place" as it were! Dr. Newton remembers when one of his teachers, Major Virgil (Postie) Armstrong, taught him about eight dimensions of reality existing in the same space. It took him many months before he could even "chew" on this idea and a year before he could "swallow" it and another year before he could fully "digest" it. Now he is most comfortable with this concept, having a general picture/feeling of how this is possible but it is hard to explicate in words. The concurrent dimensions are somewhat like a layer cake in that each layer is separated by frosting and yet still connected to the other layers, except that the layers are very thin. Completely comprehending this will necessitate a Universal wholistic perspective and may even be subject to each individual person's perspective/inherent ideological prejudices! Dr. Newton has a strong feeling that THERE IS NO NUMBERING AS TO THE NUMBER OF DIMENSIONS THAT EXIST!!

The CREATIVITY of our CREATOR APPEARS TO BE STAGGERINGLY INCOMPREHENSIBLE BY US!!!!

Anyway, in Hinduism and Buddhism it is well accepted that we remain in another dimension after our so called "death" and then we reincarnate on Earth for another chapter in our "life". Even Christianity, at its core beginnings, accepted this concept, although this was obliterated as were all overt references to reincarnation were deleted from the "New Testament" at the "Council of Nicaea" in Turkey. This is intricately detailed in the book, "The Phoenix Fire Mystery", by Head and Cranston. This book details how there are many overt references to reincarnation stored in the Vatican Library. How fortunate we are to have this information stored beyond our reach and for our elucidation/edification?

Anyway, there is an overt reference to reincarnation in the New Testament where Jesus says, "Before Abraham was, I AM". This was about the only reference to reincarnation which survived the "axe" at the Council of Nicaea. Here the Catholic Church, under the threat of death to the Pope, via threats by the Turkish King, Constantine, deleted reincarnation references in the Bible so as to appease the King's wife and Queen. AGAIN, THIS IS CONSPIRACY REALITY—NOT CONSPIRACY THEORY! The Rosecrucians certainly have always believed in the circle of rebirth/reincarnation! So they are lights years beyond the rest of humanity because they did not have theologians and clerics filling their heads with useless piffle!

Dr. Newton has recieved what he feels are Akashic inspired insights which indicate to him that WE DO NOT NEED TO DIE AND REINCARNATE ON EARTH THOUSANDS OF TIMES UNTIL WE REACH OUR ENLIGHTENMENT, as believe the Hindus, Buddhists and Yogis, if we ENTRAIN OUR CONSCIOUSNESS IN THETA/DIVINITY/SUPERCONSCIOUSNESS. This LEADS TO OUR ENLIGHTENMENT, as it were, and the REALIZATION OF OUR REFLECTIVE PERFECTION OF THE CREATOR and the

INHERENT DIVINITY and immortality that emanates therefrom. And this could be achieved, in fact will be ACHIEVED, when a person becomes a MASTER OF KRIYA YOGA PROTOCOLS—especially through the POWERFUL SANSKRIT MANTRAS listed in this book, through KRIYA KUNDALINI PRANAYAM, and through SAMADHI and KUNDALINI AWAKENING which are a natural extension of Pranayam.

It is this which allows us to meld—TO BECOME ONE WITH OUR CREATOR. Literally we are allowing OUR CONSCIOUSNESS TO BE MORE FULLY "BLENDED"/MELDED WITH THE ATOMIC FORCEFIELD OF AGGREGATED ATOMS WHEREIN THE CREATOR RESIDES!!!! And this happens by our dedication and discipline to the practices and protocols listed above. THIS HAS GRACIOUSLY SERVED TO US ON A "SILVER PLATTER" so to speak—a way to extract ourselves from "The Wheel of Karma and Reincarnation" BY OUR GOD, by God, as it were. So, once again, we see a process of "SPIRITUAL ALCHEMICAL TRANSFORMATION", where we change from the lower form of matter into the higher form of Spirit and Prana and Light!

SatGuru Sivaya Subramuniyaswami (Gurdeva) talked about karma in one of his short articles printed in "Kauai's Hindu Monastery Newletter" from April 2011. He states: "It is karma that keeps us from knowing of and reaching life's final goal, yet it is wrong to even call it a goal. It is what is known by the knower to have always existed. It is not a matter of becoming the Self, but of realizing that you never were not the Self. And what is the Self? It is Parasiva. It is God. It is That which is beyond the mind, beyond thought, feeling and emotion, beyond time, form and space. When karma is controlled through yoga and dharma well performed, and the energies are transmuted to their ultimate state, the Vedic Truth of life discovered by the rishis so long ago becomes obvious."

So this is what the author was more or less conveying in the previous paragraph. WE PURIFY OURSELVES THROUGH YOGA, WHICH

MEANS UNION IN SANSKRIT, WITH OUR CREATOR. Our reunion/"blending"/melding with the Creator is re-established and WE RE-BECOME OUR ESSENTIAL SPIRITUALLY DIVINE SELF! This is just way too cool AND SO DOABLE when the requisite effort is tendered!!!!

Dr. Newton keeps being pulled back to the pictures he has seen in his consciousness that show our atoms are perfect micro energy forms that cannot be destroyed and our bodies are perfect macro energy forms which likewise should not be destroyed since the macro is comprised of the micro. And he keeps coming back to the fact that Jesus, Babaji Nagaraj and the other Yoga Siddhas/Avatars have been in state of Soruba Samadhii (immortality) for thousands years in the same body. The author is also aware that such Avatars as Satchi Sai Baba, Sri Aurabindo, Neem Karoli Baba and SatGuru Sivaya Subramuniyaswami (Gurudeva) have come to teach us and uplift humanity and yet they let their bodies die and then reincarnate here again, even though they could obviate this process.

As we enter Theta and the even deeper Delta consciousness, can we possibly wipe our "bad Karma" (misdeeds to others) away? Could we achieve immortality of the body and concurrently work away our "bad Karma"? These things certainly are not beyond of the realm of achieveable so long as we create it to be so by unveiling our inherent perfection via the protocols listed in this book! This was shown to us through Gurudeva's article. It clearly and definitely REVEALS THAT WE ARE NOT TRAPPED IN OUR KARMA. The disciplined practice of the Kriya Yoga protocols, over time, will reveal us as perfect beings we are. Certainly these things can be programmed into the subconscious via Theta Consciousness Programming!!!! THERE IS CLARITY, THEN, OF WHAT WE NEED TO DO! And the means to do so has already been provided in Chapter Four in the "Theta Consciousness Healing"™ protocols!!!!

NEITHER CHRISTIANS NOR MOSLEMS OR JEWS NEED OR DESERVE TO GO TO HELL, the DEVIOUS CONTROL

MECHANISM DREAMED UP BY THEOLOGIANS AND CLERICS TO ENSNARE and ENSLAVE PEOPLE within the power structure they have created! Some people with insight have posited that EARTH, ITSELF, MIGHT BE HELL since there appears to be a lot of SUFFERING and a lot of FIRE and BRIMSTONE are belched FROM VOLCANOS. This appears to be a reasonable astrolocality for the place of Hell. The location thereof certainly is not delineated in any human text and the author has not found any location, thereof, in the Akashic Records

Furthermore, IS OUR CREATOR SUCH A NASTY PRESENCE and nihilistic as TO COMDEMN US TO AN ETERNAL FIERY FATE for our purported transgressions? Does not this make the Creator to appear capricious and vindictive? This would violate the "loving" God we have been told which exists! HELL IS A STRONG CONTRADISTINCTION, CONTRADICITION, and CONTRAINDICATION of OUR CREATOR!!!! The author knows with certainty that when he places trees and plants in the ground that he ONLY WANTS THEM TO THRIVE! ARE NOT WE LIKEWISE, IN A SENSE, PLANTS BEING CARED FOR BY OUR CREATOR, WHO LIKEWISE WANTS US TO THRIVE?

Even if your children were not perfect, would you want them to suffer endlessly? WOULD YOU RIP A PLANT OUT OF THE GROUND BECAUSE IT HAD A FEW DEAD LEAVES? Would the Creator desire this likewise? But if your children were perfect, could they experience such damnation? Probably not! Nobody is going to the "Hell dimension"—not Hitler, not Stalin, not Mao, not Jeffrey Damher. YOU CAN ELIMINATE THE HELL TRAVEL AGENCY! Of course, if you are into flambe of your body, have a go at it?

Mary Baker Eddy, in "Science and Health with Key to the Scriptures", states most emphatically that "Heaven can be created on Earth." Additionally, it appears to the author from all of the available evidence about the life of Mrs. Eddy from "Miscellany", "Miscellaneous Works" and accounts from people who knew her very well that her later years of her life were spent in the splendor of heaven and Divinity, even as she resided here on Earth! That is because she knew that heaven was a state of mind as she explained in the concept that we could have heaven on Earth, here, right now! THE HEAVEN TRAVEL AGENCY IS EAGERLY AWAITING PASSENGERS! Only our consciousness is preventing our ticket from being issued, irrespective of what many Christians and Moslems believe to the contrary—that only a select few will reach this goal! THE AUTHOR WANTS TO HELP YOU DIG YOURSELF OUT OF THIS HUGE MANURE PILE!

In Review:

You CANNOT DIE even though your body can take a different form in ANOTHER DIMENSION, of which there are at least fourteen as well as alternate dimensions!

These concurrent dimensions are SIMILAR TO A THIN LAYER CAKE in which the layers are separated by frosting but still connected as one whole cake!

Hindus and Buddhists believe you go to another dimension after death and reincarnate. Christians believed in this before the Council of Nicaea in Turkey, where such concepts were eradicated. However, this concept of rebirth has always been part of the Rosecrucians!

THERE IS NOT INHERENT NEED FOR US TO KEEP REINCARNATING as long as we ESTABLISH OUR CONSCIOUSNESS IN THETA which allows us to perceive our reflective perfection of the Creator and hence the revelation of our Divinity and immortality. The way we obviate the need for rebirth is through our disciplined practice of the Kriya Yoga protocols listed in this book! This confirmed through Satguru Gurudeva.

This concept of immortality can also be revealed through Quantum Physics where we know that ATOMS, WHICH ARE PERFECT MICROFORMS OF ENERGY should ultimately lead to PERFECTION ON THE MACRO LEVEL OF ENERGY which would constitute humans forms.

This is the ULTIMATE ALCHEMICAL TRANSFORMATION, which means changing from a lower or material form to a higher spiritual and Pranic form of light!

NOR DOES ANYONE NEED OR DESERVE TO GO TO HELL, although there are some people who feel that Earth is Hell because of apparent widespread suffereing and a lot of fire and brimstone as manifested by volcanos.

"HEAVEN CAN BE CREATED ON EARTH" AS WAS PROCLAIMED AND LIVED BY MARY BAKER EDDY, founder of Christian Science and she did so for herself!

YOU CAN ELIMINATE THE HELL TRAVEL AGENCY!

THE HEAVEN TRAVEL AGENCY IF EAGERLY AWAITING PASSENGERS! Only your consciousness is preventing your ticket from being issued!

CHAPTER ELEVEN

WHAT HAPPENS WHEN THE SHIITE (EXCREMENT)—NOT
THE MOSLEM SECT—HITS THE FAN? THE BREATHAIRIAN
CHRONICLES (Living Without Eating Food)

Mitch Battros, author of "The Earth-Sun Conncection" talked about a comparison of Solar Cyle Four and Solar Cycle Twenty four that we are immersed in at this time, discussing this on the 6-13-2011 "Coast to Coast" radio show. He indicated that the GLOBAL WARMING MYTH IS ABOUT TO BE FROZEN OUT OF EXISTENCE by an impending Ice Age"! This is cross validated by the great scientiest, Dr. Eben Browning, who also came to this same conclusion over twenty years ago after studying about a hundred years of climate data. Also, the EARTH IS VERY CLOSE TO HAVING ITS MAGNETIC POLES SHIFT. Geologist's have looked at strata of rock and have determined that this already happened about 10,000 years ago. IT IS KNOWN AS A FACT, although there is basically a media "blackout" on this topic, THAT THE MAGNETIC FIELD ON OUR EARTH IS WEAKENING AND THE MAGNETIC POLES ARE IN A STATE OF FLUX, right now as this is statement is being written!!!!

Additionally, soon our satellites and electrical energy grid are going to be in grave danger of being compromised and rendered inoperable by solar spikes and flares from the Sun! Additionally, although Battros did not mention, or possibly the author missed him saying this, that as active volcanos on Earth are spewing volcanic ash into the atmosphere, this factor lowers the Earth's mean temperature! The author remembers Dr. Browning also talking about this and how the production of foods would become much more difficult!

The scenario for mass death events of people is a real possibility now in light of widespread earthquakes, tsunamis, floods, tornados, hurricanes, erupting volcanos and "HYPERDIMENSIONAL" (aka "torsional) ELECTROMAGNETIC ENERGY EMANATING FROM THE CENTER OF THE "MILKY WAY" GALAXY catalzying catacylsmic events on Earth. Actually many millions of children are dying from starvation RIGHT NOW! This scenario of Earth calamties has happened before on Earth and likely on Mars and other planets in our solar system. In the case of Mars, it is hard to ignore the devastation that occurred there in the past from the NASA photographs around the New Cydonia area and from the pictures of a devastated temple from other Mars mission photos.

Anyway, when the temperature of the Earth declines even only several degrees, the growing of food becomes problematic and the amounts of food produced is minimal or non-existent. Unfortunately, the Ostrich routine/protocol will not aid you in dealing with this situation and will only worsen your plight! THE AUTHOR IS MOST CERTAIN OF THIS AND COMPARABLE HISTORICAL EXAMPLES MAKE THIS SELF EVIDENT to all people EXCEPT THOSE WITH OSTRICH HOLE "VISION". Unfortunately, the author sees so many "ostriches" that their numbers are uncountable!

So how do we deal with this predicament? First and foremost, we must always and this must be repeated—WE MUST ALWAYS KNOW THAT WE ARE CONNECTED TO THE LIGHT (Hey Resh Chet) by a GOD WHO WILL ALWAYS "be there for us" (Ayin Resh Yod) and this ALLOWS US TO OVERCOME OUR FEARS (Mem Nun Daled). This is an important spiritual, mental and emotional framework as to how we can deal with our situation/new set of circumstances. And these things will become obvious to you as they are now to Dr. Newton as you assiduously practice Kriya Kundalini Pranayam, the Tai Chi "Standing Meditation", the "Backflow Meditation", the "Gayatri" and Mrityonjaya" Sanskrit mantras, and as you study "The 72 Names of God from Exodus 14: verses 19-21, as you study "The Emerald Tablets" of Hermes Trismegistus, as you study Mary Baker Eddy's "Science and Health With Key to the Scriptures", as you study "The Patterns on the Trestleboard: The Truth About Self" by Paul Case Foster, "The Yoga Sutras" by Satguru/Siddha Patanjali and "The Bhagavad Gita".

If you are skeptical about this, Dr. Newton understands your doubt. But he is only writing this book because these things he is writing about so dramatically changed his own life. THIS BOOK IS NOT ABOUT SELF-AGGRANDIZEMENT BUT RATHER THE SHARING OF MANY PROFOUND THINGS THAT ALLOW FOR AN ADVANTAGEOUS SHIFT IN OUR CONSCIOSNESS that Dr. Newton has encountered and experienced!! His approach is to reject the Illuminati cult in that he believes—no he actually knows that THERE IS ENOUGH PROSPERITY AND HAPPINESS FOR ALL PEOPLE—NOT JUST A FEW PRIVILEGED, selfish, greedy plutocrats and oligarchs (self proclaimed illumined elite individuals)!!!!

Also, the existing capitalist system, which some people feel is actually a derivation of socialism, as has been well chronicled in many issues of the "American Free Press", must be changed so that there is a more even distribution of wealth. Not in a socialistic manner but certainly not where one percent of the population has a stranglehold on ninety nine percent of the money/wealth. Certainly as detestable, and more importantly grossly inaccurate, is the saying, "There is not enough room for everybody at the top—you must know and accept your place in life." Why should one individual of equal ability have a lower "station" in life and be paid less than a comparable person with a higher position who has higher wages?

Could it be that this is the way the Illuminati (equal to cabal and cult status) is better served by this arbitrary hieracrhial and/or economic caste system? More compliant slaves make better workers!!!! This is akin to letting illegal aliens flood your country, who will work for lower wages and with marginal working conditions and will not complain about such!!!! THIS IS MORE THAN JUST AN INTERESTING PARALLEL BUT AN ACTUAL PARALLEL SCENARIO! Governments and corporations love compliant, docile slaves as citizens and workers!!!!

Secondly, until you demonstrate the fulfillment of your actual "light/ energy body" and "breathairanism", EAT LESS FOOD—EAT LESS FOOD. Most Americans eat too much food. Actually, AT LEAST 99% OF AMERICANS, INCLUDING DR. NEWTON, EAT TOO MUCH FOOD! Obesity is the rule now rather than the exception. A scarcity of food might be our plight for some time because with the impending Ice Age and and a lot of "natural disasters" and flooding, just detailed above in this chapter, imperiling the production of foods. When you eat, take smaller bites and chew your food thoroughly; GOOD MASTICATION of your food will make it MORE DIGESTIBLE, make nutrients more available, fill you up with the consumption of less food and create more Prana/life force likewise. This will be discussed in more depth in this chapter

By doing this you will EAT LESS and you WILL EAT LESS WITHOUT GOING ON A DIET THAT IS NOT LIEKLY GOING TO WORK IN THE LONG TERM ANYWAY! Drink more water and you will eat less food. DRINKING PURE, HIGHLY OXYGENATED WATER (H2O2), as produced by the "John Ellis Water Machine", WILL CURB YOUR APETITE EVEN MORE! When your body is more in a "LIGHT STATE", in that it is exhibiting properties of MORE LIGHT AND LESS ILLUSORY MATTER, THE LESS LIKELY YOUR BODY IS TO BE DAMAGED BY DISASTERS AND BY LACK OF FOOD!

If you eat foods high in fiber, such as whole grain or sprouted grain breads that have three to five grams of fiber, you will eat less food and be better nourished and eliminate blood sugar "spikes". If you eat cereals such as

Oatmeal, Shreeded Wheat and Bran flakes, among others, you can get food with five to ten grams of fiber. Eat pasta instead of Rice because although it is not high in fiber, it breaks down slowly and blunts "sugar spikes" that Rice can cause (pasta generally has two grams of fiber and Rice has one gram or less). This will help you eat less food and be better nourished and eliminate blood sugar "spikes. Focus on eating local grown organic vegetables. Eliminate eating all meats and poultry and substitute fish in their place. Do not consume pasteurized dairy foods but consume their raw counterparts. Otherwise, YOU ARE EATING FOOD DEVOID OF NUTRITION since PASTEURIZATION KILLS ALL ENZYMES, VITAMINS and MINERALS. This is science fact, regardless of whether you believe it or not!

Do not eat vast amounts of fruit; Citrus, Bananas, Tomatoes, Apples, Pineapples, Grapes and Avocados are the most beneficial for you. For nuts, raw Almonds are supreme, seeds are very good and Peanuts are good. Eat a lot of high Postassium foods including Bananas and Potatoes, because Potassium helps in the transmission of electricity and the Prana contained in our bodies, and may even generate such. Do not drink carbonated beverages (they deplete Oxygen and thus Prana) and substitute this with highly oxygenated water as produced by the "John Ellis Water Machine" that creates distilled, detoxified, highly oxygenated water (H2O2). Do not drink water that is treated with "Chlormine", which destroys digestive lactobacilli or which has been flouridated because aluminum flouride is toxic and actually makes bones more brittle (the "John Ellis Water Machine" removes these undesirable characteristics). John Ellis says and John Ellis is correct when he says that drinking more water will allow you to eat less food. He is correct in this statement and the MORE OXYGENATED OUR WATER IS, THE BETTER FOR US!!!! H2O2 is produced by the "John Ellis Water Machine" so it exactly what your body requires, whether it be it a "light" or material body!

DO NOT EVER EAT SOY PRODUCTS OTHER THAN MISO. Soy is loaded with phytic acid which is TOXIC TO HUMANS, can play

HAVOC with the THYROID GLAND and is loaded with estrogen with feminizes men and causes breast cancer other problems in women. Always substitute Whey for Soy since Whey has almost as much protein as Soy and will also enhance immune system functioning.

So, you WANT TO EAT FOODS HIGH IN FIBER SINCE THEY ARE LOW GLYCEMIC and will eliminate "sugar spikes" which release high levels of insulin and cortisol which highly contribute to humans becoming overweight. Focus on vegetables alkalizing to the body like Broccoli, Cabbage, Garlic, Onions, Peas, Spinach, Sweet Potatoes, raw Tomatoes, Algaes and Wheat Grass and Potatoes even though they are slightly acidic and probably are alkaline if eaten uncooked. Also eat alkalizing fruits such as Apples, Avocados, Bananas, Dates, Figs, Grapes and Raisins, Citrus, Nectarines, Pineapples, Melons and uncooked tomatoes but no plums or prunes as they are very acidic. For nuts eat Almonds, raw Pumpkin and Sunflower seeds and some Peanuts even though they are slightly acidic. For flesh protein eat Chicken breast (free range, organic) or even better, Fish even though it is slightly acidic but easy to digest.

Try to eliminate the eating of all flesh foods, even fish. You don't need nearly as much protein as you have been "brainwashed" to believe! WHEN DR. ADKINS, THE MAJOR PROPONENT OF A HIGH PROTEIN DIET DIED, HIS HEART AND ARTERIES EXHIBITED THE INCREDIBLE DETERIORATION, rife with arterial and coronary plaque; this was reported in the "American Free Press". So basically, Dr. Adkins hastened his own death via his flawed, high protein-high meat protocol!!!!

There is a commendable diet from Dr. Joel Fuhrman which calls for the eating of Green foods, Onions and Garlic, Mushrooms, Berries, and Seeds (GOMBS). Not only will use lose weight with this eating protocol, Cancer, likewise, cannot exist in your body since it will be alkalized!

If you can eliminate flesh food, so much the better you. Beyond a doubt, cattle need approximately ten to nineteen pounds of feed to create one pound of meat and this is truly a waste and misallocation of grain foods. Additionally, the cattle are routinely given antibiotics to keep them "healthy" and steriods to make them grow faster. They are also given Soy as feed and as we have just discussed, this is toxic and cancerous. If you still love your beef and burgers, you might say that these risks are so small that you can ignore this information. But, on the contrary, these substances potentize up to twenty times in strength than the initial dosage given to the Cattle. Additionally, all cooked meat will putrify in your intestines because cooking kills the Cathespin Enzyme contained therein which allows it to be digested. This is thoroughly documented in "Enzyme Nutrition" by Dr. Edward Howell. If you ignore these facts please do not complain if you suffer from Colon Cancer or Crohn" Disease or Colitus, which are basically inevitable for "dedicated" eaters of meat!

Pigs, which will eat anything including their own or other sources excrement, are in fact "unclean" as the Bible classifies them. Pork is loaded with worms and parasites and is cured with nitrates, none of which are nutritional necessities—at least the last time Dr. Newton checked on this. Chickens and Turkey are given feed laced with Arsenic to eliminate lice and other parasites in the feed. Well at least Arsenic has nutritional properties! REALLY? DON'T THEY PUT ARSENIC IN RAT POISON?

Chickens are given routine antibiotics and raised in extremely cramped and unsanitary conditions and given growth hormones. At the chicken slaughter houses they are packaged and distributed with Salmonella and E-Coli bacterias intact! Free range and organic poultry usually circumvent bacterial infection but this is a small percentage of the total of Chicken meat consumed! You can thank the FDA and the U.S. Department of Agriculture for their perverse proclivity in allowing routine unsanitary conditions that exist in all slaughter houses! Can this really be ignored? Apparently by them it can!!!!

For sweeteners, use real Maple Syrup, Date sugar, Stevia and the best of all, XYLITOL and ERYTHROL because they are low glycemic sugars and prevent tooth decay! For spices and seasonings use "Herbs de Provence", hot Peppers, Cinnamon, Curry, Ginger and Sea Salt. For cooking oils, use extra virgin Olive oil but NEVER CANOLA OIL because it is TOXIC TO HUMANS since it comes from rapeseed (even the name of this is suspect), as it were!!!! A seed that rapes your body!? And NEVER USE SOY OIL, as Soy has been discussed as a nasty and dangerous substance in this chapter!!!!

Why do you want alkalizing foods? This is because,**neither viruses or bacterais or fungi or cancers can exist in an alkalized body of 7.3 or higher!!!! IN AN ACIDIC BODY, ALL OF THESE THINGS THRIVE!!!!.** Additionally, which type of battery has more energy, a Nickel-Cadmium or an Alkaline? Obviously it is the Alkaline battery is more energetic and so does an Alkalized body have more energy. And while Dr. Newton does not have any research that would validate the idea that an ALKALIZED BODY CARRIES and/or ATTRACTS MORE PRANA THROUGHOUT THE BODY FORM, this is information from Akashic/atomic records that he trusts and would not distribute without a reasonable certainty of the accuracy thereof!!!!

Now, transitioning to BEING A BREATHAIRIAN IS VASTLY SUPERIOR TO EATING FOOD WHICH IS A HIGHLY INEFFICENT AND WASTEFUL WAY TO NOURISH YOURSELF, at least from a certain perspective of efficiency. This process of eating equates to two pounds of food in and two pounds of poop out. But as Dr. Newton was searching the internet on this subject, his intution and other facts lead him to know that although several people around the world and in India have CLAIMED TO HAVE EATEN NO FOOD OR WATER FOR MANY YEARS, the assertions related thereto simply are not valid in most cases! Does that make the concept or practice of Breatharianism inherently invalid and/or dangerous? Certainly not, within certain parameters. CERTAINLY THE MOST IMPORTANT PARAMETER IS THAT YOU SHOULD

START THIS FROM A STATE OF HEALTH OR OTHERWISE YOU SHOULD AVOID THIS AS MANY ANECDOTAL EXPERIENCES WOULD CONFIRM! On the other hand, there are many experiences of PEOPLE REGAINING THEIR HEALTH THROUGH A REGIMEN OF JUICE FASTING!!!! The anecdotal testimony regarding this is significant—not only Jack LaLanne!

For Breatharianism to work, you should first have pure air (non-poluted) with a high Oxygen content. Big city air is polluted and has about ten percent Oxygen content which makes it too dirty and deficient for our purposes. Air by large bodies of water can have a twenty percent Oxygen content which more suits our purpose assuming the air is clean, without pollutants. Why is the OXYGEN CONTENT such an important factor? It is more than likely A MEANS BY WHICH PRANA ENTERS THE HUMAN BODY and it may even POTENTIZE PRANA IN THE BODY. And the idea of being a Breatharian is to nourish yourself with Prana/Chi/life force as opposed to food—in a sense Divine Food (light-Prana) versus denser human food which contains less light and Prana.

Some people, related to this practice, believe that our Sun is a source of Prana for us. And other people feel that Prana is carried in the light spectrum of all colors. Both ideas are more or less equally valid since atoms and photons comprise all sources of light, including the Sun, and are an electro-magnetic means by which Prana is transmitted.

Other people believe that staring at sun will pull more Prana into the body and while this is true it is not to be recommended until you are actually manifesting literally a "light body" since your eyes could be damaged in multiple ways. However, absorbing Sun through your body, other than the eyes, would also be effective. People using sunscreen might inhibit this since recent studies have shown that it blocks the absorption of Vitaman "D" from the Sun. So likewise, sunscreen appears to also block Prana!!!! Again, although dermatologists will be outraged by this statement, maybe their outrage should be directed at themselves rather than the author for stating factual truth AND THEMSELVES FOR IGNORING SUCH!

Remember, as was discussed in previouly in Chapter Seven, that the Sun is considered as a significant source of "anointing oil" (a rejuvenating factor). Also this applies to Bindhu, Monatomic Gold, H2O2, Aloe Vera, hot Peppers, and Occinum Sanctum (Holy Basil). These can all be factors making the transition to Breatharianism a more easily facilitated reality!

Creating a "light/energy body" has already been discussed in earlier chapters including Pranayam, Samadhii, Kundalini awakening, Sanskrit mantras, the "Backflow Meditation" and the Tai chi "Standing Meditation". These listed practices put the practitioner of them in Theta/Divine/Superconsciousness and infuses the body with considerably more Prana than it previously contained. This will help facilitate an actual "LIGHT/SPIRIT BODY", THE ACTUAL REALITY OF WHAT WE REALLY ARE!

Why would the body ever be in state of less than optimum Prana? Several reasons come to mind including the following: First, remember earlier where we encountered Rabbi Berg's explanation of our apparent imperfection when he says that we agreed to incarnate here on Earth in a "game" where we come to Earth within a "veil" where we FORGOT ABOUT OUR REAL ESSENCE/PERFECTION and our challenge would be to reconnect with our "Divine nature".

Secondly, there is an emotional component to this equation. Coming down to Earth, in "a veiled consciousness", a lot of confusion besets us until we get our "bearings" here and are fortunate enough to be introduced to sources of Truth such as Mary Baker Eddy, Hermes Trismegustis, Paul Foster Case, Kriya Yoga and "The 72 Names of God", "The Bhagavad Gita", "The Yoga Sutras" and even this book, as the author will humbly submit. In the process of confusion and mostly likely frustatrations of dealing with what looks like a miasmic (infested/toxic) situation, THE

NEGATIVE EMOTIONS OF ANGER, FEAR AND DOUBT (which we have already discussed as a component of sickness and disease) CREATE A CONDITION OF DIMINISHED PRANA. Many of these EMOTIONS MAY BE COMING TO US FROM A SOURCE BEYOND OURSELVES CARRIED IN OUR DNA FROM OUR RELATIVES AND ANCESTORS and affecting us in our daily lives, WITHOUT OUR ACTUAL KNOWLEDGE THEREOF!!!!

Thirdly, INCARNTING HERE ON EARTH could likely be the most CONFOUNDING EXPERIENCE IMAGINABLE! This is meant in a literal sense as well as figurative way. THE MAGNITUDE OF THIS STATEMENT CANNOT BE UNDERESTIMATED OR DISMISSED NOR THE EMOTIONS WHICH ARE ELICITED AND ATTACHED THERETO! Fortunately, for us, WE HAVE MAPS and PATHWAYS TO EXTRICATE OURSELVES FROM THIS SITUATION. Most of them are listed in the paragraph above and are synthesized in Chapter Thirteen. Mary Baker Eddy, in "Science and Health With Key to the Scriptures" states emphatically that GOD NEVER ASKS US TO DO MORE THAN THAT WHICH WE ARE CAPABLE OF DOING (this might be close to a direct quote but the author is using his memory records and there is no copyright infringement intention)! ALWAYS KEEP THIS IN MIND AND IT WILL SERVE YOU WELL AS YOU CONFRONT LIFE'S CHALLENGES which could be coming to us all in a very intense manner!

Apologies are offered for what appears to be sidetracking away from the topic of this chapter but it is a necessary and intregal background part of our discussion on Breathairianism and you will she why immediately!

Some Breathairians feel that "LIGHT BLOCKAGES" in the body INHIBIT THE FACILITATION of this BREATH BASED PROTOCOL. These "light blockages" are most likely the result of emotional stress. This appears to be fact based, especially considering the emotional component just discussed above. The more highly charged your body is with Prana/

Chi/life force, the more Prana your body puts in storage keeping you in Theta/Divine consciousness. And it literally makes your body "lighter" by two factors—EMANATING MORE LIGHT FROM THE BODY AND ACTUALLY FORMING THE BODY WITH LESS PHYSICALITY/ MATTER AND MORE SPIRIT/ENERGY. As a reult of this process the BODY BECOMES AN ENERGY/LIGHT FACILITATOR AND ATTRACTANT! SO, SHEDDING YOURSELF OF THE NEGATIVE EMOTIONS OF ANGER/FEAR/ BETRAYAL OF YOURSELF BY THE CREATOR, ALONG WITH THE PRACTICES DESCRIBED IN THIS BOOK—ALLOWS LIGHT/PRANA TO POUR UNIMPEDED INTO YOUR BODY—HENCE A TRANSFIGURATION INTO THE LITERAL "LIGHT BODY" as per Jesus and Babaji Nagaraj, among others!

Certainly, Babaji Nagaraj and possibly Jesus (because of his sojourn to India) were practitioners of Kriya Kundalini Pranayam. As stated in Patanjali's "The Yoga Sutras" and the "Bhagavad Gita", PRANAYAM ELECTRICALLY MAGNETIZES OUR SPINAL COLUMNS AND NERVES AND TRANSMITTED TO OUR BODY'S CELLS and INFUSES SUCH WITH LIGHT, WHICH IS MORE NOURISHING THAN FOOD!!!! This would appear to be the MOST CRUCIAL ELEMENT THE ALLOWS THE TRANSITION TO BEING A PRACTICING BREATHAIRIAN!! So once again, the author will say that this is another reason that you are benefitted by being instructed in Kriya Kundalini Pranayam!!!!

Now, some Breathairians claim that they refrain from water as well as food. However, unless you have attained Soruba Samadhii such as Jesus or Babaji Nagaraj or his Kriya Siddha counterparts, who are MahaAvatars, Satgurus and Sihhas, this will most certainly lead to dehydration and a premature demise of your existing body. WATER, ESPECIALLY PURE, HIGH OXYGENATED WATER (H2O2), as produced by the "John Ellis Water Machine", is most likely a POWERFUL RECEIVER AND TRANSMITTER OF PRANA which is THE INDISPENSIBLE

COMPONENT OF "LIGHT/ENERGY BODIES". ONCE YOU ARE IN SORUBA SAMADHII, PRANA IS ENTERING THE "LIGHT/ENERGY BODY" IN UNHINDERED AND BOUNDLESS AMOUNTS and YOU NO LONGER NEED THE PREVIOUS PRANA DISPERSAL MODES PROVIDED BY BREATHING, OXYGEN, BLOOD AND WATER.

So unless you are on the threshold of Soruba Samadhii (which is an everlasting state as opposed to the temporary state of regular Samadhii) you should not refrain from water but you can exist long periods of time without food because the large amounts of PRANA NEED TO DIGEST AND ELIMINATE FOOD CREATES A "DRAG" ON THE BODY, somewhat like an anchor!!!! WHILE THIS IS DR. NEWTON'S GOAL and a work in progess, HE IS NOT TELLING YOU TO BECOME A BREATHAIRIAN OR RECOMMENDING SUCH. THIS IS YOUR PERSONAL DECISION.

Certainly IF YOU HAVE FEARS OF malnourishment or lack of blood sugar, YOU WILL FAIL in your quest to become a BREATHAIRIAN, even before you start! Dr. Newton IS SURE THAT this is an ACCELERATED PATHWAY in the process of creating the "LIGHT/ENERGY BODY" but not suited to all or maybe even very many individuals! THIS AN ADVANCED PRACTICE, NOT SUITABLE FOR NEOPHYTES! COMPRENDE (do you understand)?

Also, for Breathairianism to work more effectively, you need a really clean environment which our cities today simply do not provide. We talked about needing unpolluted air and we talked about the necessity of having highly oxygenated air. Additionally, we talked about needing highly oxygenated water. But we also need an ENVIRONMENT FREE OF ELECTRO-MAGNETIC POLUTION. This is specifically radio and television frequency waves, electrical power radiation, atomic radiation, radar and microwave radiation and ELF radiation as dispensed by our HARP field antenna complex in Alaska and those in Russia and China.

Unfortunately for us, "the deck is stacked against us" by technology "run amuck" but with ingenuity we can find the right conditions or so the author is being told Akashically! WE ARE ALWAYS CONNECTED TO THE LIGHT (Hey Resh Chet) AND SO WE ARE DIVINELY ENABLED! And from Akashic insight it has been revealed that Negative Ion Generators would counteract many of the negative effects listed above and there is scientific validation regarding this premise! Also, there are devices from "Pyradyne" such as the "Nuclear Receptor" which can deflect these "negative energies". "Metaforms" also has similar devices.

Now, we have discussed the immense benefits of Kriya Kundalini Pranayam breathing. And as was mentioned previously in this chapter, it just so happens that THIS IS AN ESSENTIAL, if not THE ESSENTIAL ELEMENT, in the SUCCESSFUL TRANSITION to BREATHAIRIANISM, even though nary a one of websites on this topic mentions such! Remember, in Chapter Four, we covered that the Prana pulled into the body during Pranayam can create a condition of "LIQUID LIGHT" in the body which is a bodily NOURISHING FACTOR covered in "The Spiritual Science of Kriya Yoga" by Goswami Kriyananda. And then in "the Bhagavad Gita" and "The Yoga Sutras", we covered how inhaled Prana, during Pranayam, flows through the spinal column and nerves and MAGNETIZES THE CELLS IN THE BODY AND INFUSES THEM WITH LIGHT AND THEREBY NOURISHES THEM IS A SUPERIOR FASHION TO FOOD. So, THIS IS THE SECRET TO THE REAL PRACTICING OF BREATHARIANISM WHICH NO OTHER SOURCES SEEM TO REVEAL, at least of which Dr. Newton is aware!

The author is only too aware that he has more or less repeated himself, several paragraphs previously on this subject. Why would he do so? Dr. Newton knows that people do not often absorb information on their first exposure thereto at the conscious level. So like a truly competent teacher, at times he will repeat the same thing is a different manner! The author is trying to circumvent the "prejudice filters" which many poeple use to dismiss new information and concepts!!!! AND CERTAINLY

THE CONCEPT, and even more so, THE ACTUAL PRACTICE OF BREATHAIRIANISM IS EXTREMELY ALIEN TO "MAINSTREAM THOUGHT" AND UNDERSTANDING!

How could we measure the purported benefits and effects of Pranayam? We already discussed how you can measure the increased oxygen saturation of the body from Pranayam with a Pulse Oximeter. We also already talked about measuring the increased electromagnetism in the body with dowsing rods. And if a subject infused huge amounts of Prana into their body via Pranayam, we might also measure this with a Magnometer or an Electrometer. The point to be emphasized here is that THE AUTHOR DOES NOT MAKE UNSUBSTANCIATED CLAIMS BUT RATHER OFFERS CORRESPONDING VERIFICATION! Since Dr. Newton has had his own share of "being driven off of a cliff" by so called experts, he does not wish you to experience the same!

There is a self-proclaimed Breathairian, Wiley Brooks, who says you cannot attain Breathairian consciousness until you have consumed alot of Mc Donald's Hamburgers and at least a liter of diet Coke and then, and only then you are ready to say five phrases that will allow you to be successful in this practice. Truly, it is hard to envision this protocol as a clean environment for the body considering that the hamburger, since it has been cooked, will putrify in your intestines (check Dr. Howell's book, "Enzyme Nurtiriton"). And the diet Coke will definitely create a state of acidosis in the body, among other undesirable side effects such as oxygen depletion. The author knows of no dedicated, practicing Kriya Yogi or Yogini who would use this protocol and additionally, IT IS A RATHER CRUDE AND INEFFECTIVE PROTOCOL COMPARED TO PRANAYAM!

Dr. Newton can understand the protocol of the Amazonian Indians when they eat lots of Bananas before they ingest a hallucinogenic concoction that allows them to enter the state of "Akashic consciousness". The Bananas have alot of Potassium which seems to be a Prana enhancer—something that is found lacking in the hamburger/Diet Coke regimen which is also rather devoid of Potassium, but less so if it included French fries. Maybe that is the glitch in Wiley Brooks protocols? NVL (not very likely)!

These Amazonian Indians, as a sidenote—decoded the sequence of DNA more than two hundred years before our modern scientists, which is no small feat and yet THIS CAN ROUTINELY OCCUR AT THE THETA/ AKASHIC LEVEL OF CONSCIOUSNESS into which these Indians are entering using a hallucinagenic concoction. This is detailed in the book, "The Sexy Serpent". This is somewhat of a digression but tangentially related to our topic.

Some extremely prescient points have been made by Jack Davis in a Breathairian posting on the internet. He points out that more energy is used in digesting food than the resultant energy contained in the food itself, as Dr. Newton delineated earlier in this chapter. He also points out that people want to sleep after eating a very large meal and as such this would indicate/validate the tremendous amount of Prana/energy required to digest food. Additionally, Davis reveals that the body is 65% Oxygen, 18% Carbon, 10% Hydrogen and 3% Nitrogen and that these chemicals are sufficiently provided in our air and therefore we can breathe these "chemical nutrients" into our body. This could very well be hard to refute unlike the hamburger-diet Coke regimen, even though few, if any people have accomplished this.

Another good source on Breathairianism besides Jack Davis is Jasmuheen who claims that she is sans food most of the time, only eating a handful of food occassionaly. She is likewise internet accessed by "Goggling" "Breathairian". Davis points out that our body is about 70% water and Dr. Newton would say that is why you can get by without food but not water, until the realization Soruba Samadhii (immortality), because the body needs this as mechanism of substitute nutrition! BE AWARE, THERE HAVE BEEN ASSIDUOUS DEVOTEES OF BREATHAIRIANISM THAT HAVE DIED PREMATURELY! Dr. Newton is not attempting to scare or dissuade you from Breathairianism but rather to inform you so that you do not proceed as some careless dunkoff fanatic! Also be aware, THAT CARDIOLOGISTS WILL TELL YOU THAT YOUR HEART WILL BE SEVERLY DAMAGED BY THE BREATHAIRIAN PROTOCOLS OF LITTLE OR NO FOOD. At the same time, NEUROLOGISTS AND NEURO-SURGEONS WOULD TELL DR. NEWTON THAT HIS BRAIN WOULD BE DAMAGED BY SAMADHI AND YET IT HAS ONLY BEEN ENHANCED THEREFROM (although after reading this book there will be some doubters as to the veracity of this statement)!!!! The ultimate determinator of this must be the reader of this book and/or their doctors?

AT THE END OF THE ALCHEMICAL PROCESS OF CREATING/ CATALYZING THE ENERGY/"LIGHT BODY, WE WILL NEED TO CEASE EATING FOOD AND WILL NOT NEED TO EAT FOOD. Of this, the author is certain, beyond doubt! And so if there are FAMINE CONDITIONS on Earth, FOR A PRACTICING BREATHAIRIAN, this becomes IRRELEVANT—YOU REMAIN IN A STATE OF LIBERATION and without stress!!!!

In review:

BE PREPARED FOR THE "SHIITE" TO HIT THE FAN because of the electromagnetic Solar flares and spikes bombarding the Earth! Also, physical disasters and other astronomical factors could well createa new Ice Age as discussed by Mitch Battros and Dr. Browning. This could make food very scarce, so we should learn and practice EATING LESS FOOD, EAT LESS FOOD, EAT LESS FOOD, EAT LESS FOOD!

To be successful in this, EAT FOODS THAT ARE HIGH IN FIBER and FOODS THAT ALKALIZE! Drinking WATER that is HIGHLY OXYGENATED AND PURIFIED (such as that produced by "The John Ellis Water Machine" will make you eat less food and increase the Pranic content of your body!

Also, "The 'GOMBS' Diet", the eating of GREEN FOODS, ONIONS and GARLIC, MUSHROOMS, BERRIES and SEEDS is highly recommended to LOSE WEIGHT and to be "ANTI-TUMORIC"

Ideally, you can weather the coming famine using a BREATHAIRIAN PROTOCOL of none to very little food and consuming highly Oxygenated water or any water you can get.

It is quite likely that our electrical transmission grid and our satellite systems will be knocked out of commission by solar flares. The government already knows of this possibility, as do the electrical utility companies!

Breathairians can nutrify the body with Oxygen which is a powerful distributor of Prana and Pranic force. It is possible to nutrify the body in this manner!

Additionally, we know from "The Yoga Sutras", "The Bhagavad Gita" and Goswami Kriyanada that through the PRANAYAM BREATH WE BRING MAGNETISM AND LIGHT DOWN THROUGH OUR SPINAL COLUMN AND NERVES AND THIS NUTRIFIES OUR BODILY CELLS BETTER THAN FOOD! This is from sources that are thousands, if not millions of years old!

A Breathairian protcol of eating little or no food could be achieved BUT CERTAINLY NOT WITHOUT DRINKING WATER until the onset of Soruba (continual) Samadhi!

DO NOT BE OVERWHELMED ABOUT THE TEST WE WILL FACE! OUR CREATOR IS ALWAYS WITH US (connecting us to the light [Hey Resh Chet], as a certitude (Ayin Resh Yod) and this positions us to overcome our fears (Mem Nun Daled) and restore things to their perfect state of energy and light (Aleph Kaf Aleph)

WHAT MORE COULD YOU NEED? EVERYTHING (PERFECTION) IS ALREADY HERE AND EVERYWHERE BECAUSE GOD IS! Practice and study the protocols already systematically discussed in this book to allow this to come to fruition in your life

AS MARY BAKER EDDY SAYS IN "SCIENCE AND HEALTH WITH KEY TO THE SCRIPTURES", GOD NEVER ASKS MORE OF US THAN WE CAN DO. Therefore, the TASK FACING US IS MORE THAN ACHIEVEABLE! Enjoy your experiences. AND CONTINUALLY GIVE THANKS TO YOUR GOD FOR WHAT HAS BEEN AND WILL BE PROVIDED FOR US!!!!

AT THE END OF THE ALCHEMICAL PROCESS OF CREATING/ CATALYZING THE ENERGY/"LIGHT BODY", WE CAN STOP EATING AND WILL NOT NEED TO EAT FOOD!

FAMINE CONDITIONS LEAVE A PRACTICING BREATHAIRIAN IN A STATE OF LIBERATION, UNLIKE PEOPLE WHO ARE OBESSED WITH EATING FOOD!!!!

CHAPTER TWELVE

WHAT IS MORE DIVINE, HUMANS, ANIMALS, PLANTS OR MUSIC? KNOWING YOUR PLACE WITHIN THE SCHEME OF DIVINITY!

The answer to this chapter, IN ORDER OF DIVINITY (the highest to the lowest) would be MUSIC AT THE HIGHEST, next are PLANTS AND TREES, followed by ANIMALS and THEN HUMANS. This is CERTAINLY CONTRADICTORY TO CHRISTIAN, ISLAMIC AND JEWISH TEACHINGS because they believe that Man has "dominion over the whole Earth". Please note that the MEANING OF "DOMINION", at the time of the Old Testament, meant "STEWARDSHIP" or "CARETAKING"—NOT DOMINATION OR SUBJUGATION OR DECIMATION OR DESECREATION!!!!

MUSIC is undoubtedly "THE UNIVERSAL LANGUAGE", as many sources have described it. Most certainly, MUSIC CAN LIFT US TO BLISS and euphoria which are STATES OF THETA, Divinity and Superconsciousness. Certainly the SONIC VIBRATIONS which emanate FROM MUSIC can AFFECT US profoundly at the EMOTIONAL LEVEL. A culture devoid of music is probably not a culture at all or a very pathetic one at best. Dr. Newton has listed selections of music in Chapter Three which strongly inducive tin creating Theta/ Divinity/ Superconsciousness state of consciousness in which humans become awesome or better! Not only thought and intention can manifest templates that are realized into actual creation, but sound has the same properties to create the same things. Virtually every religious tradition states or implies that God created through "the word", which when uttered is "sounds".

Included within SINGING, and probably THE STRONGEST PART, is CHANTING and the RECITATION OF SANSKRIT MANTRAS. So we've already thoroughly discussed "The Gayatri" and "Mrityonjaya" Sanskirt Mantras in Chapter Three, as well as the "Ram Mantra" and the "Babaji Mantra". There are many other of these Sanskrit mantras which you can learn in Kriya Yoga training, available from Babaji'sKriyaYoga.com. When these Sanskrit mantras are chanted in a circle and in unison for several hours during a YAGNI (fire) ceremony, the volume of PRANA FOCUSED into the circle will put some of the PARTICIPANTS into a DEEP THETA consciousness. And this is the DIVINE CONSCIOUSNESS or DIVINE MIND! This is the natural high which many of us may have been seeking **and it can easily be created by us!!**

PLANTS AND TREES also convey to us, in a manner of speaking, a universal yet unheard language auditorily. Conceiving of existence on this planet without such wonderful presences is almost incomprehensible. The most amazing thing that Dr. Newton has learned from his sixty plus years in the discipline of horticulture is that PLANTS AND TREES ALWAYS DO WHAT THEY ARE SUPPOSED TO DO AND ALWAYS THRIVE WHERE THEY ARE SUPPOSED TO THRIVE. AND THEY OFTEN REFLECT THESE TWO TRAITS EVEN IN SITUATIONS WHERE THEY SHOULD NOT SURVIVE! How many humans do you know that come close to doing this. For Dr. Newton, he could probably count all qualified people on less than all of the fingers of one hand.

PLANTS AND TREES SOOTH US EMOTIONALLY AND KEEP US IN A STATE OF BALANCE BECAUSE OF THEIR INHERENT DIVINITY! Exactly how plants and trees do this is hard to specifically describe. But it has been detailed in Peter Tompkins "The Secret Life of Plants" and "Secrets of the Soil" that PLANTS HAVE SENTIENCE—that is, they actually have feelings and consciousness! And they seem to have the ABILITY TO COMMUNICATE with each other as per the movie "Avatar". This movie is much more than a psychedlic or phantasmagoric fantasy and it surely reveals the inherent and SYMBIOTIC CONNECTION

BETWEEN PEOPLE AND PLANTS and plants between plants. This has also been detailed in Peter Caddy"s book, "Perelandra", about a special organic garden in Scotland created on terrible, basically unarable soil. This has been subsequently covered by Michaelle Small Wright's book, "Perelandra Garden workbook". Dr. Newton entered the field of landscape contracting because he would garden after his job in a grocery store and he noticed that it had an intense calming effect upon his "high strung" emotions.

One of the worst things imaginable that can occur is when a LESSER FORM, LIKE HUMANS MUTILATES or deforms a HIGHER FORM, LIKE PLANTS and TREES. Plants that are cropped/trimmed into UNNATURAL FORMS IS NOT ONLY A FORM OF MUTILATION/ DEFORMATION, BUT IT ALSO literally HURTS AND INSULTS THE PLANT AND THE CREATOR. With TREES that are SEVERLY TOPPED OR OVERLY THINNED OF THEIR BRANCHES OR ARE PRUNED AT NON-JUNCTION POINTS, the same thing applies. As a certainty, the Creator never made a square plant nor has a genetic manipulation by man. NATURE HAS A NATURAL "RANDOMNESS" and "FREE FLOW" TO IT THAT IS WELL DISPLAYED IN THE PLANT KINGDOM. This is what makes Nature and plants so interesting. CONSIDER THIS WELL BEFORE YOU MUTILATE A PLANT INTO A SQUARE SHAPE or you plant a long boring hedge that is constantly being trimmed into unnatural shapes!

This is why Ammachi (or Amma), a holy woman, Avatar, from India states we should be ". . . . DEDICATED TO HELPING NATURE . . . ." because nature is ". . . . DEDICATED TO HELPING US . . . .". "BY LOVING AND SERVING NATURE WE ARE WORSHIPPING GOD ITSELF". The author will state categorically and without equivocation THAT THOSE POEPLE WHO MULTILATE PLANT FORMS INTO UNNATURAL SHAPES ARE INCAPBLE OF RESPECTING NATURE/GOD until they stop such DESTRUCTIVE ACTIONS!!!!

Especially in OLDER TREES centuries and millenia old, THERE SEEMS TO BE A WISDOM AND PERMANENCE AND INTELLIGENCE WITH WHICH WE CAN COMMUNE AND COMMUNICATE!!!! If you have ever hugged a very large tree you may have felt this! NO, YOU WERE NOT IMAGINING THIS! Again, this concept is well portrayed in the movie, "Avatar".

Also the obessive complaining about trees dropping leaves and needles is so petty and is nothing more than human's, and highly disfunctional ones at best, trying to "control" something superior to themselves when they are completely devoid of control of their own person—codependent cubed, so to speak! Fallen leaves serve a function of cooling or warming tree roots and providing nutrients from mulch as the leaves decompose. ON ALL AREAS, OTHER THAN LAWNS AND PATIOS, LEAVES SHOULD BE LEFT TO ACCUMULATE. This is both horticulturally correct and giving due deference and respect to our Creator! TAKE SOME TIME TO THINK ABOUT WHAT HAS JUST BEEN SAID BEFORE YOU SUMMARILY DISMISS IT! Truly, there is no human who is more insightful than Nature itself because NATURE IS GOD and trumps all of our human ignorance!!!! And likewise, GOD IS IN NATURE!!!! This may be PANTHEISTIC, which bothers many people, but nevertheless IT IS SCIENTIFICALLY VERIFIABLE SINCE GOD IS ENCOUNSED IN THE ATOMIC FIELD AND EVERYTHING IS COMPRISED OF ATOMS!!!! After this, there should be little argument about the foregoing **scientific** statements!

For those people who consider it outrageous that trees could be more divine than mankind, consider the following: Trees create oxygen, sequester carbon, remove toxins and pollutants from the air, create shade, provide refuge for birds and small animals, deplete almost no resources taking their nourishment from the soil, provide us with beautiful forms to view, provide fruit for us to eat and are an emotionally palliative for our unbalanced emotions. On the other side, people deplete oxygen, create carbon, create and spew forth toxins and pollutants, kill birds and small animals, deplete huge amounts of natural resources, live much shorter lives than trees, cannot create fruit other than progeny which are not normally consumed as food and are often emotionally conflicted and unbalanced. *The ultimate factor is that trees can exist just fine without man but man cannot do likewise. Also, trees naturally improve soil structure whereas man naturally depletes and destroys soil IN VIRTUALLY EVERY QUALITATIVE MEASUREMENT, TREES DISPLAY A CLEAR SUPERIORITY TO HUMANS!!!!*

Now as to ANIMALS, ONCE AGAIN, THEY PRETTY MUCH ACT WITHIN THE TEMPLATE OF DIVINITY WITHIN WHICH THEY WERE CREATED. It is very easy to COMMUNICATE TELEPATHICALLY with animals THROUGH PICTURES from your consciousness to thier consciousness. THEY ARE INHERENTLY PSYCHIC and communicate with each other, intra-species and inter-species, and with humans. As for domesticated pets, in most cases they are extremely loyal even when they are being abused. Such abuse or belittling of your animal is a blatant insult to it and again, our Creator. Additionally, when one animal kills and eats another animal species, it only does so within an "as needed" basis! Human hunters, often ignore this parameter of necessity/impending hunger and need for food!

In the case of HUMANS, it has already been discussed that most Christians, Moslems and Jews believe that MAN HAS DOMINION OVER THE EARTH, believing that everything should be SUBSERVIENT TO MAN. However, as was previously discussed NOTHING COULD BE MORE DISTORTED AND INCORRECT THAN THIS ASSERTION, because the word "DOMINION" was DEFINED as "CARETAKER" or "STEWARD" at the time of the writing of the Torah and Bible! THE DIFFERENCE BETWEEN THESE TWO THINGS IS AS STARK AS THE DIVISION BETWEEN DAY AND NIGHT. Certainly, the Illuminati cult feels they should dominate everything on this planet including you! A caretaker's job is to take care of something—not abuse it, not destroy it, not mutilate it, not disrespect it BUT RATHER

NURTURE IT! Personally, Dr. Newton would rather see "PLANET GAIA" ("Mother Earth") nurtured rather than the manifestation of "PLANET EXCREMENT" (a barbarian plunder and toxification of our planet which has transpired over a long period of time). RESPECTING AND LOVING NATURE DOES NOT INCLUDE MUTILATING IT AND THE CLEAR CUTTING OF FORESTS AND SPEWING POISONS IN A "HITHER, NITHER" MANNER!!!!

It is past time for humanity to extricate itself from the mountains of excrement, both literally and figuratively, that have been created. Let go of the pathetic standards of the "I'm only an imperfect human being" and begin feeling like and acting from the "perfect man" of "Science and Health with Key to the Scriptures", "The 72 Names of God", "The Emerald Tablets", "The Patterns on the Trestleboard: The Truth About Self", "The Bhagavad Gita" and "The Yoga Sutras". These sources have been recurrently discussed throuhout this book. THERE IS A FUNDAMENTAL NECESSITY FOR THIS—THE SURVIVAL OF OUR PLANET AND THE UNVEILING OF ITS PERFECT FORM, OF WHICH WE ARE AN INTEGRAL PART!!!!

YOU KNOW YOUR PLACE IN THE UNIVERSE BY RESPECTING AND NURTURING ALL OF GOD'S CREATIONS! And by following this behest/axiom, we ourselves are blessed therefrom BECAUSE WE ARE IN RESONANCE—AN ATOMIC VIBRATORY RESONANCE— WHICH MORE FULLY CONNECTS US WITH OUR CREATOR!!!! This is akin to Number "6" in "The Patterns on the Trestleboard: The Truth About Self" by Paul Foster Case where we see the beauty of all creation both small and large. But actually our higher "vibratory resonance"/ spiritual transformation is the result of RESPECTING ALL OF GOD'S CREATIONS!!!! This is something we have a self interest in fostering!

In Summary:

Man's "dominion over the Earth does not mean subjugation but rather "stewardship" or "caretaking"

Music and Sanskrit Mantras SUCH AS "GAYATRI", "MRITYONJAYA", "RAM" and "BABAJI" are the highest level of Divinity because they exhibit "sonic perfection". Also, any culture without music would most likely be a pathetic one, at best.

Plants and trees are the second highest level of Divinity because they always thrive where and how they should and many times even exist where they are not suited to live! How many humans can say this?

Plants and trees soothe us emotionally and help keep us in a state of balance because of their inherent Divinity!

Incorrectly trimming trees and plants and mutilating them into unnatural forms is an insult to the plant and tree and an insult to the Creator!

People and trees and plants are tied together by a type of sentience such as depicted in the movie, "Avatar"! These concepts have been chronicled in Peter Tompkins books, "The Secret Life of Plants" and "Secret of the Soil". Additionally these ideas have been discussed in Peter Caddy's book, "Perelandra" and Michele Small Wright's book, "The Perelandra Workbook". It is especially easy to communicate with large and old trees in a telepahtic manner!!!!

Complaining about the mess of falling leafs is the result of disfunctional humans lack of understanding of the importance of this process to a tree and is insulting to the Creator!

When all of the qualities are totaled and compared to humans, the superiority of trees becomes starkly self evident.

Animals pretty much live within the Divine template by which they were created. Telepahtic communication with them by humans is easy and they communicate between themselves in this manner. They should never be abused unless abusing Divinity is a good thing!

Again, having "dominion" over the Earth does not include "subservience". Rather it includes "stewardship" and "caretaking" and there is an incredibly stark difference between these concepts!

There is a vast difference between respecting and nurturing "Planet Earth" as opposed to a barbarian plunder and toxification of "Planet Excrement"!

It is time to stop justifying human mediocrity and to begin to live within the Divine templates of behavior listed in "Science and Health with Key to the Scriptures", "The 72 Names of God" from "Exodus", "The Emerald Tablets" of Hermes Trismegustis, "The Patterns on the Trestleboard: The Truth About Self", "The Bhagavad Gita" and "The Yoga Sutras".

YOU KNOW YOUR PLACE IN THE UNIVERSE BY NURTURING AND RESPECTING ALL OF GOD'S CREATIONS and we are personally benefitted by doing so, as is the Creator!

CHAPTER THIRTEEN

TYING IT ALL TOGETHER TO CREATE YOUR PERFECT SELF
AND "LIGHT BODY"!!!! ARE YOU SURE I CAN GET THERE—
ACTUALLY ACHIEVE THE AGENDA OF THIS BOOK?

THE ANSWER TO THESE QUESTIONS IS YES AND YES. Over time, as Dr. Newton has talked about fragments of this book to many people over the years, he has been scolded, ridiculed, belittled, excoriated, derided and TOLD THAT HE WAS CRAZY and SOMETIMES WORSE, including being an "anti-Christ"! Nevertheless, he has moved forward, all the while thanking the people who told him he was "crazy" because he knows the following saying: WHEN NEW IDEAS ARE FIRST REVEALED, THEY ARE CRITICIZED, RIDICULED and DERIDED. NEXT THESE IDEAS ARE ATTACKED and/or VIOLENTLY OPPOSSED and maybe even LEGISLATED OUT OF EXISTENCE. **FINALLY, AFTER THE THE PASAGE OF ENOUGH TIME, THEY ARE ACCEPTED AS SELF-EVIDENT!!!!**

WHY LET OUR INHERENT PREJUDICES "SHORT CIRCUIT" THE PROCESS OF LEARNING, KNOWLEDGE WISDOM AND DIVINE CONSCIOUSNESS? **"PREJUDICE FILTERS" ONLY LEAVE US INHERENTLY DIMISHED AND LESS DIVINE!!!!** We are truly are more than pendejos or dunkoffs or schmucks or putzs, or we would not have reached this point in the book, of course unless we are reading the last chapter first? Let's consider a real life situation where "prejudice filters" do not serve our best intersts!

Dr. Newton has discussed with some Christian Scientist's how it was revealed to him that "atomic force" was the essence of "Spirit" that Mrs. Eddy talked about in "Science and Health . . ." and he could tell, even though they were polite to him in this discussion, that they thought he was totally "looneysville". He knew this because he could read their thoughts "like a book". And the author knows that they thought like they did because Mrs. Eddy states emphatically that the world is not affected by "atomic force" and this is because early physics was obsessed with the material nature of the atom. Whereas, Mrs. Eddy rejected the existence of matter in any form AND SHE WAS CORRECT in so doing!

Without the slightest hint of "wishfull thinking", the author is positive, without doubt, that at this point in time, Mrs Eddy would agree with his depiction of atoms as Spirit and not as matter. Mrs. Eddy never defined Spirit in low level abstractions—only that "Spirit is God" and infinite. And then God is defined with terms such as "omnipotent" and "omnipresent" and "omniscient" which are all true but still defined with high level abstractions. In the chapter of "Recapitulation" in "Science and Health . . .", Mrs. Eddy describes God as beyond corporeality, Divinity, with supremacy, limitless Mind, Spiritual, Soul, Principle, and all Life, among other qualities but these are still vague and high level abstractions. Dr. Newton is BASICALLY EQUATING SPIRIT WITH ATOMS, ENERGY, ELECTROMAGNETISM, LIGHT AND VIBRATIONS (SONICS) and these are lower level abstractions and considerably less ambiguous considering that we can smash atoms now in atomic colliders and see them in Electron (Helium Ion) microscopes and we can measure all of the qualities of atoms with scientific instruments and meters. Now Dr. Newton is equally sure that Mrs. Eddy would not agree with his views on sexuality, described in Chapter Three, but that is not a problem for him.

Dr. Newton is asking you to consider that WE CAN LEARN SO MUCH IF **WE REMOVE OUR "PREJUDICE FILTERS"**, as the author has worked assiduously to do himself. Please consider doing likewise, yourself!

DOING SO WILL PUT US ON THE "TRACK" TO DIVINITY, THETA CONSCIOUSNESS and SUPERCONSCIOUSNESS in THIS LIFETIME—IN THE HERE AND NOW!!!! Otherwise, our heads are just "stuck in the mud". And mud is a rather nasty substance that makes working in it and with it very, very difficult!

After digression, the point is that my Christian Science friends could have had an ephiphany if they had been **sponges** ready to **absorb new things and viewpoints**. Are you, the readers of this book, READY TO DO THE SAME? If you are, the ANSWER WILL BE "YES AND YES" for you in relation to the question at the beginning of this chapter. Dr. Newton is anxiously anticipating that more people to "throw off the shackles" and "soar into the heights of DIVINE CONSCIOUSNESS! ADDITIONALLY, HE WANTS TO AID THIS PROCESS, NOT FOR SELF-AGGRANDIZEMENT BUT THE THE BENEFIT OF HUMANITY! When humanity is benefitted, the author is uplifted likewise!

IF YOU FEEL THESE POINTS HAVE BEEN BELABORED, YOUR ARE CORRECT. But Dr. Newton knows that he is fighting the "PREJUDICE FILTERS" in your SUBCONSCIOUS and THE CONSCIOUS MIND ITSELF AND THAT A PART OF YOU IS VICIOUSLY FIGHTING AGAINST THE CHANGING OF YOURSELF. Dr. Newton has full memory of this similar battle within himself. THE AUTHOR EMPATHIZES YOUR PREDICAMENT! WITH The TEMPLATE or MAP WHICH HAS BEEN REVEALED TO YOU THROUGHOUT THIS BOOK, YOUR PATHWAY IS CLEAR, IF YOU ALLOW IT TO BE SO! Maps to Divinity and its perfection have been revealed herein!

So how becomes "THETA/DIVINE/SUPERCONSCIOUSNESS/ LIGHT CONSCIOUSNESS" and the resulting "LIGHT BODY" of **ALCHEMICAL TRANMUTATION**?

The following is a **SYNTHESIZED** and **INTEGRATED MAP** and **PATHWAYS** to this goal:

THE FOLLOWING ARE MAPS AND PATHWAYS OF PRACITCES/ DISCIPLINES AND ARE SPIRITUAL ALCHEMICAL **CATALYZING AGENTS** (STUDIES/SOURCES THAT ARE LISTED). STARTING AT NUMBER TEN BELOW ARE THE "**CHEMICALS**" OF THE **TRANSFORMATIONAL PROCESS.** THIS IS A SYNTHESIS OF CHAPTER THREE:

1.

KRIYA YOGA ASANAS are poses (stretches) and counter poses (counter stretches) that prepare the body for Kriya Dhyana Meditation, Kriya Kundalini Pranayam, Samadhi and Kundalini Awakening through helping to properly align our spinal column, among other things, SO THAT PRANA CAN MORE POWERFULLY ENTER OUR BODIES!!!!

2.

KRIYA DHYANA YOGA is a specific system of "CONTROLLED" MEDITATIONS that will us allow to focus our minds like a "laser". This you can learn from Dr. Newton's Yogi, Govindan Satchianada reachable at Babaji'sKriyaYoga.net via the internet—just Google it!

3.

KRIYA KUNDALINI PRANAYAM is the "**royal road**" **to breath control/life control,** fuller **Oxygenation** of our bodies, enhanced **Prana** (energy/Spirit/electromagnetism) assimilation and **Bindu** accumulation. Once you master three rounds (forty eight repetitions) of Pranayam with a time of thirty to forty seconds or more for each repetition, you are at a level Theta/Divine/Superconsciousness and YOU ARE **REACTIVATING YOUR "LIGHT BODY"** and will be truly blessed by attaining this (NO BULL EXCREMENT BUT RATHER PRANA ENHANCED)! Again, you can learn this again with Yogi, Govindan Satchianada through

Babaji'sKriyaYoga.net or you can learn it in one of Dr. Newton's seminars which allow you to more fully access the practices in this book.

THE AWESOMENESS OF KRIYA KUNDALINI PRANAYAM IS THE MULTI-MODALITY APPROACH AS IT BRINGS US TO THETA AND LIGHT BODY CONSCIOUSNESS through the Pranic breathing, through the SITA-USHNA, through the IDA-PINGALA and BINDHU and definitely through the EKA NYLAI. It takes longer than the Tai Chi "Standing Meditation" or "The Backflow Meditation" and is more than worth the extra effort involved because IT ALLOWS US TO NOT ONLY MASTER OURSELVES BUT OUR SURROUNDINGS!

IF YOU HAVE HEART OR RELATED PROBLEMS, DO NOT PERFORM PRANAYAM OR SAMADHI OR KUNDALINI AWAKENING!

4.

SAMADHI is your reward for becoming a "master" of Pranayam. KRIYA YOGA SIDDHA,SATGURU AND MAHAAVATAR PATANJALII, IN "THE YOGA SUTRAS", SPECIFICALLY RECOMMENDS SAMADHI FOR THOSE PEOPLE WHO WISH TO ACHIEVE "PERFECTION". In this state of suspended breath and heart cessation, a clarity consciousness of our Mind occurs and we are even deeper in Theta and "light body" consciousness than in only Pranayam. It should be emphasized that this is not a holding of your breath. It does not work that way BUT RATHER IT WILL AUTOMATICALLY UNFOLD NATURALLY after three rounds of Pranayam when you attain a thirty to forty second cycle for each breath. The breath will be shallow or cease and your Heart will stop beating or only very lightly. LITERALLY YOUR BODY IS BEING SUSTAINED BY PRANIC OR HYPER-PRANIC FORCE AND WE CAN EASILY ACCESS THE AKASHIC RECORDS VIA OUR DEEP THETA-DELTA LEVEL AND OUR BODY IS INFUSED WITH EVEN MORE LIGHT THAN PRANAYAM. WE ARE IN A STATE OF BLISS/euphoria. Once again, it will be stated, that

Patanjali, in "The Yoga Sutras", highly recommends Samadhi for those who wish to achieve perfection! DO NOT PERFORM SAMADHI IF YOU HAVE HEART OR RELATED PROBLEMS!

5.

KUNDALINI AWAKENING is usually the result of the mastery of PRANAYAM and SAMADHI but not necessarily so in the case of some people and Dr.Newton, but they are a sure PATHWAY thereto! DO NOT DO THIS IF YOU HAVE HEART OR RELATED PROBLEMS. This definitely **THIS IS THE MOST DANGEROUS AND INTENSE PRACTICE THAT WE CAN UNDERTAKE**!!!! And yet, you will NEVER BE CLOSER TO GOD THAN IN THIS STATE, other than Soruba Samadhi, where you have attained immortality of the body!!!! For the author, these experiences were exhilating and yet disorienting for a period of time!

6.

"THE GAYATRI MANTRA", THE MRITYONJAYA MANTRA, THE "BABAJI NAGARAJ" MANTRA, THE "RAM" MANTRA and other Kriya Yoga SIDDHA MANTRAS, spoken in SANSKRIT, a "sacred language", WILL CHANGE YOUR BODY MORE TO A STATE OF LIGHT AND MIND MORE TO A STATE OF THETA/ DIVINITY/ SUPERCONSCIOUSNESS through the SONIC VIBRATIONS which emanate therefrom. They are performed 108 times continuously as a Catholic Rosary. This constitutes one round and you should do at least two to three rounds if you are only concentrating on one of these mantras. Your spiritual transformation may be gradual with the recitation of the Sanskrit mantras or it could be rapid! THE KRIYA YOGA SIDDHA, PATANJALI, IN "THE YOGA SUTRAS", UNEQUIVOCALLY RECOMMENDS THE **RECITATION OF SANSKRIT MANTRAS FOR THOSE PEOPLE WHO WISH TO ATTAIN "PERFECTION"**. Remember, "Sanskrit" means "perfect form" so you are working from INHERENT PERFECTION with this language! THE VALUE OF THIS CANNOT BE UNDERESTIMATED!!!!

7.

THE **TAI CHI "STANDING MEDITATION"** can be quickly mastered and assmilated into our daily routine. You can access the feeling of the Chi/Prana/life force energies in your hands and spine and maybe other places. With long sessions of this meditation (thirty minutes or more) you will definitely be anchored in THETA CONSCIOUSNESS as well as beginning the process of REACTIVATING YOUR "LIGHT BODY"

8.

THE **"BACKFLOW MEDITATION"** can be learned very quickly and would be used in place of "Kriya Kundalini Pranayam" until you have been initated into the Pranayam protocol.

9.

KEEPING YOURSELF IN A STATE OF GENERAL AND SPECIFIC **HAPPINESS**. When you are happy through your practices and activities, you are stronger because somehow, more Prana is entering your body. This can be proven conclusively through KINESOLOGICAL MUSCLE TESTING by pushing down an arm or trying to separate your thumb and index finger when they are conjuncted with your other index finger. **Invariably, positive and happy statements test incredibly stronger than negative and hostile proclamations**. All of the recommended practices and statments will make you happier because they are based in Theta Consciousness which is Superconsciousness and Divinity (which are the essence of the Creator)!!!!

THE FOLLOWING ARE MAPS AND PATHWAYS OF STUDY AND CONTEMPLATION AND ARE LIKE CHEMICALS THAT ARE ALCHEMICALLY CATALYZED BY THE PRACTICES AND DISCIPLINES LISTED ABOVE:

10.

Studying "SCIENCE AND HEALTH WITH KEY TO THE SCRIPTURES", by Mary Baker Eddy, will give you insigts into

DIVINITY/DIVINE MIND/THETA CONSCIOUSNESS/SUPER CONSCIOUSNESS and the "SPIRITUAL/LIGHT BODY". There are weekly lessons that you can purchase from the Christian Science Publishing Society which will aid your metaphysical progress. This is accessable via the internet or from a Christian Science Reading Room at any Christian Science branch church which are all over the world. You can also purchase "Science and Health . . . ." from any Christian Science Reading Room. The branch churches also hold Wednesday and Sunday services. THIS PATH OF METAPHYSICAL STUDY CANNOT BE OVER RECOMMENDED! Dr. Newton is well versed in Mrs. Eddy's teachings, so much so that he has memorized large segments thereof. Remember please, Metaphysical (beyond the physical or matter) is what we delving into in this book!

11.

Studying "THE 72 NAMES OF GOD", from Exodus 14, verses 19-21 will "**blow your socks off**" if you undertake this as a daily routine. TRULY, THERE IS NOTHING IN THE BIBLE OR TORAH CAN GIVE YOU MORE INSIGHT INTO METAPHYSICAL DIVINITY OTHER THAN CHRISTIAN SCIENCE! You can access the names of God and books on this subject from the Kaballah Center in Los Angeles, California. PLEASE DO NOT LOOK FOR THESE NAMES IN THE BIBLE BECAUSE THEY ARE NOT THERE because they are written in Hebrew. Also, rementioning this, Dr. Newton has laid out a protocol for using "The 72 Names of God" for Theta Consciousness Healing in Chapter Four.

12.

Studying "THE EMERALD TABLETS" of Hermes Trismegustis will also provide you with another powerful template/pathway for metaphysical illumination/ elucidation and Theta and "light body" consciousness. You should SAVOR HERMES' MESSAGE AND MEMORIZE it completely. "The Emerald Tablets" are a LIVING TEMPLATE AND PATHWAY TO THETA/Divine/Superconsciousness and the "LIGHT BODY" and it is synthesized into two paragraphs and can be assimilated into your conscious memory without an excruciating effort. The Emerald Tablets" come to us, from several sources and various translations, and the most beautiful of these is available from "The Builders of the Adytum", the organization founded by Paul Foster Case and accessible via the internet.

13.

Studying "THE PATTERNS ON THE TRESTLEBOARD; THE TRUTH ABOUT SELF", by Paul Foster Case is yet another pathway for metaphysical understanding and very powerful at that! This also is distributed by "The Builders of the Adytum" that was founded by Mr. Case. COGITATE UPON ITS MESSAGE AND MEMORIZE IT. It is comprised of eleven statements of metaphysical truths which can be easily disgested into your consciousness. This is also available from the "Builders of the Adytum".

14.

Studying "THE YOGA SUTRAS" by MahaAvatar, Satguru and Kriya Yoga Siddha Patanjali will give you basic and suble insights to Kriya Yoga, which is considered "THE ROYAL ROAD TO ENLIGHTENEMENT". DO NOT IGNORE THIS TREATISE JUST BECAUSE IT IS NOT IN YOUR COMFORT ZONE because we can wipe away our ignorance and ineffectiveness through applying its concepts!

15.

Studying "THE BHAGAVAD GITA" translation by Avatar Parmahansa Yogananda will also bring you TREMENDOUS ILLUMINATION REGARDING KRIYA YOGA and is essential to uplift you into immortality!

16.

Studying "THIRUMANDIRAM ", by MahaAvatar, Satguru and Kriya Yoga Siddhar Thirumoolar will give you synthesized information about Kriya Yoga and the nature of our Creator and is available from "Babji'sKiryaYoga.net

THIS ENDS THE BOOK FOR NOW AND THE CHAPTER ALREADY IS A SUMMARY, MAKING A RE-SUMMARY REDUNDANT!

PLEASE USE THIS BOOK TO RECLAIM YOUR FREEDOM AND PERFECT "GOD NATURE" . . . . Namaste!!!!

EPILOGUE

This book keeps expanding upon itself as it has been being written by the author. The process has been very enlightening for him and he also hopes it has the same effect on you. Dr. Newton makes no claim to great intelligence, although he did at one time, because after many years he realizes that ALL INTELLIGENCE, CREATIVITY and PROBLEM SOLVING COME DIRECTLY TO US FROM THE CREATOR. And the MORE FULLY OUR CONSCIOUSNESS IS FIXED IN THETA CONSCIOSNESS, THE MORE INTELLIGENT AND CREATIVE WE WILL BECOME. Also, virtually ALL INVENTIONS AND ARTISTIC INSPIRATION SPRING FORTH FROM THE THETA REALM be they in Alpha and Theta consciousness, daydreaming or in the dimension of sonomulence (sleep).

Additionally, the creation of Spirit/energy/light enhanced body comes from all of the Theta practices/protocols listed and discussed throughout this book. Practicing Kriya Yoga Asanas prepares your body to perform Kriya Dhyana meditation and Kriya Kundalini Pranayam more effectively. Kriya Kundalini Pranayam prepares you for Samadhi. Kriya Kundalini Pranayam and Samadhi prepare you for Kundalini Awakening. These things aggregated, as well as Sanskrit mantras such as "The Gayatri Mantra", "The Mrityonjaya Mantra", "The Ram Mantra" and "The Babaji Mantra" prepare you for Soruba Samadhi which is the perpetual manifestation of the immortal "light body" and Theta/Divine/ Superconsciousness/ Bliss/ Euphoria/Cosmic Enlightenment, which are the ULTIMATE SPIRITUAL ALCHEMICAL TRANSFORMATION AND THE RESULTING TRANSFIGURATION!!!!

So we have been given the practices, studies that support and enhance our practices and maps and pathways to achieve that which we have been exposed. THUS WE HAVE BEEN TRULY BLESSED BY OUR CREATOR! This map and it paths to our inherent perfection synthesized in the phrase "Aleph Kaf Aleph" (restoring things to their perfect state) from "The 72 Names of God" from the Book of Exodus. It is also includes "The Yoga Sutras" and "The Bhagavad Gita, "Thirumandiram", "The Emerald Tablets", "The Patterns on the Trestleboard: The Truth About Self" and "Science and Health with Key to the Scriptures". Through a preponderance of ancient and modern sources, this concept of perfection has been presented. From a critical mass of information from Physics, Quantum Physics and Quantum Mechanics, Particle and Plasma Physics WE KNOW THAT ATOMS, OF WHICH WE ARE COMPRISED, HAVE NO MATTER BUT THEY HAVE A TREMENDOUS AMOUNT OF ENERGY OR SPIRIT AND PRANA! **If atoms comprise all of creation, as they in fact do, then it is virtually impossible for the cells that comprise our body to deteriorate. SUCH DETERIORATION IS ONLY POSSIBLE IF ATOMS DETERIOATE and they do not appear to have such qualities! THEREFORE OUR BODIES BECOME IMMORTAL ONCE OUR CONSCIOUSNESS CAN PERCEIVE THIS ESSENTIAL REALITY!!!!**

It has also been revealed that THERE IS A POWERFUL PRIVATE ELITIST CULT (Illuminati) AND MANY RELIGIONS AND MANY GOVERNMENTS THAT DO NOT WANT YOU TO KNOW YOU ARE PERFECT BECAUSE YOU WOULD BE ABLE TO SEE THROUGH THE FALSE MIRAGES AND ILLUSIONS AND IMAGES THEY PORTRAY TO YOU AND YOU ARE NOW ABLE TO UNCOVER AND DECIPHER THEIR PROPOGANDA AND THE FALSE UTTERANCES CONTAINED THEREIN. The author cannot control how you will react to all of this. But if you are "fed up" enough with being sick, underpaid and less than abundant, THE **PATHWAYS TO YOUR FREEDOM HAVE BEEN ILLUMINATED!!!!** What are YOU going to do in regard to this? TTATOD, (Time to awaken to our

Divinity) **and reclaim it!!!! OUR SPIRITUAL TRANSFORMATION AND OUR EARTH TRANFIGURATION CAN ONLY OCCUR IF WE CREATE SUCH. THE MORE PEOPLE INVOLVED, THE SHORTER THE TIME SPAN WILL BE REQUIRED FOR OUR CREATION OF "HEAVEN ON EARTH"!**

Can the Illuminati cult be unprogrammed from the Earth? Yes it can and the process has already begun. The illusory power of "Evil" and "sin", which can be equated with ignorance, can and always will eventually be destroyed and/or unmasked. Mary Baker Eddy knew this as an unwavering certitude. The author genuinely wishes Mrs. Eddy was/is here to aid us in our transformation!!!! **But in a sense, she is!**

When this process occurs is DEPENDENT ON A CRITICAL MASS OF INDIVIDUALS PERCEIVING AND CREATING THIS SCENARIO WITHIN THE "MASS CONSCIOUSNESS"/"COLLECTIVE CONSCIOUSNESS"! That is our "cold, hard reality"!!!! Irrespective and regardless of this, **WE ARE TRULY BLESSED, EVEN BEYOND OUR BEST COMPREHENSION, TO HAVE THE THETA CONSCIOUSNESS PROTOCOLS THAT ALLOW US TO TRANSFORM OUR LIVES AND BE HEALED AND ABUNDANT AND AWESOME by achieving the IMMORTALITY OF OUR EXISTING BODY!!!!** So ACTUALLY OUR REALITY IS WARM AND ENJOYABLE WHEN WE ARE "TUNED INTO" THE THETA FREQUENCY" OF OUR CREATOR IN OUR BODY OF SPIRITUAL ENERGY! **A higher frequency of consciousness elicits the satisfying outcomes that we are all craving and deserving thereof!!!!**

DR. NEWTON, WILL BE GIVING WORKSHOPS AROUND THE USA, REGARDING THE PRACTICAL APPLICATION OF EVERYTHING CONTAINED IN THIS BOOK, INCLUDING THE KEY PRACTICE OF KRIYA KUNDALINI PRANAYAM. Check the webside listed in this book for locations and dates. YOU CAN ALSO LEARN THE KRIYA YOGA PROTOCOLS FROM THE AUTHOR'S kRIYA YOGA TEACHER AND HIS AUTHORIZED TEACHERS BY CONTACTING: "info@babajiskriyayoga.net".

ALSO, DR. NEWTON'S FIRST BOOK, "PATHWYAS TO GOD: EXPERIENCING THE 'LIVING GOD' IN YOUR EVERYDAY LIFE" IS FINALLY BACK IN PRINT, UPDATED AND IS ACTUALLY FOUNDATIONAL FOR THIS BOOK, IN SOME ASPECTS. "Pathways" is an invaluable resource for "energy healers", "bodyworkers", crystal and gemstone healers, Acupuncturists' and the "like" AND APPLICABLE TO EVERYONE AND EVERYTHING!

SPIRITUAL ALCHEMICAL TRANSFORMATION FORMULAS:

Below, are listed FORMULAS SHOWING the inter-relation of the MAPS and PATHWAYS in a FORMULAIC MANNER which manifested itself through Dr. Newton in February 2011, FROM THE "AKASHIC RECORDS":

THE FOLLOWING FORMULA IS A HEBREW TRANSLITERATION BECAUSE THIS COMPUTER DOES NOT HAVE HEBREW SYMBOLS (ALPHABET); HEBREW IS READ FROM RIGHT TO LEFT BUT THIS FORMULA IS GIVEN LEFT TO RIGHT SINCE IT IS SANS THE HEBREW SYMBOLS:

FROM "THE 72 NAMES OF GOD" FROM EXODUS 14, VERESES 19-21:

Connecting to the Light (Hey Resh Chet) + The certainty that God is Always with us (Ayin Resh Yod) + Allows us to see the big picture (Aleph Nun Yod) + Allows us to overcome our fears (Mem Nun Daled) = Restoring things to their perfect state (Aleph Kaf Aleph) and perfect health (Mem Hey Shin).

"The Emerald Tablets" of Hermes Trismegustis + The Patterns on the Trestleboard: The Truth About Self "+ "Science and Health with Key to the Scriptures" + "The 72 Names of God" from Exodus + "The Yoga Sutras" + "Bhagavad Gita" + "Thirumandiram" = limitless Light + limitless Substance and Abundance + Omniscience (unending wisdom and knowledge) + Immortality of the body via the "light body".

The Sanskrit symbols OM and AUM = vibrational, sonic and musical perfection, resurrecting and catalyzing the perfect atomic creation on Earth.

A.
Kriya Yogic knowledge + the Tao + Hermetic Traditions ("The Emerald Tablets", "The Patterns on the Trestleboard: The Truth About Self" and Asclepian knowledge, the works of Manley P. Hall, et. al.) + Enochian knowledge + plus Kabbalistic knowledge ("The 72 Names of God from Exodus 14, verses 19-21 + plus the Science of Christianity (Christian Science) + Physics + Quantum Physics + Quantum Mechanics = a map to Theta/Divinity/ Superconsciousness and the manifestation of the perfect man in a metaphysical body (an immortal "light body" as opposed to matter which inherently decays)

B.
Kriya Kundalini Pranayam + the Tai Chi "Standing Meditation" + Kriya Dhyana meditations + Kriya Yoga Asanas + the "Backflow Meditation" + the Sanskrit Mantras of "Gayatri", "Babaji Nagaraj" and "Mrityonjaya" + "The 72 Names of God" from Exodus 14, verses 19-21 + toning and chanting + drumming percussion + crystal and gemstone energetics + pyramid energetics + yagni (fire ceremony) + Tantric sex + Samadhii + Kundalini awakening = A MAP OF PATHWAYS for the THETA/ LIGHT CONSCIOUSNESS BODY.

C.

Overcoming your fears (Mem Nun Daled) of moving forward + removing impending obstacles (Yod Chet Vav) on the "Theta/light body" pathways = Christian Science spiritual/metaphysical healings + "Theta Healing" + Theta Consciousness Healing + Samadhii + Kundalini awakening unleashed = all spiritual and "personal" needs manifested + limitless Spirit/ energy/ life force/Prana/Chi and living in a "field" of "Limitless Light and Euphoria and Ecstacy.

A.+B.+C. (from jus t above)= connecting to the light (Hey Resh Chet) + Light/Theta consciouisness + the spiritual/energy "light body" + Atomic and Akashic knowledge + living in consonance/union with the Creator!

$$\frac{A+B+C}{\text{Limitless light}}$$ = the true nature of God's perfect creations, piercing the veil of apparent imperfection of (Maya/mortal mind) wherein limitless light extinguishes the illusion of dense matter and all that is left is the Spirit/Energy of The Creator.

Ancient traditions + physics + Quantum physics + quantum mechanics + plus the techniques assoicated with the ancient traditions = "light body" activation and consciousness + Theta-Delta consciousness and Divinity/ Superconsciousness!

On 9-25-11, the following was revealed to Dr. Newton:

$$E=mc2 \quad + \quad E=mv2 \quad + \quad E=pa2 \quad =$$

(Energy=mass light squared) $+$ (Energy=mass velocity squared) $+$ (Energy=prana aum squared)

A pure manifestation of light and vibration with Divine Mind/ Theta Consciousness'/ Cosmic Consciousness/ Super Consciousness/Soruba Samadhi and the manifestation of the immortal "light body", wherein we become remolded and reunited knowingly with The Creator!

BIBLIOGRAPHY

"The Bhagavad Gita", Parmahansa Yogananda, Self Realization Fellowship

"Principia", Sir Isaac Newton

"The Hundreth Monkey", Ken Keyes

"The Yoga Sutras", Satguru, MahaAvatar and Siddha Patanjali

"Fabric of the Universe", Dennis Postle

"Science and Health with Key to the Scriptures", MahaAvatar Mary Baker Eddy

"Origin of the Universe: The Scientific Evidence for the Existence of God, Dr. Hugh Ross (internet source)

"The Bridge to Infinity", Bruce Cathie

"Beond the Bridge to Infinity", Bruce Cathie

Physicist Max Planck, from various internet sources

"The 72 Names of God": Technology for the Soul", Rabbi Yehuda Berg, The Kabbalah Center

"The Emerald Tablets", Hermes Trismegistus, Builders of the Adytum

"The Patterns on the Trestleboard: The Truth About Self", MahaAvatar Paul Foster Case, Builders of the Adytum

Information from Louis Contant from internet source and Builders of the Adytum

"The Secret", Rhonda Byrne

"Fabric of the Universe", Valery P. Kondratov (internet source)

"The Confiration of Nine Energies of Egyptian Traditions", Valery P. Kondratov (internet source)

"The Geometry of a Uniform Field", Valery P. Kondratov

"You Can Heal Your Life", by Louise L. Hay

"The Effects of Telomerarse Activity", Dr. Nadaraja, "Kauai's Hindu Monastery Newsletter", June 2011

Various articles, "The American Free Press"

Various articles, "The Barnes Review"

Various books and lectures by Tom Bearden

"Sound Signature" literature and manuals by Sharry Edwards

Various articles by the "DInsbaugh Society"

"Theta Healilng", Vianna Stibal

"The Death of Death, Satguru, MahaAvatar and Siddha Babaji Nagaraj, Babaji's Kriya Yoga

The seminar on "Light Speed Learning", Thomas and Jane Morton

"How to Know Higher Worlds", Rudolf Steiner

"The Life Power", by Louis Contant and Paul Foster Case, Builder's of the Adytum lesson

"Meditations on the Pssadi", MahaAvatar Paul Foster Case (internet source)

"Babaji's Kriya Yoga, Jan Ahlund and Yogi Marshall Govindan Satchidanada

"Kundalini: The Evolutionary Energy in Man", Gopi Krishna

"Source Field Investigations", David Wilcock

Various lectures by Richard Hoagland of the "Enterprise Mission"

"The True History and Religion of India", Swami Saraswati

"The Vedas"

"The Upanishads"

"The Spiritual Science of Yoga", Goswarmi Kriyananda

"Challenging Materialism" Jay Lakhani in "Hinduism Today, July, August, September 2011 issue

"Paracelsus: Selected Writings", Paracelsus

"Dr. Dean Ornish's Program for Reversing Heart Disease", Drs. Dean Ornish and Liu

"The Ramayana", SatGuru, MahaAvatar and Siddha Valmiki

"HUMAN RACE: The Lion Sleeps No More: Get off Your Knees", David Icke

"The Four Corners Vortex", Richard DeWolf on the "Coast to Coast" radio show, June 5, 2011

"The Noetic Effects of Sin", Dr.Michael Jensen (internet source

"The Sirius Mystery", Robert Temple

"Anointing Oils", William Haney on the "Coast to Coast" radio show, June 20, 2011

"Vitamin 'D'", Nora Gidowski, on the "Coast to Coast" radio show, June 21, 2011

"The Stairway to Heaven", Zecharia Sitchin

"The Twelve Planet", Zecharia Sitchin

"The Lost World, Zecharia Sitchin

"The Herbal Physicians Desk Reference"

"The Akashic Experience, Ervin Lazlo

"Earth Changes Media", Mitch Battros (Internet source) and "Coast to Coast" radio show

"The Earth-Sun Connection", Mitch Battros

"The Browning Newletter" and climate change video, "Climate and the Affairs of Man", Dr. Eben Browning

"The Death of Ignorance", Dr. Frederick Bell

"Breathairianism", Jack Davis and Jasmuheen (internet sources)

"Secrets of the Soil", Peter Tompkins

"The Secret Life of Plants, Peter Tompkins

"The Findhorn Garden", The Findhorn Community

"The Perelandra Garden Wookbook, Michaelle Small Wright

"Information Theory and the Origin of Life, Dr. Hubert Yockey

"Pathways to God: Experiencing the 'Living God' in Your Everyday Life, Dr. Robert J. Newton

"The Secret of Sion", William Henry

Please check Dr. Newton's website, "A Map to Healing and Your Essential Divinity Through Theta Consciousness" for upcoming classes and seminars in your area.